For Tom
Best Wishes to
a true friend —
Merry Christmas and a
Happy New Year 1973-74!

BOUND AND GAGGED

BY THE SAME AUTHOR

Continued Next Week
World of Laughter
Kops and Custards (with Terry Brewer)

BOUND AND GAGGED

The Story of the Silent Serials

Kalton C. Lahue

CASTLE BOOKS ★ NEW YORK

For Frank Leon Smith and Spencer G. Bennet —
The Last of the Mohicans.

Acknowledgments

To all those who wrote me after the publication of *Continued Next Week,* and especially Samuel Peeples, my warmest gratitude. The letters, interviews and materials provided by Spencer G. Bennet, Joe Bonomo, Louise Lorraine, Ethlyne Clair, Mary Horsley, Nan Boardman, Robert F. Hill, Ernie Westmore, Ford Beebe, Wilfred J. Horwood, Alan Brock, Edith Hutchison, Arline Pretty, Jack Hoxie Jr., Priscilla Dean, Frank Lackteen, Edmund Cobb, Richard Thorpe, and especially Frank Leon Smith, were instrumental in compiling this story of the serials. I wish to thank Samuel K. Rubin for permission to print excerpts written for *The Classic Collector,* Milton Luboviski for his unfailing optimism, Kent D. Eastin for his usual fine cooperation and John Hampton for his foresight and dedication in preserving the silent film. Appreciation is also extended to Sam Grossman, Nick Fiorentino, Bob Cooper, Don Overton, Bill McKenstry and many others for making it possible for me to view serial footage from their private collections. And special thanks to Shirley I. Fisher for her devotion to reproducing the materials brought to her with the request—"Needed yesterday."

Contents

Introduction

The perfect serial never existed. All of the better ones possessed elements of the kind desired by intelligent producers, but *none* ever contained all of these elements. The genre was established for the purpose of making money. Although the ideal might have been a fine adventure story, told with the same dramatic restraint found on the legitimate stage, the problems involved in putting such on the screen were complicated. If he knew his business at all, the producer realized that exhibitors and audiences liked an action approach which sacrificed story quality for stunts. This was especially true after the serial medium became stabilized in the thrill-and-stunt cliché.

The power and glory of the stunt should not be taken lightly. A verdict of "too highbrow" from exhibitors could have meant the life or death of a substantial investment; a risk few wished to take. The monsters, horror characters, clutching hands, evil eyes and all other ultra-dramatic devices served to reinforce the reckless physical action and exaggerated the struggle between evil and the forces of good as represented by the hero.

In the twenties, only Pathé attempted to present chapter plays for adult audiences, and toward the close of the period even Pathé fell down on this ideal. Universal and the independent producers went after the most effect for the least money. There are many different ways to define and characterize a "good" serial. From the purist viewpoint, few existed. From the audience's seat, I think it would be fair to define such a chapter play as one which had a reasonably logical story and worked in suspense, action and thrills in a combination which created an exciting experience.

It is my contention that this is the only fair basis by which a serial should be judged. After all, it was put on the screen for the sole purpose of earning money. Serial producers were not after awards for artistic achievement; they were in the business of entertaining people and if those who left the theaters were pleased with what they had seen, the producer had succeeded.

The silent serial is a part of a vanished America; an America that many of us look back at fondly and muse, "Those were the good old days." Others cry out that we do not have the time to look behind us; we must forever face the future. To those people I can only say—you don't know what you've missed in life. Read on.

BOUND AND GAGGED

Mary Fuller, the Edison actress who started it all. Viewers were fascinated by her monthly tribulations as serialized in *McClure's Ladies World* and released to the screen as *What Happened to Mary?* (1912).

1

The Spellbound Multitude

Of all the distribution practices evolved by early motion picture producers, perhaps the most distinctive was the silent serial. Today, it occupies a rather unique position in American cinema history. Little has been written about it, save for the occasional bits about Pearl White and Ruth Roland.[1] Its history is largely shrouded in darkness, obscured and overlooked by film historians in favor of what they feel to be more substantial accomplishments of the film industry. In truth, this is indeed a shame, for there was much drama as well as pathos connected with the manufacture of serial thrillers. To a certain degree, the miniature world of the serial accurately reflected the maelstrom which was the realm of motion pictures prior to the arrival of sound. In addition, serial making represented a down-to-earth approach to one of the fundamental obligations of the movies—entertainment.

Scarcely ever was there mention of that abominable word which Hollywood was to later preempt as its own—art. The approach used was entertainment in exchange for money and those who adhered intently to this dictum were seldom disappointed. Pathé, the undisputed leader over the years, was equally well known as "The House of Serials." Until 1925, few chapter plays bore the proud rooster trade mark unless their quality was of the highest.

Of necessity, the silent motion picture serial must be considered as a separate and complete movie endeavor. The writing and production were

---

[1] To date, the literature of the silent serial has been insignificant. The following articles have appeared in *Films In Review*: "The Serial Lovers" (Miller and Ray), Edward Connor, August–September, 1955; "The Man Who Made Serials" (George B. Seitz), Frank Leon Smith, October, 1956; "40 Years of Cliffhanging" (Spencer G. Bennet), George Geltzer, February, 1957; "The Truth About Pearl White," Wallace E. Davies, November, 1959; "The 2nd Greatest Serial Queen," Geltzer, November, 1960.

Charles Clary is one Hindu villain who does his best to know all, see all, and tell nothing. *The Adventures of Kathlyn* (1913).

Some terrible evil is surely afoot as Charles Clary schemes with the station master in *The Adventures of Kathlyn* (1913).

A knock at the door! What outlandish fate awaits Kathlyn Williams in this first episode of *The Adventures of Kathlyn?*

but a part of this endeavor. Equal stress must be placed on publicity, promotion, sales and exhibition of the product. These latter areas had as much to do with the success of many serials as did the quality of the film itself. Many advertising budgets alone exceeded the production costs of the chapter plays being marketed.

Another consideration which is necessary to place before the reader, prior to moving into the various aspects of serial production, is the time-change factor. Frank Leon Smith has formed a good definition of this, and in a letter he explained, "Truth about one period is not necessarily truth about other periods and generalities about any enterprise—and in particular, the movies—are very, very dangerous." The point which Mr. Smith has made is simply that as soon as something was accepted by the majority in the business as being a fact of life, the rules of the game had changed and the fact was no longer valid.

This is best exemplified by a quick look at the early serials. Many will argue that *What Happened To Mary?* (1912) was not the first serial. Others disagree and state that although it was not a true cliffhanger, it started the entire trend. Let me point out that serial standards, as we now conceive of them, did not exist at that time. Development of what is most often considered to be the true serial format, the cliffhanger, was still in the future. The script of the Mary Fuller chapter play (written by Horace G. Plympton, General Manager of the Edison studios) contained a great deal of exciting physical action in the chapters. This action could have been broken up by the ending of a chapter, but it wasn't. It remained for *The Adventures Of*

A long journey is ahead for Kathlyn Williams as she decides to locate her missing father in this scene from Chapter 1 of *The Adventures of Kathlyn*, the serial that introduced the to-be-continued chapter play.

Lure of the Circus (1918) found Eddie Polo (center) facing danger in a circus setting.

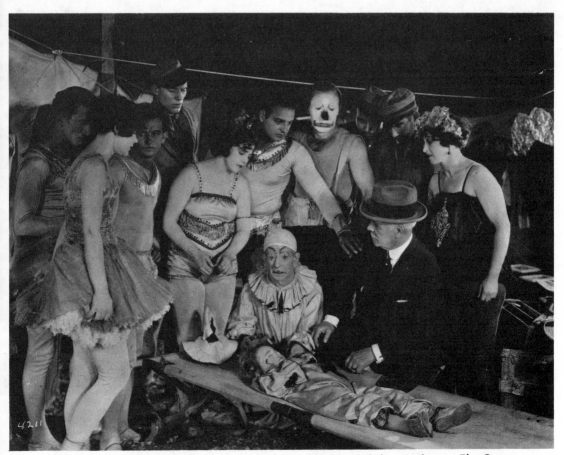

Joe Bonomo and Louise Lorraine want to know what caused the accident in *The Great Circus Mystery* (1925). (Courtesy Joe Bonomo)

A rare scene taken directly from a frame of the only reel known to exist of Charles Hutchison's first serial effort, *Wolves of Kultur* (1918). (Courtesy Wilfred J. Horwood)

Kathlyn (1913) to introduce audiences to a colorful device as a logical development of the serial format. This was the "hold-over" suspense which teased the viewer about the next exciting episode.

Certainly, at the outset no one quite knew how to go about the architecture, engineering and construction required in a serial. Trial and error proved to be the only method, as one can determine from viewing what remains of the early chapter plays. The progress from complete chapter to cliffhanger was steady but not rapid. The genre was fluid for quite a few years and didn't become standardized until after many, many serials had been made by a variety of firms.

Contrary to what some writers would have the reader believe, the serial makers were not aware of what they were doing all of the time; they did

George Larkin pays homage to Cleo Madison, the love of his life, in a scene from an early reel of *Trey O' Hearts* (1914).

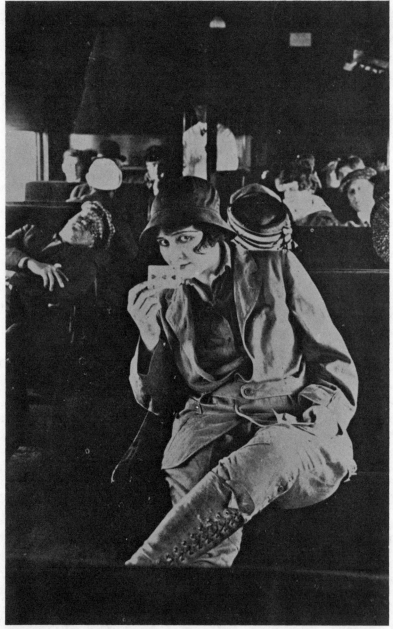

Cleo Madison, as the evil twin sister, contemplates the macabre significance of *The Trey O' Hearts.*

not have full autonomy over their end result nor could they hope to be on top of the job at all times. Each and every serial was a separate and complete adventure and nearly every one ever made was done as the product of a serial enterprise which had a separate existence in the organization of a parent company. This was true, in part, because serials were a distinct and rather lowly department within all of the major producing firms. Serial practitioners often were on a lower social scale than those who worked in features. It was not until the days of Republic Pictures, in the era of sound, that serials became somewhat socially acceptable.

Bearing this in mind, one can credit the origination of the serial format to William Selig, but refinement of the techniques by such craftsmen as George B. Seitz, Henry McRae, Robert F. Hill and Spencer G. Bennet,

Ella Hall gazes wonderingly at the sights of the big city as the evil schemers look on. From *The Master Key* (1914).

among others, helped to assure its development, popularity and survival. It possessed a peculiar appeal all of its own. From the vantage point of the producer, the chapter play meant continuing profits on a rather low investment. The exhibitor might depend upon a successful serial to draw patrons who would not otherwise pay the price of admission just for the feature attraction. It also served a definite commercial purpose—exhibitors used it to draw and hold audiences on off-nights during the week. To the audience, it represented the extreme of a human failing—curiosity. What would happen next?

In an era of rapid innovation in a young industry, the serial actually regressed in order to advance. Early chapter plays placed the major emphasis on a strong plot line which was crisscrossed with sub-plots; and although at times the pace was rapid, stunts were performed as an integral part of the story. Later serials were to emphasize the stunt angle in preference to a solid plot and they depended upon rapid action for action's sake. In short, the later serials utilized action in lieu of a plot in a surprisingly large number of cases. A thin story line could be stretched out and supported by the use of an endless number of hair-raising affairs.

The chapter play really came into its own with the development of the aforementioned cliffhanger ending. The standard treatment was to place the star in extreme jeopardy at the end of the chapter in order to evoke interest in the next installment. In many cases, the script writers outdid themselves and dreamed up such a dreadful peril that logic alone could not hope to bring the star out alive. Logic was dispensed with in such cases and the sharpened pencils took over. When an effort was made to extricate the leading character from such a position, the end result was very often banal and quite unbelievable. In some instances, the desperate plight of the star was simply overlooked in the succeeding episode, as though it had never happened. Producers often depended a great deal on the weekly interval between screenings to deaden the memory of the audience and a gross lack of continuity appears in many of the silent serials when seen today.

A case in point was *Lure of the Circus*, the 1918 Eddie Polo serial. At the close of one episode, Eddie was most securely bound and a time bomb was set to explode in forty-five seconds. The villains rushed out the door to safety. Death was a certainty for the star and no fan could possibly believe that he would escape in any logical manner. This proved to be a correct assumption for the opening scenes of the next chapter showed Eddie free and the bomb disarmed with no explanation whatsoever of how the miracle occured.

Among the early serials, several came from the pens of such noted fiction

Harry Houdini's one serial was really quite fascinating, but *The Master Mystery* (1919) didn't fare too well with fans; the master magician solved problems like this one all too easily. Truth is stranger than fiction but Houdini's insistence on reality seemed to strain the credulity of the audience. (Courtesy Alan Brock)

EPISODE N°. 5

White supremacy was the moral of *The Yellow Menace* (1916). Edwin Stevens portrayed the monstrous Ali Singh, a fanatical Oriental bent on destroying the United States. (Courtesy Alan Brock)

writers as Arthur B. Reeve, John Fleming Wilson, Elsie Van Name and Louis J. Vance. The seemingly inexhaustible demand for material brought many new names into the fold, and Grace Cunard, Cyrus Townsend Brady, E. J. Montague, Garfield Thompson, Gilson Willets and Frank Leon Smith turned out some highly original material. Many of the later serials came from the pens of hack writers and abounded with clichés. This was especially true of a number of the state right releases made and distributed in the mid-twenties. They utilized cheap casts, routine plots and poor production values in an attempt to cash in on a good thing.

Although not undiluted thrillers as were their counterparts in the days of sound, the silent serials were rich in imagination, story and action. The serial writers took advantage of all the usual paraphernalia of mystery and melodrama—trap doors, sliding walls, secret passages, tunnels, underground lairs and the like. Jeopardy was an integral part of the chapter play, in the form of explosions, wrecks, quicksand, vats of acid and many others. The ultimate in speed and power—trolley cars, automobiles and fast locomotives —were all used to give punch to the drama. When the airplane came of age, it too was put to work regularly.

Many serials made use of hooded villains and masked heroes. The Clutching Hand, Silent Menace, Phantom Menace of Mad Mountain, Wolf-Devil, Hooded Terror, Purple Shadow, Faceless Terror and even such mundane heavies as The Frog and The Claw paraded across the screen to do battle with The Laughing Mask, Riddle Rider, Mystery Rider, Vanishing Rider, Lion Man, White Horseman and The White Rider. The chapter plays took advantage of popular athletes, using Jack Dempsey, Gene Tunney, James J.

This impressive set gave *The Jungle Goddess* (1922) production values far above the average independent serial.

Jungle Goddess set. The elephant serves to emphasize the enormity of the goddess.

Corbett and Benny Leonard in starring roles. Vaudeville headliners such as Houdini, J. Robert Pauline and Lucien Albertini tried their luck. One independent producer made an unsuccessful attempt in 1927 to sign Babe Ruth and Lou Gehrig, offering them $40,000 to star in two proposed serials.

Nearly every serial with a heavy emphasis on mystery made use of some weird or elaborate set. A subterranean chamber served as the meeting place for the master criminals in *The Mystery of 13* (1919). Craig Kennedy's laboratory was filled with scientific gadgets, gauges and knobs used in combatting the Clutching Hand in *The Exploits of Elaine* (1914). Doctor Blakely's deranged victims were locked away in an underground prison in *Officer 444* (1926). An elaborate set was specially designed and constructed to simulate a moving mountain for *The White Horseman* (1921).

One of the more intricate ones appeared in *Wolves of Kulter* (1918). Actually, it was a series of sets installed at the Crystal studio and constructed to operate mechanically at the touch of hidden buttons and levers. As it appeared on-screen, the set was an old bookstore with thousands of volumes on the shelves. One entire section of the shelving was made to swing open, revealing a complete workshop containing switchboards, electric motors, revolving steel saws and other tools, along with a perfect model of a radio-torpedo. A section of the workshop floor dropped down, acting as an elevator to the depths of an underground passageway. The dampness of a cryptic vault buried deeply beneath the city was simulated by running water and the passageway led to a council chamber which contained an electrically

Independent serials like *The Jungle Goddess* often contained a daring scene like this for the adult viewers. Such an unreserved display of feminine pulchritude usually served only to bring forth the wrath of censors.

controlled steel chair. All this in order that Sheldon Lewis might checkmate Leah Baird!

Of course, sets such as this were dwarfed by the more elaborate and expensive ones used in the sound cliffhangers—such as *Flash Gordon* (1936) —but the production values found in many of the well-made chapter plays of the latter twenties were above average for their time. One way in which a costly appearance was imparted to a routine serial was by the use of expensive sets that had been constructed for use in one of the feature or spectacle productions of the day.

The successful continued picture demanded a unique type of star. A movie star was seldom so much an actor or actress as an attractive personality that

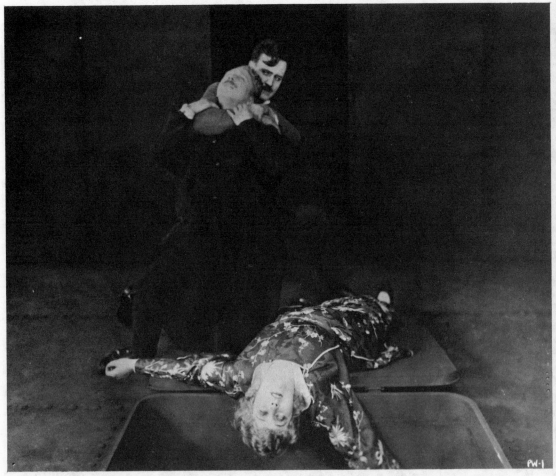

Walter McGrail barely managed to save Pearl White in *The Black Secret* (1919) and it was only Episode 4!

lent itself well to the screen. Only a few were able to make the transition from serial to feature and back again with some measure of regularity and success. Neither Ruth Roland nor Pearl White won many fans or critical acclaim for their features, but both were top chapter-play stars. Conversely, both Lillian Lorraine, a leading Broadway attraction of her time, and Billie Burke, a very fine actress, failed in their serial attempts. Although the vehicles which they used in their efforts played a role in the failures, stage reputations were of little value in front of the serial camera—which demanded a technique of its own. From the point at which Helen Holmes destroyed her serial image, her career went downhill with amazing rapidity, ending with independent features and bit roles.

Double-barrelled trouble faced the villain as Arline Pretty and Henry G. Sell investigate the old Amory mansion in A Woman in Grey (1920). (Courtesy Arline Pretty)

Anne Luther and George Larkin in a moving moment from *The Lurking Peril* (1919). But the action was about to begin. Larkin possessed what the script writer described as "an unusual sort of brain," and in a moment of extreme financial stress had sold a diabolical old professor the right to dissect his head after death. With the professor trying to kill him off in each episode without suspicion beclouding their friendship, Larkin was in deep trouble for 15 chapters. (Courtesy Alan Brock)

In the later silent period, Allene Ray scored as one of the most valuable properties that Pathé ever signed to a contract. Although her early features were fairly well received, she would never have tasted the heady wine of success had it not been for the chapter plays. It was also her good fortune to have the best writers and directors which Pathé possessed.

Surprisingly, many of the stars who are well remembered today for their serial feats actually appeared in a small number of continued plays. Neva Gerber made a large number of short westerns and features, but her fame

Irene Castle faced herself in this dual scene from *Patria* (1917), the vitriolic Hearst "preparedness" serial. (Courtesy Alan Brock)

rests chiefly on eleven serials made over a period of nine years. Grace Cunard starred in only five. Marie Walcamp appeared in six. Even more interesting is the fact that the fame of many rests upon a select number of serials in which they were co-starred. Francis Ford is most often associated with Miss Cunard and although they made a wealth of short films together, they made only four serials as a team. Neva Gerber made her greatest hits with Ben Wilson. William Duncan made several fine serials with Carol Holloway, but he hit his finest stride with Edith Johnson and they became a team in real life, as well as on the screen.

Even though Louise Lorraine and Eileen Sedgwick made numerous appearances before the camera, who would recall them today had it not been

Mollie King, tormented by *The Mystery of the Double Cross* (1917), hurries toward freedom. Some thought that Pathé intended to build her up as a new Pearl White but Mollie left pictures instead. (Courtesy Alan Brock)

for their serial careers? Miss Lorraine made eleven over a ten-year span and Miss Sedgwick turned in twelve in as many years. The same can be said for the male stars. Separate Elmo Lincoln and Charles Hutchison from their serial feats and they would be forgotten to all but the serious cinema addict. Art Acord and Eddie Polo are recalled today for a small number of interesting features and short subjects, but in reality their fame was made everlasting by serial roles.

What does all this imply? Was there some sort of magic about the serial which made ordinary people into giants? I think not; but the chapter play did possess a peculiar charm that features and short subjects lack. This was a built-in and unique publicity advantage—each chapter was plugged hard and this in turn kept the fans coming. A typical serial received ten to fifteen times more attention than the average feature or short subject. A star could make two or three during a given year and rest assured that his or her appearance in a community would last throughout the year. The same number of features might receive eight to ten weeks' playing time during the same year.

How does one explain the success of the profusion of continued pictures that paraded forth on the silent screen? More than any other reason, I believe that they filled a definite void in many lives. They appealed directly to a simple, yet profound, audience need for entertainment having a kind of unbelievable and magical quality about it. Appealing mainly to the senses, they avoided the so-called "realism" which abounds in cinematic presentations of today. There was enough realism in each individual life as it was. The screen became an instrument of escape and the serial a method. Although adults often laughed themselves helpless at the antics on the screen, down deep inside a measure of respect for the humdrum quality of their own lives kept them returning for the following chapters.

The youngsters stared in wonder at the screen and daydreamed; their imagination placed them in the stead of the hero or heroine and established a response pattern which held forth into adulthood. How many moviegoers of yesterday fondly remember the Saturday afternoon matinee and the sense of anticipation that the latest installment of their favorite serial created as they stepped up to the box office to deposit the thin dime held tightly clutched in their sweaty little palm! What a surprising number of sophisticated people of today recall the wild excitement with which they viewed the serial chapters! Perhaps the years have smoothed many rough edges from memories but there is little doubt that at the time the serial appealed to a large number of people in a positive manner. Beyond this possible explanation, I have never met or heard of anyone who could, with the authority of knowledge, explain the basis for public acceptance of the silent serial.

Until about 1920, serials played in all kinds of theaters across the nation. As audiences became more selective, and the trend toward glamorous movie palaces became apparent, the serial found itself relegated to the cheaper houses and second-run theaters. In the late twenties, Pathé's sales were almost entirely to second-run houses which played them with the cheaper features. It was to remain this way until 1930, when Universal's fabulously successful *The Indians Are Coming* was booked into the Roxy for a Broadway first run.

The audiences were one of the factors that helped place the serial in the cheaper houses; they were made up largely of children and women from

1914 until roughly 1919. Immigrants were especially pleased with serial chapters as they could easily understand the action, and the language barrier was broken by the fast-moving plot. Concurrent with the return of our soldiers from Europe, the audiences began to change. They had lost much of their zest for the action which this elemental story technique provided. The middle class had discovered the movie as an entertainment form only to shy away from chapter plays. As a result, the serial shifted to those houses which held the type of audience it pleased best—children and those people without too sophisticated or demanding tastes.

From 1925 until the arrival of sound, the path of the silent serial became steadily rougher. The profusion of cheaply made state right chapter plays

Thomas Chatterton is close to discovering who had stolen *The Secret of the Submarine* (1916). (Courtesy Alan Brock)

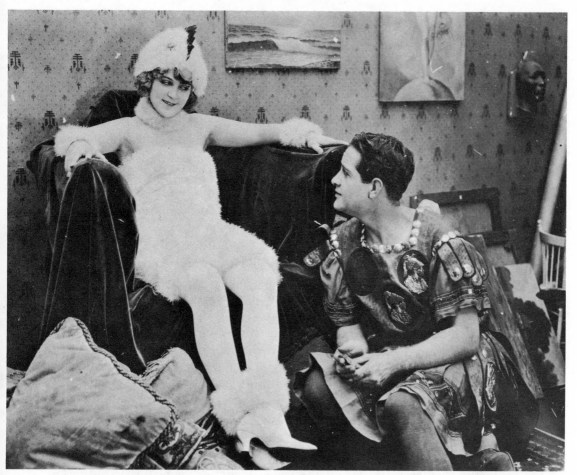

Eileen Percy and Jack Mower in the opening chapter of *The Third Eye* (1920). The serial title referred to a camera lens which had captured a murder on a movie set. The "weenie"? The scrap of film which incriminated Warner Oland. (Courtesy Alan Brock)

was another of the many factors which combined to lessen the popularity of the serial. Children were now the main audience and the thrillers began to bend over in an effort to appeal to them, in turn alienating adult audiences. Censorship, as we shall see, had taken its toll by restricting villainy to a predictable pattern. Longer features and the beginning of double bills were aiding in the demise of short subjects. A large number of the great serial stars were no longer active and only Allene Ray was able to establish a reputation by serials alone. Constantly rising production and exploitation costs coupled with declining box-office receipts to lessen the profit margin.

In reality, a fertile field had been well plowed. Aside from the efforts of Nat Levine and the Pathé team of Smith and Bennet, very little original material was reaching the chapter play screen by this time. Vitagraph had disappeared. Although the production staff at Universal hesitated several times, it continued to grind out pale imitations which failed to live up to expectations. The great days of Arrow were over. Truly, the serial had fallen upon evil days. Well-worn themes and action sequences were given time-tested treatments to become undistinguished and cliché-ridden releases.

One of the finest examples to point up the entire problem of the serial plot in the latter twenties was the last silent—first sound Universal epic, *The Indians Are Coming* (1930). Boasting a large budget ($160,000), a competent cast headed by Allene Ray and Tim McCoy, and directed by the venerable Henry McRae, this western adventure story was based very loosely on the William F. Cody story "The West That Was." One only needs to view the first few chapters to find a recapitulation of all the clichés which had plagued the western film for years and which are still available to undiscerning audiences today, on both television and the widescreen. In this respect, time has treated this serial rather well.

Although it is both interesting and amusing to view today, when placed in context with the period of production, *The Indians Are Coming* should have been rather disappointing to the audiences that helped make it a smashing financial success. Each chapter made a point of providing but one exciting situation and missing a couple of chapters here and there did not really matter, as the plot moved ponderously through twelve chapters. The novelty of sound undoubtedly accounted for its excellent reception at the box office, as little else about it was outstanding.

To a great extent, originality had disappeared from the serial screen by the late twenties and even the excitement and thrills commonly associated with the chapter plays was on the wane. It almost seemed as if the serial had already died but was being denied a decent burial.

Censorship had played a role of undeniable proportions. The serial concept felt the heavy blows almost from its conception. Those pious individuals who wished to "protect" their fellow man were unsparing in their attack. Although there was much agitation through the years that the silent serial flourished, a Federal Censorship Board was never established. The censorship movement was mainly restricted to local communities. Chicago was the pioneer, passing an ordinance which became effective November 19, 1907. The Superintendent of Police issued permits until 1912 when more comprehensive legislation placed the authority in the hands of an individual especially appointed to the post.

In the beginning, the ordinance restricted only that considered to be "immoral or obscene" but succeeding years saw the scope of this legislation widen. In 1919, the Chicago board examined some 8,000,000 feet of film, rejecting seventy pictures and cutting over 110,000 feet which it considered to be objectionable.[2] Pennsylvania followed the example set by Chicago in 1911 with the creation of a state board but it was not until 1915 that it became active and effective.

Each board was self-sustaining. The producer of a film who wished to circulate it within the jurisdiction of the board was required to pay a fee for each reel to be used and to submit the film for consideration. Pennsylvania charged a flat $2.00 per reel, which brought in an annual revenue of nearly $100,000 in 1920. This was more than ample to maintain the necessary facilities and staff required to do the job.

From the start, the industry vigorously resisted all attempts to institute

[2] Ellis Paxon Oberholtzer, *Morals of the Movies*, Penn Publishing Company, Pennsylvania, 1922.

Jim Gordon (Mark Strong) failed miserably in this attempt to dispose of Ruth Roland in *The Tiger's Trail* (1919). (Courtesy Larry Edmunds Bookshop)

Perilous situations like this made Pearl White the audiences' number-one favorite. As *The Lightning Raider* (1919), she performed many such stunts. (Courtesy Larry Edmunds Bookshop)

Jack Mower has had enough from Leon Kent as Allene Ray (wearing a wig over her blonde hair) looks apprehensive over what might happen in *Ten Scars Make a Man* (1924). (Courtesy National Film Archive, Great Britain)

Having failed to save the heroine from abduction, Charles Hutchison decided that a *Double Adventure* (1921) was the best way to effect a rescue. (Courtesy Larry Edmunds Bookshop)

censorship on its product. Members of the Motion Picture Patents Company were assessed varying sums to defeat those proposals that seemed most likely to succeed. Lobbyists and attorneys were employed in abundant numbers to ward off threats across the nation. Exhibitors were harangued at their annual meetings to resist all efforts at control of the screen. The end result found an organized and well-financed industry able to avoid the "reformers" who sought strict controls. As a result, many censorship boards degenerated into plush political posts. The actions of certain well-known censors such as Major Funkhouser of Chicago merely served to injure the movement and prevented it from gaining sizable momentum.

The closest that censorship ever came to being effective on a national scale

Allene Ray's blonde tresses were hidden under a black wig which was hidden in turn under a head dress in *The Fortieth Door* (1924).

Following *The Trail of the Octopus* (1919), Ben Wilson rescued Neva Gerber from this perilous situation at the opening of Chapter 2. Note the unusual idol set which slid back to reveal an underground escape route.

came with the National Board of Review, a New York City organization which depended upon voluntary cooperation, for it had no way of imposing its will on producers other than to refuse the use of its seal of approval. Those who favored the Smith-Hughes bill of 1915, which would have brought a Federal board into being, openly charged the National Board of Review with being a small group controlled by and directly interested in the industry. Even the House Committee on Education in 1916 noted the inefficiency and inadequacy of the Board, but the proposal met with defeat nonetheless. The industry was thus able to maintain an "open" screen, and with the

Although serial heroes were supposedly strong and bold, today's viewers might consider them somewhat inept. This was the usual fate for Tony Moreno in his Vitagraph serials, but by the time his first one (*The Iron Test*, 1918) was completed, Tony had learned how to free himself from the clothes line binding. (Courtesy D. Elmo Brooks)

establishment of Will Hays as the head of an organization formed by the major companies it depended upon "self-regulation."

Clearly, there were many violations of good taste in the early silent pictures but as the screen matured, the major producing firms became more careful, and by the early twenties a surprisingly large number of such violations could be attributed to the independent showmen who were out to make a dollar in a hurry. All, however, seemed bent on reflecting the changing moral standards of the nation. Many scenes of drunkenness openly scoffed at Prohibition. Sex became a prime box-office ingredient, but on the other hand, many censorship boards were "scissor-happy" and often cut for the sake of cutting. The effectiveness of such a board quite naturally depended

A popular serial character, Tarzan was played by several actors in the twenties. Frank Merrill's look of grim determination is sufficient to reassure the viewer that *Tarzan, the Mighty* (1928) will survive this peril of Chapter 9. (Courtesy D. Elmo Brooks)

almost entirely upon the good sense of the person or persons who held the position but the few gave the many a bad name in the public view. The majority of the rules and regulations governing the actions of censors quite clearly spelled out the range within which their activities were to be conducted and a zealous person such as Major Funkhouser of the Chicago board was able to alter a film to fit his conception of what it should be.

The Pennsylvania State Board of Censorship provided one of the best examples of the stringent standard imposed upon the industry. Among other things, it firmly condemned white slavery, prostitution, immoral assaults, the drug habit, nudes, abortion, vulgar comedy, drunkenness, crime, prolonged love scenes and any subtitles which used objectionable or suggestive language to convey covert ideas about these topics. Broken into twenty-four sub-sections, this comprehensive code could be, and often was, interpreted so as to severely restrict the film producers. While directing *Pearl of the Army* (1916), Edward Jose chided Ralph Kellard about his amorous advances toward Pearl White. Walking up to the actress, Jose grabbed her and told Kellard, "You've been kissing her for the Pennsylvania Board of Censors, now kiss her like this for the rest of the country"; and he proceeded to demonstrate what he meant.

The serial was one of the prime targets of the early censors and they made their points felt in quite an effective manner. Many objections were brought forth against the fact that a villain was able to continue his nefarious activities week after week, unhindered by the forces of good until the final episode. True, cohorts of the villain were captured each week, but this did not satisfy those critics who frowned on the chapter play. It was also considered wrong to place the hero or heroine in jeopardy, to remain there for a week before a rescue was effected. What apparently disturbed censors the most was the rousing reception with which children greeted each chapter.

Many objections centered around the emotional impact of a serial installment. Those who condemned this form of entertainment complained that children were exposed to two reels of hair-raising thrills, improbable as they might be, and left on a high pitch of emotion after watching evil apparently triumph over right and justice. A large number of voices cried out that this was a contributing factor to juvenile delinquency and it seemed all too easy to find a prison warden or law enforcement officer who would blame the motion picture for the large number of offenders in his care.

Warden McKenty of Eastern Penitentiary, Pennsylvania, staunchly supported the movement for censorship in 1915 with the following statements made in front of a legislative body considering the necessity of censorship in the state. "I do not think, I know that criminals are made in the picture houses. I study the cases of those who come to me. I ask the men how they

Surrounded by soldiers, Pearl White realized that her pistol was no match for their rifles. Here is a peril worthy of the name, from *The Black Secret* (1919). (Courtesy Bettmann Archive, Inc.)

were started on the paths which brought them to me and they say through the motion picture."

Warden McClaughrey of the Iowa state prison at Anamosa had appeared before his state legislature in 1913. His testimony was built around the idea that although the motion pictures did not directly teach crime, they illustrated a huge variety of criminal acts. According to his view, these acts were suggestive of the possibilities of crime and made such appear more attractive.

In light of the large number who fondly recall the silent serials with all of their vicarious thrills, I would venture that much of the noise raised about censorship of the chapter plays was nonsense. Other areas of screen entertainment, especially those which capitalized on sex, were more deserving of the attention of censors. Of all the serial chapters that I have viewed, none have been in as poor taste as some of the better Mack Sennett comedies, which often crossed the border into vulgarity.

Many early serials specifically identified the villain as a member of a particular minority group. *Patria* (1917) is an outstanding example, for

Robert Leonard tells Ella Hall of the starving condition of the miners. She decides that it is time to locate *The Master Key* (1914).

it clearly placed the villainy on the shoulders of the Mexicans and Japanese. *The Yellow Peril* (1916) featured an Oriental villain, as did a number of Pearl White epics. *The Perils Of Pauline* (1914) and *The Diamond From The Sky* (1915) referred to gypsies in what was felt to be an unfavorable light. By 1920, the insistence of pressure groups opposed to this had made it very difficult for a producer to specify the identity of the villainous element. Thus, the serial was removed another step from reality.

A very popular form of chapter play has often been quite loosely called the "crime serial." Thrillers fitting into this general category dealt with a criminal mastermind out to rule the world. In many cases, these were masked villains whose identity was withheld to the very end. A crusade by the cen-

The poor old lady knows well that Frank Lackteen is up to no good in *Into the Net* (1924). (Courtesy Frank Lackteen)

sors culminated in the early twenties with the disappearance, for the most part, of the masked villain. This did away with one of the most valuable tools of the serial writer. Writers began watching the work of their competitors to see what new villainy fellow scripters were able to develop and then proceeded to imitate it.

On top of these developments, the scandals of the early twenties (Arbuckle, Reid and William D. Taylor's unsolved murder) gave added public weight to the efforts of censors and caused many firms to shy away from the more imaginative and mystifying plots. Universal began to concentrate on hiding violent action in "historical" serials in an effort to avoid criticism. Other firms began to avoid plot by substituting stunting action. Some of the serials

Thrills like this made Pearl White Queen of the Serials.

became nothing more than a showcase for quick action which often defied logic.

Of all the serial-producing companies, Pathé and Vitagraph showed the greatest taste and restraint in its product. Few of their serials were subjected to the scissors and a number were even cited by groups which advocated control. This is a well-earned tribute to the men who put these chapter plays together. Neither George B. Seitz nor Spencer G. Bennet ever allowed objectionable material to obscure their vision of clean, thrilling installments which would appeal to everyone.

William Duncan, who directed the bulk of his Vitagraph footage, came forth with his reply to critics of the serial in a 1919 statement:

Crane Wilbur and Pearl White in the best-remembered serial of them all, *The Perils of Pauline* (1914). Although only a few chapters had a cliffhanging ending, this serial propelled Pearl White from near-obscurity to everlasting fame.

Donald MacKenzie, director of *The Perils of Pauline*, in makeup for his role as "Blinky Bill," the terror of the Seven Seas.

Will Pearl White believe the fantastic story Paul Panzer and Francis Carlyle have concocted? The hand belongs to the scourge of the high seas, "Blinky Bill" (Donald MacKenzie), who's weaving a tale of romance and treasure that spells trouble for our heroine in Chapter 3 of *The Perils of Pauline.*

Villainous Paul Panzer (center) and his henchman Francis Carlyle (left) enjoy scheming with Donald MacKenzie as they plot the third of *The Perils of Pauline.*

Screen banditry delivers an important message to the impressionable minds of youth. Talks of eliminating wicked characters from the screen is as sensible as talking of eliminating evil from the Bible. Good stands out in a more illuminating light when contrasted with evil. Youngsters do not attempt to imitate the bad men of the screen. Instincts tell them to imitate the hero, who is always a man of virtue.

If a screen hero had nothing to accomplish, he would have no place on the screen. Because he does overcome obstacles and eradicates crime, he is a hero in the minds of the movie audiences. No reputable producer screens crime as a virtue. Rather he shows that crime does not pay and criminals always come to a bad end. Is it logical to believe that a boy seeing a hero rewarded and the bandit punished, would choose to enter a career of crime?

He might imagine himself a detective, policeman, ranger or a peace officer of some sort, but he could hardly be expected to imagine himself as a desperado.

When crime is rightfully pictured on the screen, it teaches a powerful lesson for good. The only banditry which should be eliminated is the sort repulsive to human intelligence and refinement, or crime wrongfully extolled as a virtue.

Duncan's statement should have been sufficient rebuttal to the charges placed against the serials, but still critics continued to complain.

Having built a foundation for the serial's mystique, let's part the curtain of the past and step into its adventurous world, meeting some of the men responsible for writing and directing the silent chapter plays. At the same time, we'll look briefly at the companies who made them, how they were constructed and sold to the public, along with some of the actors and actresses who are still remembered by the moviegoer of yesterday.

Crane Wilbur welcomes Pearl White on board for a final clinch as the twentieth chapter of *The Perils of Pauline* comes to a close.

2

The Empire Builders

Of the major firms involved in the entertainment medium of movies, Pathé's position was most nearly unique. Before the silent period was over, it had become known as "The House of Serials" and the rooster trademark on its product was readily identified the world over as a sign of quality. Yet, for all this success, Pathé was never a producer of motion pictures in the same manner as Universal or the other giants which survived the turbulent and hectic early days of growth in a bitterly competitive arena.

Charles and Emile Pathé had established themselves at an early date in France and quickly moved into business on an international scale. They began in a small way, exhibiting films, and soon worked their way into the field of film processing which remained a mainstay of their operations from beginning to end. Watching the misfortunes that befell the early producers, especially Méliès, Charles Pathé felt that the real profits lay in the field of distribution. It was a safer operation and allowed someone else to risk and absorb production costs. As a result of this theory, Pathé directed his energies toward the building of an enormous overseas sales organization. At the same time, however, Pathé had to produce some films and these French releases were also handled by the American branch. A large and modern processing plant was established in Bound Brook, New Jersey. Studio space was erected in Jersey City and Louis J. Gasnier arrived from France to take charge of production.

Pathé soon branched out and acquired a $75,000 studio in Edendale (California), placing James Young in charge. Westerns and some comedies were made in both studios, but Pathé did not become a force to reckon with in the industry until the acquisition of Eclectic and its nationwide distribution system gave the company a firm foothold in the American market. The Motion Picture Patents Company, which Pathé had joined, controlled Eclectic's distribution through the General Film Company. The General exchanges were floundering by this time, deeply involved in lawsuits and internal management problems.

Pathé quickly saw that if he relied on the system as it was then functioning, he would be stymied in his efforts to build the kind of organization he felt necessary for success. Thus in an open letter, addressed to the General Film Company and dated May 9, 1914, Pathé announced the establishment of exchanges in sixteen leading American cities. A radical departure from established procedure, this action amounted to open defiance of the trust. However, Pathé explained his actions in simple terms which could not be argued. For public consumption, the reason given was that General Film had not lived up to its agreement concerning release of the Pathé Weekly. Therefore, according to Pathé's reasoning, the move was not a fight but a logical

Although *The Million Dollar Mystery* (1914) was a smash hit, its successor, *Zudora* (1914), confused and bewildered audiences. It was the second and last serial starring James Cruze and Sidney Bracy.

development to help General Film fulfill its obligations in a more efficient manner. The International Film Service, which produced the Hearst News Pictorial, later merged with Pathé (December 28, 1916) and the disputed newsreel became the Hearst-Pathé News. A contract was arranged with Theodore and Leopold Wharton to produce in the Pathé studio and a legend was about to begin. The first offering proved to be the fabulous *Perils of Pauline* (1914).

The first of the great serial teams, Francis Ford and Grace Cunard, made only four chapter plays but are still remembered today for the fast-moving, action-packed thrills they provided for audiences. Acting was not their only forte, for they were also capable writers and directors. Here they discuss a scene from *Adventures of Peg O' The Ring* (1916.) (Courtesy John Hampton)

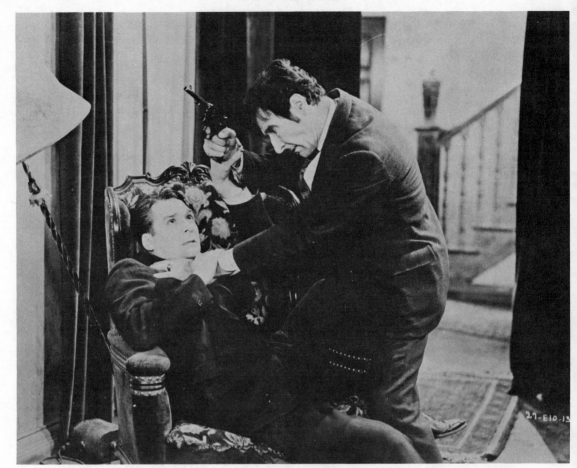

Pathé's reigning hero of the twenties, Walter Miller, struggled desperately with Paul Panzer, Pathé's original villain, in the closing episode of the final Pathé serial, *The Black Book* (1929).

Soon after this, the theory of operating strictly as a releasing firm with no built-in production units of its own was put into practice. Partially due to the outbreak of war in Europe, the American branch of Pathé quickly found that it couldn't acquire enough film to meet its obligations. A Pathé Film Committee had been established to consider and act on the wares of independent producers. If the Committee liked the film, it was bought at Pathé's price. The independent was at a loss, for where else could he obtain such excellent distribution of his product? He might turn to Universal or some of the other large companies but Pathé was *the* releasing house in terms of prestige and marketing ability.

As the demand continued to grow for a product that was not forthcoming

Anders Rudolf has convinced Louise Lorraine and Malcolm MacGregor that they're not welcome. The once-popular Vitagraph comedian, Hughie Mack, is at the left in this scene from *The Silent Flyer* (1926), Nat Levine's first serial production.

from the independent producers, Pathé decided to subsidize production in order to acquire what it desired. In some cases the company advanced the necessary money to begin production, but each arrangement was individually tailored to existing circumstances. The majority of cases found a producer taking most, if not all, of the preliminary risks, and gambling on the Pathé Film Committee to approve the finished product for purchase.[1] This worked to both advantage and disadvantage for Pathé. Once a serial was started, it was highly desirable for Pathé to contain the production. This became even more pronounced in the twenties when Pathé's policy was to advance the initial production costs upon the signing of a contract and then to make

---

[1] The Committee was strict in the matter of approval. In 1915, a vote of NO GOOD was handed down on the early chapters of an Arrow series, *Who's Guilty*, forcing the firm to reshoot.

regular payments for finished episodes which were accepted. As we shall see, this technique often worked against the company's best interests.

Among the early suppliers of product were Balboa and Astra. H. M. Horkheimer formed Balboa in 1913 at Long Beach, California. A reasonably successful producer in the theatrical world, he decided in 1912 to look into the motion picture business. This investigation convinced Horkheimer to invest his $7,000 in plant and equipment. Staffing the firm with personnel hired mainly from Selig, he opened shop and brought his brother Elwood into the fold. The early history of Balboa is now hidden by time, but Horkheimer once claimed that he had suffered many financial reverses at the outset and it was only because of the generous nature of his employees that Balboa managed to survive in the bitter struggle. This generous nature

Ethlyne Clair is in trouble again. But Walter Miller can't be far away in *Queen of the Northwoods* (1929). (Courtesy Spencer G. Bennet)

Wracked by pain from an injury incurred in her first serial and plagued by poor eye-sight, Pearl White's ability to make *Plunder* (1923) amazed even her close friends.

took the form of employee investments and deferred payrolls until such time as the market turned favorable.

Whatever the case might have been, the year 1915 found Balboa turning out a weekly output of 20,000 feet of negative film. A favorable contract to produce for Pathé release had been successfully negotiated in December 1914. Technically, the product was superb. The photography, printing and processing were way above the average quality of the time. Perhaps much of the credit for this belongs to a select group of employees who had remained with Balboa from the start. William Beckway was chief cameraman, Robert Brotherton was chief chemist and his sister, May, headed the editing department. John Wyse, as stage manager, might have shared in the blame

Joe Bonomo's final silent serial, *The Chinatown Mystery* (1928), found him cast as Joe Masters, secret service agent; it featured many old serial favorites in a rousing battle of wits with the arch-fiend, the Sphinx. (Courtesy Joe Bonomo)

for other aspects of Balboa's product but it seems logical that the lack of production values should be placed at the doorstep of the Horkheimer brothers. They did everything possible to cut corners and skimp on costs. Story values were nil and the dramatic aspect was simply shoddy.

Neal of the Navy (1915) just barely eased by the ever-omnipotent eye of the Pathé Film Committee. Harry Harvey had taken the job as director on a bonus basis. Balboa wanted the serial completed in twelve weeks, and to this end set forth a $500 incentive. Harvey did the first eight episodes in six weeks and made it under the deadline to collect the extra money. The serial showed it. Many of *The Red Circle* (1915) chapters were rejected outright, with retakes ordered. Balboa supplied only four of the early serials which carried the crowing rooster trademark.

A far more important production unit was Astra, formed in 1916 by Louis J. Gasnier, George B. Seitz, Edward Jose and George Fitzmaurice. Astra possessed all of the assets of Balboa and none of its liabilities. In addition, it had one of the finest serial craftsmen, Seitz, in charge of production plus the services of Pearl White. Taking over the studio in Jersey City, Astra was soon turning out some of the best of the early Pathé serials. It was an important unit in other ways. A number of the people connected with Astra went

The serial screen's first great villain, Paul Panzer, blocked J. Robert Pauline in his attempt to reach Peggy Shanor and De Sacia Saville. *The Mystery Mind* (1920) was Panzer's last major serial role and the beginning of a long road to obscruity.

William Pike was invaluable to Herbert Rawlinson and Marguerite Marsh. He furnished the detective atmosphere by rubbing his chin in the best Watson-Holmes style in *The Carter Case* (1919).

Anne Luther forgot to present a visiting card. As a result, she is in a dangerous position in *The Lurking Peril* (1919).

"If any harm comes to Miss Van Norton you are responsible," cried Ned. A former silent comedian, George Ovey (right) helps restrain William Desmond as Eileen Sedgwick is spirited away in *Strings of Steel* (1926).

on to greater fame in the chapter-play realm. Bertram Millhauser and Spencer G. Bennet were two of the production staff who became famous in the twenties.

Before Astra disbanded, it had turned out ten serials and firmly established Pathé as the leader in the field. Near the end, Seitz discovered that the profits of the two Astra serial units had been wasted on the four feature production units and he decided to get out. Pathé gave him Pearl White and he formed his own company which proceeded to make seven top serials for Pathé release before it also closed shop. Seitz's undoing was ironic, for it was a feature film, *Rogues And Romance*, which he shot abroad with his own money. The film was a box-office failure and it dragged him under. Ultimately, he reopened his studio to do three Hutchison chapter plays and Miss White's finale, *Plunder* (1923).

Among other important sources of early serials which helped Pathé gain recognition was the continuation of product from the Wharton brothers. Theodore Wharton had entered the business as a writer for Edison in 1907. A season with Kalem followed, and when Pathé opened its American studio,

ANTONIO MORENO
"THE INVISIBLE HAND"
A VITAGRAPH SERIAL
EPISODE NO. 4
"GASSED"

JOHN SHARPE UNEXPECTEDLY RUNS INTO
HIS ENEMY, IRON HAND.

Antonio Moreno didn't mean to fall into the clutches of his nemesis Iron Hand, but it meant another chapter of excitement for his fans, who followed the exploits of *The Invisible Hand* (1920). (Courtesy Larry Edmunds Bookshop)

he became one of their first directors; but he moved to Essanay in 1911. Two years later, he opened the Essanay Ithica studio and when it was given up by the company, he and his brother Leopold kept it open and produced for Pathé and independent release. Under various film names (Star Company, Feature Film Company, International Film Service and Wharton, Incorporated), they released seven productions including four with Miss White and the famed *Patria* (1917).

Diando (D & O) was formed by a brilliant young executive and interpreter for Charles Pathé (Douglas) and the father of Baby Marie Osborne. A short-lived unit, it contributed the shortest full-fledged Pathé serial on record, *Terror of the Range* (1919). Upon dissolution of the company, Astra took over Diando's Glendale studio. Other early sources of product

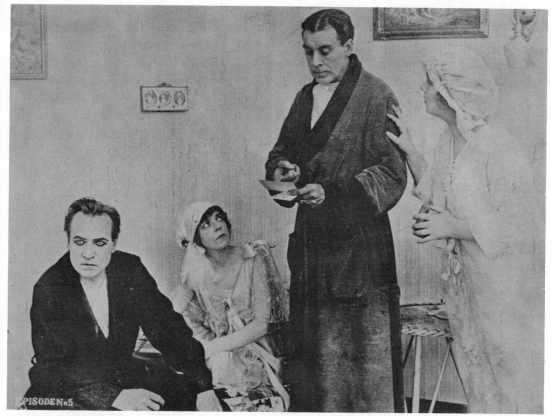

A hasty conference between heroes and heroines in *The Yellow Menace* (1916), a white supremacy serial starring Edwin Stevens as Ali Singh. From the expression shown here, the conclusions seem to run the gamut from "I think we've got him" to "Ah, what's the use?" (Courtesy Alan Brock)

were Brunton and Western Photoplay. The latter was controlled by Joseph A. Golden and served to introduce Charles Hutchison to the episode thrillers. Ruth Roland formed her own company which was financed mainly by Pathé. This carries the Pathé story roughly to 1920.

From this point on, Pathé began to display a curious mixture of ineptitude and sound critical judgment in its business dealings. On the one hand, it continued to subsidize production to such a degree and in such a manner that it approached the ridiculous. Producers such as Malcolm Strauss, C. W. Patton, Tom North and Schuyler Gray brought in ideas for serials which resulted in contracts and even advances on production costs, depending upon the case. After the signing of such a contract, the so-called producer could then go to a bank and get a large loan to start him off. This meant in effect that no actual cash belonging to the producer was at any time tied up in the effort. In addition to this, the studio and office space had to be rented, as Pathé had given up its Jersey City studio and Seitz had closed his.

All this meant that no actual financial responsibility was incurred or assumed by the independent producer. As if to compound this sometime grievous error, the entire production responsibility was then turned over to Pathé personnel with Seitz responsible for direction and Frank Leon Smith for story and script treatment. The producer therefore became a profitable bystander while the success of the venture fell entirely upon the skill and integrity of the Pathé people. On top of all this, extravagant cost

Lamar Johnstone meant business in *The Secret of the Submarine* (1916), as Hylda Hollis discovered. This was the first of the "preparedness" serials which preceded America's entry into World War I. (Courtesy Alan Brock)

Eileen Percy and Warner Oland in *The Third Eye* (1920). (Courtesy Alan Brock)

estimates and padding — plus cutting corners, shaving and trimming costs and even chiseling at times — stood the independent producer to good monetary advantage, as these areas were his responsibility and many rose to the occasion.

Pathé overlooked the fact that Seitz was not only an expert, but was honest. After he closed his studio, he became a mere hired hand who worked for and through independents as a Pathé staff man. Pathé was much more concerned with "financial responsibility." For example, C. W. Patton was a wealthy retired cattleman. This led the home office to associate him with the desired qualities of responsibility and reliability and thus they contracted with him to bring in various serials. All that he had to do was to post a performance bond, and as explained earlier, Pathé furnished the money and talent. He could hardly lose.

Each of the twenty-two chapters in *The Diamond From the Sky* (1915) found Irving Cummings fighting for his life.

On the other hand, Frank Leon Smith became quite disgusted at the manner and degree to which Pathé was actually exploiting itself for someone else's benefit. He finally managed to drive the point home to Elmer Pearson (vice-president and general manager) that Pathé was only kidding itself to the tune of huge sums. Pearson agreed and with nothing in the form of a written contract, Spencer G. Bennet and Smith became the actual producers of a number of the Miller-Ray epics beginning with *Play Ball* (1925). They made their chapter plays for the actual costs. All bills were sent to a unit accountant furnished by the home office and the two were on salary. They eliminated the traditional chiseling and padding and earned the respect of their crew, who followed the example they established. The entire unit worked hard to keep costs to a reasonable minimum, consistent with quality. After finished episodes were viewed by the Pathé Film Committee, a bonus was given to both men based on the number of Good and Nearly Good votes cast.

Thus, it can be seen that from the start, Pathé's policy opened avenues of opportunity for financial gain both for itself and for the individual producer. That it worked rather well cannot be denied. The Pathé Film Committee stood in judgment and kept quality at a high level throughout most of the silent period. A certain number of duds crept by, especially toward the end of the twenties, but Pathé usually had a large investment to protect. It also cannot be denied that the system worked against the company and its best interests in the long run. The total cost picture was often much higher than it should have been and ate into the huge profits more than necessary.

The Universal Film Manufacturing Company was the brain child of Carl Laemmle, the one-time clothing store manager from Oshkosh, Wisconsin. Laemmle had worked for his brother-in-law, Samuel Stern, and envisioned the day when he could go into business for himself. In 1905, armed with a savings account of $2500 and full of determination, he appeared in the Chicago office of Cochrane Brothers, an advertising agency concerned with clothing promotions. He had become acquainted via mail with Robert Cochrane and thought highly of his friend's advice.

While conferring with Cochrane in Chicago, Laemmle stumbled onto one of the Hale's Tours locations. Highly impressed with the apparent future of this device, he sold Bob Cochrane on his thinking and by 1906, they were involved in the exhibition of motion pictures. In the next few months, they entered the exchange business and headed on a collision course with the Motion Picture Patents Company. Formed in December 1908, the trust had rapidly organized the industry along lines established by J. J. Kennedy. Laemmle didn't agree with Kennedy and in April 1909 announced that his growing system of exchanges had gone "independent."

This helped to create a market for independently made films, but by midsummer it was evident that such production could not satisfy the market for a new product. Foreign films were used by the independent exchanges as a stop-gap measure. Although they prospered, audiences were not satisfied with the imports. The demand encouraged formation of many early independent producers among which were firms destined to play a large role in Laemmle's future. Rex was founded by Edwin S. Porter and William Swanson. P. A. Powers, a dealer in talking machines, hired Joseph A. Golden as his director and opened Powers Picture Plays. David Horsley went into business first with Centaur, then Nestor.

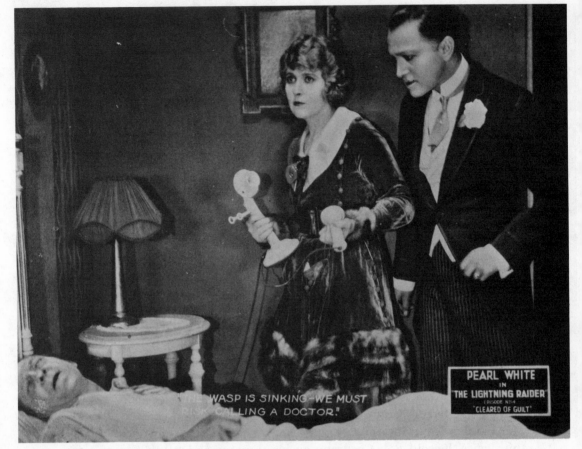

"THE WASP IS SINKING—WE MUST
RISK CALLING A DOCTOR."

PEARL WHITE
IN
"THE LIGHTNING RAIDER"
(EPISODE NO. 4)
"CLEARED OF GUILT"

With William Burt dying, Pearl and Henry G. Sell had to make a hard decision in *The Lightning Raider* (1919). (Courtesy Larry Edmunds Bookshop)

Under these circumstances, Carl Laemmle decided to go into production. The Independent Motion Picture Company (IMP) was established in the fall of 1909 by Tom Cochrane, another of the ad agency's members. Sent to New York City to make pictures, Cochrane rented space in the Actophone studio and hired William Ranous of Vitagraph as IMP's first director. This was to be the beginning of the Universal organization that would soon become one of the dominant forces in the industry.

In the meantime, Laemmle had been harrassing the Patents Company with weekly ads in the trade papers. His aggressive actions kept him in full view of the trust, which attempted vigorously to shut down IMP by legal and other means. The formation of the General Film Company was announced

"IF YOU KNOW THE TRUTH--TELL US--WASP!"

About to expire, William Burt tried to pass valuable information to Pearl and Henry G. Sell in *The Lighting Raider* (1919). (Courtesy Larry Edmunds Bookshop)

in 1910 and it immediately took over the exchanges belonging to Patent Company members. Successful efforts were shortly made to buy out independent exchanges. It was now full-scale war. The General Film Company was out to destroy all competition and monopolize the business. Strangely enough, for all of his maneuvering and annoyance to the trust, Laemmle was not the one directly responsible for breaking the stranglehold which the Patents Company tried to institute. This was left to The Greater New York Film Rental Company, owned by William Fox. It filed the suit which eventually resulted in a dissolution order. By the time that a final decision was made in 1917, the trust had been effectively dead for three years.

Life among the independent producers was not all a bed of roses during

Under the influence of the evil "Black Order," Jean Sothern was about to kill herself when Howard Estabrook intervened in *The Mysteries of Myra* (1916). (Courtesy Alan Brock)

this time. The Motion Picture Distributing and Sales Company had been formed in 1910 to market the wares of independent producers and to pool assets in the fight against the trust. Although Laemmle had been chosen president, Harry E. Aitken played an important role. Dissension between these two men resulted in a split by 1912. In March of that year, Aitken and John R. Freuler of the American Film Manufacturing Company formed the Mutual Film Corporation. June gave birth to the Universal Film Manufacturing Company with Laemmle at its helm. A disagreement between Laemmle and P. A. Powers led to a struggle for control. David Horsley's

Nestor stock played a leading role and the acquisition of his shares gave the Laemmle-Cochrane group a controlling interest. Powers was to hold on until 1920, when he sold out for a sum reputedly in the neighborhood of $2,000,000. Laemmle had come a long way in seven short years. He was now able to consolidate his gains into one of the largest motion picture organizations ever seen.

The entry of Universal into the continued picture field was not one of choice. It was dictated by the fabulous success posed by the immediate public acceptance of *The Perils of Pauline*. Universal sales people realized at once that their release program must be able to compete with Pathé. Serial production was the only answer. A two-reel western was expanded almost over-

Arline Pretty holds villain Fred Jones at bay as she awaits the arrival of police in *A Woman in Grey* (1920). (Courtesy Arline Pretty)

It looks as if Frank Wunderlee and Frank Lackteen are about to disagree over the spoils from Sunken Silver (1925)

Little Vonda Phelps, the victim of a balloon accident, was regarded with awe by the natives. Having fallen from the sky, there was little doubt in their minds that she was truly *The Jungle Goddess* (1922).

night into *Lucille Love, Girl of Mystery* (1914). Not so well remembered today as Miss White's initial effort, Grace Cunard's work in this chapter play placed her on the road to fame. It also proved beyond the shadow of doubt that there was a good deal of gold to be mined in this area of screen entertainment. From that point on, the serial became an important item in the Universal release schedule.

Universal turned out a different kind of serial product and for apparently valid reasons. Consider the philosophy behind the firm. For all of his pious statements about quality, Laemmle was interested in this aspect of production only to the degree that it might retard sales. Whereas Pathé attempted

PEARL WHITE
IN
"THE LIGHTNING RAIDER"
EPISODE Nº7
"MESHES OF EVIL"

"AND YOU CAN SEE WE NEED
PROTECTION, CHIEF."

As *The Lightning Raider* (1919), Pearl operated outside the law, but found ample opportunities to cooperate with the police during the course of fifteen exciting episodes. (Courtesy Larry Edmunds Bookshop)

to elevate their serials in all respects, Universal did not bother with any
form of quality control in the early days. Quantity and a strict adherence to
a release schedule were the prime determining factors. From its earliest
beginnings, contrary to the trade paper exhortations made by Laemmle,
Universal was an assembly line which turned out film footage for exhibition
and did it with startling efficiency. As such, it was a valuable school providing experience in all phases of film making, but little emphasis was placed
on superiority of release material. Some of the Universal serials prior to
1920 were exceedingly good, but mainly because of the people who formed
the particular unit that made such an effort. The front office was not constantly on the search for better material. In this respect, Universal was no
better or worse than many of the other early film companies.

Harry Marvin (Crane Wilbur) holds Pauline (Pearl White) affectionately as she recounts her wild trip aboard a runaway balloon in Episode 6 of *The Perils of Pauline* (1914), the best-remembered silent serial.

It was not uncommon for a director to take a crew on location and shoot four westerns at one time, using the same cast, props, scenery, etc. These were put together in the editing room where it often happened that there was only enough usable film to form three complete pictures but with a quantity of unused footage left over. Padded with subtitles, the fourth found its way to the screen. Operating under this philosophy, a director soon found himself capable of meeting the requirements in a satisfactory manner or he looked for a new job. However, as the firm continued to grow and prosper, personnel changed and the pictures became longer and more important. More pains were taken in the twenties but even then quality never received the same emphasis at Universal as it did at Pathé.

Whereas Pathé sublet the great bulk of its production to other firms, Universal made a large majority of its own chapter plays. During its peak, the corporation had a maximum of forty-two units producing at one time and not even Paramount or Metro-Goldwyn-Mayer could challenge its output.

Of the early pioneer firms, only Vitagraph followed the serial path. Vitagraph rose to a position of prominence behind Universal for a time. Its first serial effort had been a three-episode spoof on the detective stories in vogue at the time, *The Fates and Flora Fourflush* (1915). Announcement was made of *The Goddess* in May 1915, billed as the supreme artistic achievement of the chapter-play world. Vitagraph burned its financial fingers so badly on this serial that eighteen months passed before *The Scarlet Runner* was released. Tony Moreno and William Duncan became the two most valuable serial properties which the company possessed. William Duncan entered serials in 1917 and the following year found Moreno also thrilling weekly audiences. Duncan specialized in outdoor stories with a western flavor while Moreno made mysteries. The exploits of these two stars kept Vitagraph in the chapter-play field until the end of 1921. When Duncan moved to Universal, Vitagraph dropped the serial program completely.

By this time, the firm was in a different competitive position and a retrenchment was in order prior to its sale in 1925 to Warner Brothers. Although it was one of the earliest producers, Vitagraph had never grown too large. Albert E. Smith supervised production by himself after J. Stuart Blackton left the partnership. Smith, along with Cyrus Townsend Brady, conceived and watched over the majority of the formula thrillers made by the company. With a release schedule much smaller than either Pathé or Universal, only one year saw more than three Vitagraph serials placed in distribution.

Of the other early firms, the best example of their thinking is to be found in the history of Kalem. In 1907, three men of varied experience in the picture industry decided to enter the field on their own and organized a new company. The name was based on the initials of the founders; George Kleine, Samuel Long and Frank Marion. A delightfully simple arrangement, it began with a capitalization of $600 from the pocket of Marion. Kleine contributed a camera and Long owned a building. Long and Marion were experienced Biograph men while Kleine, a Midwestern dealer in optical goods, had become the leading exchangeman in the Chicago area. This was the firm that soon established the precedent of motion picture rights to literary works with their one-reel *Ben Hur*, which eventually cost them $25,000 plus court costs.

By 1908, Kalem's original capital was bringing in profits of over $5000

weekly. This figure continued to rise during the prosperous days of the
Patents Company, for their product was made with an eye to minimum
expenditure, simple stories and quantity production. The firm's immense
success continued to grow but the fundamental change brought about by the
feature picture during 1912–13 began to indicate that a policy change would
have to be made if Kalem were to continue to prosper. As a member of the
Patents Company, its product was marketed by the General Film Company,
which was in a bad way by this time. General's ideas were old-fashioned; its
leadership would not budge and an immense effort was being exerted to
hold the line and resist inevitable progress. The golden days of the trust
were rapidly ending.

Unfortunately, Frank Marion was either short-sighted or simply decided
that this risk was too great. Kleine had left for greener pastures by then and

RUTH ROLAND
IN
"THE TIGER'S TRAIL"
EPISODE NO.2
"THE GLOWING EYES"

BELLE BATTLES WITH BULL SHOTWELL
FOR THE IDOL.

Ruth Roland could fight her own battles, as Fred Kohler soon discovered in *The Tiger's
Trail* (1919). (Courtesy Larry Edmunds Bookshop)

If Louise Lorraine had known what was ahead *With Stanley in Africa* (1922), chances are good that she would have stayed in bed. (Courtesy Louise Lorraine)

Marion's policy regarded features as a gamble which was not worth the financial investment. He had decided to continue production as long as the demand for his one- and two-reel pictures remained constant. Once it fell off, he would close the doors and bow out gracefully. Kalem opened its doors to do processing for a number of the independents, and interestingly enough, Marion invested his money in stocks, buying shares of his competitors businesses.

The Kalem studio facilities were kept to a minimum, in line with the company policy. Air-drome studios were used, consisting of adobe floors and upright beams with sun screens to direct the natural lighting. This made it unnecessary to utilize artificial light and practically did away with scenery painting. Kalem troupes were thus able to plant a company anywhere on earth, sending their footage back to New York City for handling.

Joe Bonomo and Margaret Quimby made an important discovery in Chapter 4 of *Perils of the Wild* (1925). (Courtesy Joe Bonomo)

In 1917, the assets of Kalem were purchased for $100,000 by Vitagraph. The assets were mainly in the form of negatives and a few player contracts. Whenever a star really began to shine, no effort was made to retain the personality by a higher salary. The company remains important to the serial and its history mainly because of the impetus that it gave to the careers of J. P. McGowan, Helen Holmes and a few others. The continued photoplay held little appeal to Kalem but many series pictures in one- and two-reel lengths were made. The serial was in a sense too risky. A series could end at any time easily or be extended indefinitely — as was the case of *The Hazards of Helen* and *Grant, Police Reporter. The Girl from Frisco* was twice extended in production to a total of 25 double reels.

A combination of like circumstances afflicted Edison, Selig, Lubin and Es-

Jack Mower realized at once that his hidden treasure trove had been discovered in *Perils of the Wild*. (Courtesy Joe Bonomo)

sanay. Selig's important contributions after *The Adventures of Kathlyn* (1913) were made mostly as an independent showman. Edison serial output was as limited as the other pioneer firms, although it was the Edison studio that had started the development of the chapter-play format.

A typical reaction to the increasing popularity of lengthy films was exhibited by George K. Spoor of Essanay in July 1916. When queried by the trade media as to his feelings about longer films, Spoor replied: "The public wants varied programs of one, two and three reels with features thrown in as an occasional banquet. Patrons desire the pleasant informality of dropping into a theater at any time, instead of making it a ceremony, like a stage play." Spoor's short-sightedness was legendary in the industry. Reliance, Thanhouser and American — independent firms outside the Patents Company circle — were in no better shape as a result of the sharp warfare going on with the Mutual Film Corporation. By the time that Triangle was formed in 1915, Mutual was as sick as the General Film Company and soon died a lingering death after releasing a few serials which Helen Holmes had made for its Signal brand.

A proliferation of independent showmen crossed the silent screen and a representative number of serials were produced by these small firms. Quite a few of these were one-shot affairs in which the producer sought to extract the maximum gain from a minimum investment. A good example of such was *The Chinatown Mystery* (1928). This was produced by Trem Carr (of later fame with Monogram) at the Metropolitan studio. The story was writ-

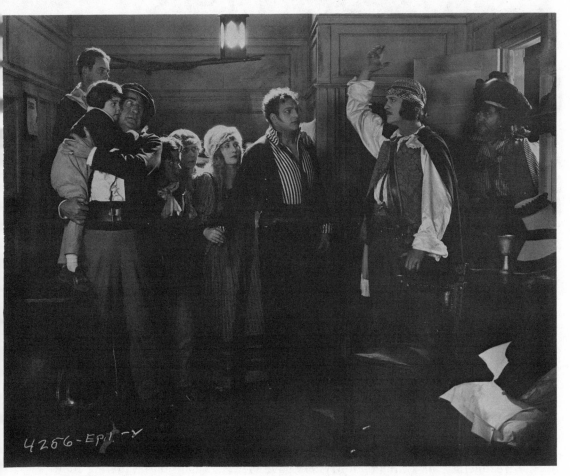

Jack Mower issued an ultimatum to the Robinson family in *Perils of the Wild* (1925). (Courtesy Joe Bonomo)

Allene Ray, J. Barney Sherry, and Walter Miller want the truth in *Play Ball* (1925) and it looks as if they'll get it. (Courtesy National Film Archive, Great Britain)

ten by Francis Ford, the old serial expert, and directed by J. P. McGowan. Joe Bonomo was hired for the lead and Ruth Hiatt, a Sennett comedienne, played the female interest with Ford also handling the villainy. This serial was really a gem in one respect, for the cast included many veterans of serial thrills, including Sheldon Lewis, Ernest Shields, George Chesebro, Jack Richardson, Grace Cunard, Rosemary Theby, Peggy O'Day, Duke Worne and Helen Gibson. Far from the typical independent serial in story and treatment, *The Chinatown Mystery* gave viewers a field day watching their old favorites in action once more, topped by the amazing athletics of Joe Bonomo.

Three independent companies led the way and their product was quite a cut above the rest. In point of time, Arrow was first. Formed by the Shallenberger brothers, it quickly gained a position of prominence within the state right field. The Shallenbergers broke into the motion picture business with an active participation in the affairs of the old Thanhouser Company. This led to a connection with the Syndicate Film Corporation, which had been established to finance and market *The Million Dollar Mystery* (1914), a Thanhouser production. In this capacity, W. E. Shallenberger was quickly impressed with the box office value of a properly done chapter play. The appreciation thus gained was carried on after the formation of Arrow.

While affiliated with Thanhouser, the Shallenberger fortunes mingled with another young man who was to stress the value of the serial as an entertainment form and profit maker. Born in Jamesville, Iowa, W. Ray Johnston was graduated from the College of Commerce in Waterloo. After his schooling was finished, Johnston went into the field of banking and real estate. It was in this capacity that he met the Shallenbergers. They introduced him to Charles J. Hite, president of Thanhouser. Hite placed Johnston on the payroll as his personal secretary and he was shortly appointed as treasurer of the Syndicate Film Corporation.

When Thanhouser stopped active production, Johnston left to join his friends at Arrow and soon became a vice-president. By 1924, he felt that his experience was broad enough to leave and form his own company, Rayart. *Battling Brewster* (1924) opened his program of chapter-play releases. The production of such films was farmed out to smaller independents with Rayart taking on the responsibility of distribution. Beacon Films, a creation of Robert Dillon and George Blaisdell, turned in chapter plays such as *The Flame Fighter* (1925), from a story written by Dillon. These were quite often on a par with the better independent serials.

On the other hand, Rayart handled some duds, such as *Secret Service Saunders* (1925). Thomas D. Van Osten, the publisher of the *West Coast Independent Exhibitor* (a trade paper), headed Califopictures, Incorporated and contracted a serial to Rayart. Richard Holt was borrowed from Gerson Pictures, another independent, to star with Ann Little; Duke Worne, the veteran chapter-play director was hired. Robert Dillon did the story, which was photographed mainly along the Pacific coast using hydroplanes, submarine chasers and many other gadgets associated with daring and danger. The later episodes shifted into the Sierra mountains for the climax. Exhibitors who had used serials for years hung their heads and cried as this one unreeled onto the screen. Audiences laughed out loud at the very moments they should have been hanging on the edge of their seats. It was that bad. Even Rayart felt that the less said about it the better.

192

Allene Ray has the drop on Frank Lackteen, whose gracious gesture in *The Fortieth Door*

Richmount Pictures Incorporated, headed by Dwight Leeper, handled the foreign market for Rayart. Leeper bought a half-interest in 1926. He was a busy individual who had held several different positions in the motion picture industry prior to acquiring an interest in the independent releasing firm. Among others, he was president of Monogram Pictures Corporation and the Photoplay Finance Corporation, which provided funds for Rayart. This purchase in the firm eventually would lead to the Monogram Pictures organization so well remembered in the sound era.

Rayart depended mainly upon Herbert Rawlinson and Ben Alexander to carry their chapter-play program. A tall, handsome native of Brighton, England, Rawlinson had arrived in the United States in 1910 as manager of

Marguerite Courtot listened intently as the Hindu mystic tried to convince her to become "The Veiled Priestess" in Chapter 4 of Kalem's *The Ventures of Marguerite*. (1915)

the Belasco Stock Company and entered films with Selig in 1911, making his first cinema appearance in *The Novice*. A long association with Universal in many society dramas never quite placed him on top. As an actor, he passed on his good looks and a flair for the "well-groomed" role. His career had consisted of parts requiring little in the way of dramatic action. Although Rawlinson's early work had been written in a way calculated to avoid action sequences, he gradually developed an athletic ability to the point of doing his own dangerous work for Rayart. Ben Alexander was a juvenile who was to win later fame on the television programs *Dragnet* and *Felony Squad*.

The third and most important of the independent serial makers was Nat Levine, who founded Mascot Pictures Corporation in 1926. Levine had

George Walsh and Louise Lorraine fell victim to slave traders while searching for Dr. Livingstone in *With Stanley in Africa* (1922). (Courtesy D. Elmo Brooks)

entered the film industry as a salesman and gradually became associated with Sam Bischoff of the California Studios. This relationship culminated in the production of a fifteen-episode thriller, *The Sky Skidder*. Distribution was arranged through the Universal exchanges and was accepted as a part of the 1926–27 Universal serial program under the release title, *The Silent Flyer* (1926). A chubby little man with somewhat imperious ways, Levine was a good showman who knew how to make money on a small investment. His secret was simple — give the public what it wanted. He was the kind of person one expected would come out on top. Working with a small capital investment, he had the reputation of being a slave driver. What made it

George Walsh discovered that the slave traders meant business. This subplot dominated *With Stanley in Africa* (1922), supposedly an historical serial dealing with the search of Stanley for the lost Dr. Livingstone. (Courtesy D. Elmo Brooks)

possible to work for Levine was the fact that he drove himself much harder than any of his staff.

Mascot received much of its financing from Herbert J. Yates' Consolidated Film Industries. Yates, an executive of the American Tobacco Company, had seen a future in movies at an early date. An association with Hedwig Labs in 1915 led to his financing of Republic Labs in 1918. The acquisition of several additional processing labs resulted in the formation of Consolidated in 1924 as a complete film laboratory service. It became the parent firm of American Records and Columbia Phonographs and also began to finance a number of independent producers. Levine was to eventually merge Mascot into Yates' Republic Pictures Corporation in the sound era.

The Mascot serial product set a high standard of quality for an independent firm. Technically, these serials were superior to those of the other independents. Story line was often sacrificed for action in that the plot was thin, but continuity was maintained by rapid pacing. Richard Thorpe, who directed many of the Mascot thrillers, has observed that once production began it moved so rapidly that the story writers were often behind in turning in scripts. There was a good deal of overtime and night work connected with Mascot filming, with no additional pay. Thorpe regarded Mascot as a good training ground for the director who wanted to learn the business and in his person, Levine had a director who could turn out entertainment with a touch of class. Although Mascot serials have often been termed "cheap," they were shining jewels compared to other independent releases and the company's reputation continued to acquire lustre.

As was the case with the small producers, Levine usually cast his chapter plays with former stars who no longer commanded steady work of any consequence at the major studios. The best example of this type of casting was found in *The Vanishing West* (1928), with Jack Daugherty, Jack Perrin, Leo Maloney, Eileen Sedgwick and Helen Gibson (one-time box-office greats) all appearing in the same serial. Mascot made good use of the talents of Yakima Canutt, an outstanding creator of dangerous action sequences. His appearance on screen always meant countless thrills for the audiences.

Such firms as that of the Weiss brothers existed at the other end of the independent spectrum. Louis Weiss was born and raised in New York City. At the age of fourteen, he went into business as a salesman, carrying a line of phonographs. Success followed and he was soon looking for new fields to conquer. His brothers, Max and Adolph, were operating movie theaters and Louis moved into the film business. Together, the three expanded their holdings into a chain of sixteen houses.

At this point, Louis decided to go into actual production and fourteen houses were sold, the remaining two leased. With the capital thus obtained,

Until well after World War I, main titles were simple and uncluttered as this one from *The Phantom Foe* (1920).

numerous production activities were brought into existence, including Artclass Pictures Corporation, Clarion Photoplays and two organizations for handling the production and distribution of the early Tarzan features and serial. Uninterested in art or even quality pictures, Artclass was active throughout the silent period and its three serial releases in the latter twenties appear to have established a new low in chapter play history. Poorly cast and ineptly directed, the stories were bad beyond belief and the screen treatment brought groans of disbelief from true serial fans.

Some firms found themselves distributing serials by a trick of fate. Such was the case with Goodwill Pictures of California. William Horsley's laboratory had done the processing and printing of two independent serials made by Ben Wilson for Davis Distributing Division with anticipated release through Vital Exchanges. The latter two firms collapsed financially and Horsley was left holding the prints and a rather large bill for the lab work. Combining with Barney Goodman, Horsley put *The Power God* (1925) and *Officer 444* (1926) on the market in an attempt to recoup his investment.

But as the twenties wore on, major serial companies went to great lengths to produce elaborate main titles for their wares, as seen by these examples taken directly from frames of the original 35mm prints.

THE RIDDLE RIDER

COPYRIGHT, 1924 BY UNIVERSAL PICTURES CORPORATION

THE WAY OF A MAN

"INTO THE UNKNOWN"

CHAPTER ONE PART TWO

PATHÉ
Presents

GLADYS McCONNELL and HUGH ALLAN
in

"THE FIRE DETECTIVE"

Adapted by   From a Story by
GEORGE ARTHUR GRAY   FRANK LEON SMITH

Passed by the   Pathéserial   Copyright MCMXXIX
National Board of Review   by Pathé Exchange, Inc.

CARL LAEMMLE
Presents

IN THE DAYS OF
DANIEL BOONE
With An All-Star Cast.

Passed by the National Board of Review.
Copyrighted 1923 by Universal Pictures Corporation.
Carl Laemmle ~ Pres.

3

Full Speed Ahead

As the motion pictures were big business, the executives who ruled the industry regarded their firms much as a textile manufacturer regarded his plant; that is, as an economic venture to gain a profit. In fact, many of the early companies called themselves "film manufacturing companies."[1] Thus, the production of any silent serial depended mainly upon the ability or desire of the producing firm to spend money in order to make money. Expenses for a cliffhanger were much the same as for a feature production. The sole criterion used by firms to judge the success or failure of a chapter play was the monetary return in excess of production costs. This particular philosophy determined the quality of most serials, and for that reason they had a certain sameness, regardless of who made them. This was true of nearly all producers, except Pathé, whose serial product was made or supervised by creative men rising to a challenge to do their best.

There were several reasons for the formula serial. The content had to be acceptable first of all to the company which produced it. At the same time, it had to satisfy the exchange which handled it, providing it was made by a company without distribution facilities. It also had to be satisfactory to the exhibitor as well as to the patron whose coin supported the theater. And above all, it must not offend the censors. With such a diverse group of interests to please, there is little wonder that many producers sought built-in safety features in their product by using a formula or stock approach. Unfortunately, this often reduced the chapter play to a common denominator which, although universally acceptable, was not at all creative.

---

[1] The following come to mind easily: The Albuquerque Film Manufacturing Co., American Film Manufacturing Co., Essanay Film Manufacturing Co., Masterpiece Film Manufacturing Co., Oz Film Manufacturing Co. and Universal Film Manufacturing Co.

Once in the can, the individual episodes were reproduced in the form of positive release prints for circulation. Due to the rather high costs of such prints, it was not economically feasible to provide enough release prints for each theater at the same time.[2] Preference had to be given to the larger houses. Thus, exchanges rented the available prints for either a flat fee or a percentage of the gross, depending upon the theater, the serial and its expected popularity.

The publicity and advertising departments were charged with the exploitation of the serial in order to bring it before the public and whet an appetite which would draw audiences. In the case of an independent production, the exchange had to gauge the appetite in order to determine the manner of booking, theater preference and proper rental fee. The best of efforts which ended in financial failure could only be regarded in terms of how much more money could have been lost had such efforts not been expended.

At Pathé, the serial genre was *big* business and a steady flow of product had to be assured. Once the contracts were signed and production began, everything had to meet a time schedule. Efficiency was the key to profit and an efficient serial production program meant having several episode scripts ready to go. The shooting of scenes on master sets and certain locations was arranged to be done at one time, regardless of the episodes in which the scenes took place. As a result, it was common practice to have quite a bit of approved film in the can prior to the delivery of the first completed episode. Naturally, editing and final polishing of the finished product was a slower affair than the actual shooting and it took much skill on the part of a team to keep ahead of a director like Seitz who could turn out fifty to eighty scenes a day, barring the inevitable retakes.

Once production was under way, the standard was to deliver one finished chapter per week (two reels). Even though it might have benefited a director to present a finished episode of 2000 to 2200 feet in order to assure action and story continuity, Pathé invariably cut each reel to 950 feet. The film reels used for exhibition had a capacity of 1000 feet and an oversize reel meant inevitable damage to the release print while it was in circulation. Another factor which entered the picture was that Pathé processed and printed its own prints. They were expensive and no more profit accrued from a full reel than from one carrying 950 feet. Thus it was that regardless of other considerations, the final product was 950 feet *with titles*. An excess of titles caused the exhibitors to suspect that money was being saved by a

---

[2] In an effort to hold costs down, Selig covered the entire nation with only twenty-four prints of *The Adventures of Kathlyn*. This economy failed to realize the serial's potential and accounts for the fact that there are no surviving prints.

Thousands of letters such as this were distributed to exhibitors by pioneer serial producers. This sales pitch was often used when early box-office returns indicated a less-
than-smashing success. But exhibitors soon became immune to such blatant deception
and the practice was discontinued. Feature producers then adopted the technique for
their own use, with more success.

producing firm. The exhibitors' attitude was simple — "the more titles, the
less pictures."

Production and payroll time for a ten-episode Pathé serial generally took
a minimum of fifteen weeks. A fifteen-episode chapter play used from twenty
to twenty-six weeks, especially if inclement weather upset the schedule. Long
production periods could and did create some ludicrous situations — a girl in
an evening gown might make an exit from a standing set and the follow-up
exteriors might not be shot until weeks later when there was snow on the
ground. In *The Phantom Foe* (1920), the villain's garb was a long overcoat

Walter Miller took his work seriously in *Queen of the Northwoods* (1929). (Courtesy Spencer G. Bennet)

of wolf fur with a high collar turned up and a fur cap. All this was necessary to hide his face and preserve the element of mystery. Propmen doubled for the villain and were dressed in a heavy coat. This was fine during the cool weather at the outset of filming, but the serial extended past the cold weather and into days blazing with heat. It was little wonder that the poor unfortunates cursed the stench and sweat of the fur coats (which had been sprayed with preservatives).

What determined the length of a Pathé serial? Certainly not story line. Frank Leon Smith, well-qualified to speak, has always maintained that any serial story could be well done in only three chapters. Thus the most logical answer would not deal with aesthetic reasons. Particular serial lengths seem to have been dictated by commercial reasons. *The Perils of Pauline* ran

Serial advertising and exploitation was a colorful adventure for theater patrons. Who could say what choice item would be given away next week? Here is an unused "Crolette," distributed by Warton, Inc. as an advertising giveaway and handed out by theatres to announce the arrival of *The Mysteries of Myra* (1916), a story of the occult. Notice the use of the term "series." Producers in 1916 had not yet evolved a strict definition for "series" and "serial," often using them interchangeably or even together in the same breath.

twenty episodes and *The Exploits of Elaine* (1914–15) cycle ran thirty-six chapters. Other Pathé releases went out in seven, nine and fourteen episodes. However, the general and most accepted length was a fifteen-episode serial consisting of thirty-one reels.

Pathé's first episode was usually three reels long in order to set the stage properly. The first three episodes were the sales chapters, introducing the cast and story and moving the entire affair off to a rushing and exciting start. As they were the samples used to secure bookings, much care was generally taken in establishing an especially strong beginning. The middle chapters might or might not be weaker, depending upon the case, but the final chapter had to be a strong one. It was as important as the beginning, for it was used to wrap up the entire affair and leave both the exhibitor and audience with a desire to see another Pathé serial.

Pathé determined from its salesmen that fifteen chapters were considered by many exhibitors to be too many and Frank Leon Smith turned out *Bound and Gagged* (1919) in ten episodes. Although very successful, both lengths were used for some time. By the middle twenties, the ten- or twelve-installment length was accepted and adhered to by Pathé as well as many independents and eventually even Universal. This served as a relief for the writer as the fifteen-chapter format could be and was a terrible strain on the scripters. If it had an exceptionally weak plot, even the most resourceful, clever and inventive writer was constantly faced with a story which wanted to end and yet had to be kept alive by artificial respiration.

This problem was not restricted to fifteen- or eighteen-chapter serials; it even affected the shorter format after a fashion. An excellent example of such a story was scripted by Robert Dillon for his Beacon serial, *The Flame Fighter*, released by Rayart in 1925. Put simply, the plot revolved around a metropolitan fire department and one fireman in particular, Jack Sparks, who battled corruption in city hall.

By means of a well-staged fire, Sparks (played by Herbert Rawlinson) was established as an unqualified hero in the opening chapters. But by Episode #3 the pace had slowed to a crawl, and as the serial approached the half way mark, the Fire Commissioner had disappeared under mysterious circumstances and Sparks had been publicly disgraced by the crooked contractors.

The remaining episodes were concerned with an effort by Sparks to acquire a copy of the doctored bids as evidence of the corruption. As staged in the serial, this took a mere four minutes of the five chapters. The rest was padding in the form of unrealistic and unmotivated fistic encounters and the reintroduction of characters via subtitles. Each even-numbered chapter went through the tedious process of "calling roll" and explaining what had happened thus far to each individual.

The final chapter wrapped up the story with a happy ending by explaining that the Fire Commissioner, sensing a devious plot on the part of the contractors, had disappeared of his own volition to force the crooks to show their hand. Even with the excess padding removed, *The Flame Fighter* would still have had a difficult time adequately occupying five chapters. It was in this kind of internal problem that the silent serial faced the most serious threat to its survival.

From its very beginning through the end of the silent serial, Pathé was

When properly assembled, the "Crolette" was supposed to possess unusual powers. To quote from the directions printed on its back, "The best results are to be obtained if two persons, preferably of opposite sex, sit in a quiet, dimly lighted room by themselves. Under the influence of certain people of particularly nervous temperament, the Crolette will be found to work to greater advantage . . . . Questions should not be of a frivolous nature . . . . those which may be answered by "Yes" or "No" will be found much more desirable. After the question has been asked you will find that the Crolette, after a few false starts, will write its message on the paper." Here you see the Crolette in action, over a half century after it was given to some theater patron.

Serial scenes like this one from *The Terrible People* (1929) upset the censors, but fans greeted them with bated breath and quickening pulses. Surely Allene Ray will escape — it's only Episode #3. (Courtesy John Hampton)

the champion and never regarded any other serial production firm as a serious threat. Pathé was the only company which consistently strove for the highest in quality. At its start, it was the company best prepared and qualified for serial success, mainly because it was basically a French firm. The American branch was headed by Louis J. Gasnier, a serial genius who possessed an extensive background knowledge of melodrama production acquired in France. The staff in the New York office was multi-national (twenty-seven languages were spoken there) and was in touch with all facets of film production, distribution and sales over the face of the earth. Gasnier originated the concept which he called the "sportaletic" American

ANTONIO MORENO
in
'THE VEILED MYSTERY'
A Vitagraph Serial
EPISODE 9
"The SLIDE FOR LIFE"

GATHERING UP THE SCATTERED
GOLD TREASURE.

Tony Moreno, Pauline Curley and Nenette de Courcy didn't realize it, but George
Cooper and Henry Barrows were the villains of *The Veiled Mystery* (1920). (Courtesy
Nan Boardman)

girl, or what we would now call the young American sportswoman. In this
role, he cast Pearl White. Pathé always had the best villains, as Gasnier
understood perfectly the importance of the Villain as the key figure in
chapter plays. Warner Oland drew a salary of $1000 weekly for his still-
remembered portrayals.

Creative talent abounded at Pathé, in the form of Seitz, Bennet, Smith,
Millhauser and Willets. They were head and shoulders above the average
practitioners of the craft. They remained loyal to the firm, in contrast to
many of the other good men who were forever moving on, seeking something better. Working hand-in-glove with the creative people, the highly

ANTONIO MORENO
in
'THE VEILED MYSTERY'
A Vitagraph Serial
EPISODE 10
"A DEMONS DEVICE"

ETHEL AND TOM SECRETED IN A TRICK PIANO.

Following the instructions of *The Veiled Mystery* (1920), George Cooper and his hench-men prepared to spirit Nenette de Courcy and her faithful friend away in a trick piano. (Courtesy Nan Boardman)

efficient New York office was well organized in the form of a Scenario Committee. This group passed judgment on every script which was up for production after a careful consideration had been made of all its aspects. The Scenario Committee went over each and every serial script – inch by inch – with the writer. Each scene, subtitle, cut, revision and correction had to be made and approved prior to the script's being released for production.

Once the scripts were approved and turned over to the talent, the Pathé Film Committee began to function. Screening all of the finished product, it gave a verdict which proved to be priceless. This served much the same function as a private preview but the opinions were frank and rendered before any paying audience would ever see it. This meant that there was still time

Although it was only Episode #2, Allene Ray was already in the clutches of the *Hawk of the Hills* (1927).

left to improve and polish if necessary prior to actual release. Members of the Scenario Committee and the Serial Sales Manager sat in judgment with the Pathé Film Committee on each screening and various executives whose functions related to publicity, promotion and advertising were also invited in.

Pathé was not afraid to lay out money, and even though it was taken for a ride at times, the company attitude and money showed on the screen in production values. The industry itself paid Pathé its due by referring to its product as having "feature quality." This quality was eagerly sought by the company executives but many were the times when they rendered a verdict of "too classic" to the production people. It was a strange paradox that although the company deliberately went after a top-quality product, the exhibitors often complained that it was "too highbrow" for their audiences. Thus you had a continual struggle in which the writer and director found themselves squarely in the middle and not certain in which direction to turn. Happily, although this double standard did exist, it did not become prominent until long after Pathé serials had been standardized in form and content as a medium suitable for family audiences. The creative serial talent kept on trying for results acceptable to adults, but reality forced the sales people and exhibitors to accept the fact that box-office money came mostly from children. Serials rarely hit the big houses, which catered to a transient trade that had not seen earlier episodes and would not see subsequent ones.

Finally, Pathé had the greatest film sales force in the motion picture world and exposure of its product reached the far corners of the globe. The product was backed up by extensive and effective advertising and exhibitors were supplied with everything that they needed to put the show over.

The situation was somewhat different at Universal which operated under a set of rules of its own. Production was all very informal in the early days. A serial unit crew at Universal in 1915 averaged only seven members. All pitched in to make the picture a success. Without union restrictions, a director was able to exchange positions with the cameraman in order to capture on film exactly what he visualized. As with many other serial-releasing firms, Universal placed the initial episodes on the market before the completed cliffhanger was in the can. Normal production time for a single installment was one working week and a unit would turn out a completed eighteen-episode serial in four months.

It was not uncommon, however, for a production unit to fall behind schedule due to a script delay or inclement weather. Universal crews did not begin a serial by shooting stock footage to weld into finished chapters. Each episode was shot by itself. This sometimes worked a hardship on meeting deadlines. When such a delay held up shooting, production became a race against time. At times, this meant beating the clock by shooting a complete chapter in one day. In such a case, it was generally shot "in the camera" and very little editing was done. The finished chapter was allowed to pass on whatever merits it possessed. Many times such an episode did very little to advance the plot and exhibitors were quick to scream to salesmen and trade papers.

Under such hurried circumstances, the film was processed, titled and shipped the same evening. This was made possible by the clever use of subtitles. As a serial chapter generally ran between 1600 and 2000 feet, the finished footage was measured and the subtitles were then lengthened pro-

portionately to fit. Addition of the 100 to 300 foot overlap from the previous chapter meant that much less work and served to refresh the mind
of the viewer as to the peril of the previous episode.[3] This process worked
both ways. When final footage was too long but it was felt that all of it
was necessary to tell the story, the needed subtitles were shortened and the
overlap was brief or non-existent. In this manner, the footage could be
made to fit two reels.

When Jacques Jaccard became ill during the production of *Liberty, a
Daughter of the USA* (1916), Henry McRae took over as director and
began shooting the twelfth episode at 1:00 P.M. By 4:30 that same afternoon, McRae had finished the chapter and during the following thirty-eight
working days (including those ruined by inclement weather), he shot seven
more completed episodes. This is speed in any man's book.

The amount of raw film stock used in a serial varied with the firm and
the talents of those shooting it. A typical fifteen-episode chapter play consisted of roughly 30,000 feet of finished footage. To produce this, the rule
of thumb was 90,000 to 120,000 feet of exposed film. Eddie Polo shot 400,000
feet for his independent *Captain Kidd* (1922), a good indication that someone didn't know exactly what he was doing. The all-time record stands at
960,000 feet for *Gloria's Romance,* the Billie Burke serial of 1916 and a
box-office failure.

A most intriguing area of serial production revolved around the actual
costs of a chapter play. A true and realistic determination of costs sets forth
a more profound mystery than any that ever appeared on the serial screen.
Serial production was an adventure in itself and attracted not only ethical
persons but also those without the slightest understanding of principles.
Chapter plays, as with any other type of screen production, held a powerful
attraction for the sincere and talented, as well as the greedy. Great opportunities for graft existed in production, where money was free-flowing and
audits were difficult. A great deal of backroom and under-the-table negotia-
ting between the producers and releasing houses was common as well as
the kickback and payola. Frank Leon Smith put it very succinctly when
he said, "How to learn about production costs when everybody lied to
everybody else?" Of course, this is a wry comment on a certain portion of
those involved in serial production, for others were very honest and busi-
nesslike about costs.

During the period 1913–18, all costs were reasonably low — casts, mate-

---

[3]This practice was introduced by Pathé in *Double Adventure* (1921) ostensibly to give the audience a chance to make the transition to a new episode with an understanding of the sequence of
the story. It had been used by Universal for several years prior to Pathé's adoption.

Allene Ray and Marie Mosquini have just started their search for *The Black Book* (1929). Miss Mosquini made hundreds of short comedies with Charley Chase and Snub Pollard before bowing out of the silent film in this last of the Pathé serials.

A serial heroine's life was not one of ease. Marie Walcamp's chapter plays invariably brought her face-to-face with a big cat. Shortly after this publicity still was taken for *The Lion's Claw* (1918), this cat turned on her. She carried the resulting scars for the rest of her life.

Ethlyne Clair's first serial role was *The Vanishing Rider* (1928) with William Desmond.

rials, labor, prop constructions and rentals. An expensive fifteen-episode serial such as *Patria* (1917) could be brought in for $90,000 during this time.
A sharp rise in all costs except cast and studio labor took place in the years
1919–23. Only the electrical union commanded real power at this time. Without an Actors Guild, the oversupply of actors kept salaries from rising out of
their low bracket, relative to other aspects of cost. This applied to all but
a handful of proven box-office attractions.

To whatever monetary gripes a star might have had, Universal replied
with publicity. If a serial leading man became restless with his salary and
went to the front office for an adjustment, he was met with a stone-faced

Harry Schumm's portrait graced the novel giveaway used to exploit *The Broken Coin* (1915). After the coin was struck, Universal extended the serial to 44 reels over 22 weeks. One recently sold for $50.00. (Courtesy Jay Guren)

Some examples of serial advertising art, from *Moving Picture World* magazine.

A Face As
Well-Known
As the "Man
in the Moon"

BURSTON FILMS Inc.
Presents
THE FIRST SERIAL DE LUXE
KING BAGGOT in
"The Hawk's Trail"
with
GRACE DARMOND and
RHEA MITCHELL

Grace Darmond
Rhea Mitchell

Directed by
W.S. VanDyke
Produced under the
Personal Supervision of
LOUIS BURSTON

The first serial of noteworthy distinction, starring
KING BAGGOT in a protean role of
10 GREAT CHARACTERIZATIONS
supported by Grace Darmond and Rhea Mitchell.
An all-star cast of twelve principals—
A story of unequalled interest—
A Phenomenal opportunity for state-rights buyers
who act NOW.

Produced by
BURSTON FILMS INC.
NEW YORK
Distributed by
W. H. Productions Company
71 West 23rd Street, N. Y.

They Begged Us To Make It A Jewel Feature!

THEY didn't want to see it—that hard-boiled Jewel Department. But they finally came in and sat thru a solid hour of "The Scarlet Streak." Then the roof shivered. They all shouted at once: "Marvelous! Wonderful! Great! A double wow-wow! Give it to us! Make it a super-jewel" they begged. "Nothing doing," was the answer, "it's scheduled as a serial, and as a serial it stays." They begged with all but tears in their eyes, they pleaded, threatened. They said we were losing a fortune to sell it at serial prices. It hurt to refuse them. But we stick to our word. It has everything you pray for—everything audiences dream about. Suspense, romance, novelty, action, and thrills upon thrills in wild profusion. It's a gold mine, a mint, a Bonanza, treasure chest, all rolled up into one and multiplied by ten —really the first great first-run serial!

THE SCARLET STREAK

starring
JACK
DAUGHERTY

with a dazzling all-star cast including Lola Todd, Al Smith, and Virginia Ainsworth.
Directed by
HENRY McRAE

One of Universal's "Lucky Six" Adventure Serials

HARRY GROSSMAN PRESENTS

CRAIG KENNEDY

The SERIAL

Story Arthur B. Reeve
by &
John W. Grey

The STARS

HERBERT RAWLINSON
and
MARGARET MARSH

OLIVER FILMS Inc.

I. OLIVER PRESIDENT
THREE HUNDRED and EIGHT EAST FORTY EIGHTH STREET
NEW YORK CITY

The GREEN ARCHER

WITH Allene Ray AND Walter Miller

As great a mystery as any Sherlock Holmes ever had to solve.

A heartless, cruel, criminal millionaire brings a castle from England, stone by stone, and erects it on the Hudson.

Does he also import the ghost of the ancient archer who haunted the historic structure in England? How else can be explained the mysterious figure which stalks the corridors at night, a deadly menace to the oppressor?

Is the charming girl who lives near by, the Green Archer? Is it her father? Is it her father's friend? Is it the handsome captain of the state troopers who is in love with the girl?

As a feature it would be great. As a serial it is a sensational, surprising triumph.

Directed by Spencer Bennet
Scenario by Frank Leon Smith
From the book by Edgar Wallace

Pathéserial

TRADE MARK

reply, regardless of whether or not he deserved more money. All such demands were countered as a matter of policy with the statement, "We won't give you more money, but we will give you more publicity." This meant a larger name on the marquee. Many egos were satisfied with this arrangement. Others wondered out loud how larger block letters on a poster would feed and clothe them. If one were deserving and so bold as to utter such an unmentionable thought, a begrudged raise often followed an agonizing hesitation during which other ointments were offered to soothe the wound.

American serials were popular abroad, sometimes earning more in foreign than domestic release. The Trans-Atlantic Film Company, Ltd. handled English distribution of Universal serials and remade titles for each serial. Here you see the episode title taken directly from a Trans-Atlantic print of *Liberty, a Daughter of the U.S.A.* (1917). Originally three reels, the first episode was recut to two.

Although Eddie Polo's role in the serial had been a supporting one, American distribution of *Liberty* brought him so much fan mail that he received equal billing with Marie Walcamp in the English release of about one year later. (Courtesy Wilfred J. Horwood)

By the latter twenties, episode costs ranged from $4000 to $10,000. A special serial such as *The Fighting Marine* (1926) was budgeted higher. In the case of this particular chapter play, the stellar attraction was Gene Tunney. He received a straight salary of $2000 per week for twelve weeks and in addition was guaranteed 25 per cent of the gross receipts. This was a very costly arrangement for Pathé, which was paying its top serial star (Allene Ray) a paltry $500 weekly.

The actual production of silent photoplays involved many problems that seldom come to mind as the images cavort across the screen. When viewing early serial chapters today, the audience is often appalled by the harshness of the scenes, that is, the relatively few tonal gradations between black and white. This was a problem which the early producers were also quite concerned about. The very early photographic emulsions were non-color-sensitive, meaning that they responded almost exclusively to the bluish light in the spectrum. Other colors appeared darker on the screen than they were in real life. An improvement called orthochromatic stock made its appearance. This was sensitive to green as well as blue, but not to red. It was with this film that a majority of the silent serials were filmed. Although the chapter plays appeared more lifelike as the twenties approached, it was due to other tricks of the trade, not to emulsion improvements.

As the art of cinematography developed, it became apparent that what appeared on the screen was an illusion within an illusion. In the early days, studio lighting was not well-developed and the slow film necessitated the use of bright sunlight. The headache of deep, dark facial shadows accentuated by the harsh tones of the primitive film stock was fought with makeup, in an effort to whiten the face. Lips also had to be emphasized. This was done in a variety of ways, depending upon the effect desired. As the eyes were regarded as unequalled instruments for transmitting emotion, mood, action and thought, their power was relied upon to a great degree by the early producers. Nothing directly could be done to strengthen their power so the treatment was confined to their setting. Thus, eyebrows and eyelashes, as well as underlids, were freely treated with a black or dark green eye pencil to throw the eye into the strongest possible relief and hold the attention of the audience.

Although film stock remained fairly constant, the quality of equipment rapidly increased. By the end of World War I, a modification of closeup and medium shots was in vogue among cameramen. Accomplished by the use of diffusion, this was in many cases a near necessity, as the sharp lens combined with the ortho film to reveal unmercifully the physical defects of featured players.

Similar tricks were resorted to regarding clothing. In many early films available for viewing today, scenes containing a large amount of white are difficult to watch because of the lack of detail. Under the concentrated rays of early studio lighting or bright sunlight, white became too reflective and cast a halo or halation around the figure wearing it. This reduced clarity and detail, and generally contributed to a destruction of the mood of the film. As techniques improved, it was found that solid whites could be controlled to solve the problem of halation. This was done by using a special backing on the film stock. Instead of white photographing as white, it appeared streaked or grey at best. It was then found that light blues, yellows and pinks gave a perfect white while red reproduced more nearly black in appearance than black itself. The shimmering white gown of the heroine, which often provoked favorable comment from the feminine members of the audience, was not white but a soft pastel. The black coat of the villain was really a dark red and probably of cheap material. Common and inexpensive textiles produced the best photographic results. Glossy and shiny materials were studiously avoided.

With the development of more skillful lighting and the placement of reflectors to yield modeling and form, makeup was reduced to a facial "toning." The combination facilitated facial expression which was more natural. A giant step forward came in 1924 with the introduction of panchromatic film. This new film was sensitive to practically the entire spectrum and recorded the proper tonal relationship. Requiring only a slight overemphasis with makeup, this film made revolutionary changes possible in lighting, settings, makeup and photography.

There were many tricks and shortcuts used to provide the thrills found weekly on the serial screen. Some were developed specifically for the serials and later used for fast-action features. Others were adaptations of techniques used by the feature directors.

Let's dissect one action scene common to many of the silent serials, as well as their counterpart in the sound era. The hero, Fearless Freddie, and the villain, Black Bart, are engaged in a desperate, last-ditch struggle atop a high ledge. Battering blows are exchanged for awhile, with Freddie eventually forcing Bart to the edge of the cliff. A well-placed final blow sends Bart reeling backward and over the cliff to certain destruction below. Freddie brushes himself off and walks over to the spot where Adoring Anne is waiting to embrace him.

An exciting exchange of fists, with certain doom as the reward for the loser, was guaranteed to keep the audience on the edge of its seats and variations of this particular scene were found quite often in the cliffhangers. How was it done? As realistic as it appeared on the screen, we know deep inside that no man could possibly survive that fall, much less stand up under such a punishing barrage of blows as we have witnessed.

As the Fighting Marine (1926), Gene Tunney's excursion into the chapter-play world treated fans to amazing demonstrations of his boxing skill and was well-received at the box-office.

Let us imagine that we were present while the scene was filmed. At the outset, the fight was carefully planned; and it was staged from beginning to end: Each man knew how and where to move so that the scene might progress as the director desired. The actors went through the sequence in normal action, but what about those smashing blows which we saw in close-ups? Freddie had tapped his opponent gently throughout the fight as the camera turned.

What we saw on the screen was given impact and speed by an editing trick. The cutter removed every third or fourth frame from the sequence

With clenched fists and six-shooter, Frank Lackteen and Charles Brinley lay down their terms in *Idaho* (1925). A stronger title would have been more descriptive of the Western chapter play. (Courtesy Frank Lackteen)

which showed moving fists. Used in moderation, this technique produced realistic effects when projected. What about the climax? Good villains were difficult to obtain, as well as being expensive. When the time came for Freddie's rush for Black Bart, ending with the conclusive blow, the cameras were stopped. Both men took up predetermined positions at the edge of the cliff and Bart leaned backward as far as possible. Freddie placed his fist on Bart's jaw and let it rest there lightly. With the cameras turning backward, he suddenly pulled it away. Bart staggered forward slightly, straightened up and they began fighting again.

When the scene was flashed on the screen, it appeared that Freddie had slugged Bart with a tremendous punch which sent the villain staggering backward over the cliff. At this point, a rapid cut-in view from another angle, usually below and at a distance, showed a dummy or stuntman representing Bart going over the cliff to his doom. Carefully handled, it was most effective.

This is not to suggest that danger was completely avoided in serial making. On the contrary, it was ever-present and at least one accident marred most chapter play efforts. Eddie Polo, an accomplished acrobat at seven who had worked for seventeen years with Barnum and Bailey before entering pictures in 1914, was seriously injured when trampled by a horse during the filming of *Bulls Eye* (1918). Marie Walcamp broke a wrist making *The Red Ace* (1917) and was badly clawed by a lion in *The Lion's Claw* (1918). Priscilla Dean fractured an arm during the seventh episode of *The Gray Ghost* (1917) and was unable to return until Chapter 12. Joe Rickson fell over a cliff in *The Purple Riders* (1921), breaking his leg in a fifty-foot fall.

As stars became more important, all possible efforts were made to avoid the possibility of injury, but even the use of stuntmen could not guarantee against an unforseen accident. Serial adventure not only made stunt doubles necessary, it also created a demand for bodies that could be destroyed. Since such a body usually represented the villain's henchman, an innocent bystander, or some other character expendable to the story, the answer was not at all complex — a dummy. What was difficult was the construction of a suitable and satisfactory substitute that would give the appearance of a life-like human. A dummy had been used as early as 1903 in *The Great Train Robbery*, but clothes stuffed with straw and thrown from a moving locomotive no longer convinced audiences in the serial days.

Early dummies had heads of plaster, and while close in appearance to human heads, they were easy to break and nearly impossible to repair. The rough handling required by a scene could destroy the illusion by shattering the plaster head. *Papier-mâché* heads came next and proved to be much more satisfactory. Less subject to inadvertant damage, they could also be patched, repainted and used over. Wigs were glued to the head, combed out and cut to whatever hair style was to be imitated.

By the twenties, property departments were mainly concerned with maximum realism from a dummy's performance and efforts were directed toward this art. Dummies had become expensive and every effort was made to retrieve them for later use. Some, the victims of many violent deaths, had a rather long screen career and were regarded quite affectionately by the property men. Other were, of course, destroyed forever in explosions and other violent action.

At the beginning of the serial period, the ballyhoo in conjunction with the

As *Daniel Boone* (1922), Jack Mower knew that Ruth Royce was lying, but he couldn't prove it until Chapter 15. (Courtesy Don Overton)

exploitation of chapter plays was original, brassy and bold. Standard accessories such as the one-, two- and three-sheets, posters, stills, slides and advertising mats were supplied in the same manner as with features. However, the serial format was much more exploitable than a feature and few opportunities were lost in those early days. Most of the publicity was created by the releasing company on a nationwide basis. Nearly every early serial had a tie-in with a newspaper chain to publish and syndicate the episode stories in an effort to attract attention. Claims regarding the success and value of this publicity quickly reached ludicrous proportions. Thanhouser's *Million Dollar Mystery* (1914) claimed that over 500 of the nation's leading papers were actively participating by featuring the stories. Universal blasted back in no uncertain terms that over 2000 leading papers in the country were running the syndication of *The Black Box* (1915).

Marie Walcamp had a bright career in serials from 1916 until she retired prematurely in 1920. A comeback attempt some years later failed, but fans still remember her as *Liberty, A Daughter of the U.S.A.* (1916). (Courtesy Alan Brock)

Contests of all types were sponsored by the releasing firms in an effort to focus attention on their product. Thanhouser ran a contest offering $10,000 for a 100-word solution to be used in the twenty-third chapter. American offered $5,000 for the best idea for a sequel to *The Diamond from the Sky* (1915). Universal offered a large sum for the secret of *The Black Box*. Many other chapter plays were advertised in the same manner and entries flooded into the companies by the thousands from across the nation. This type of exploitation, which had started with the expenditure of $25,000 in prize money in conjunction with *The Perils of Pauline* (1914), was to fade away rather quickly, to be followed in a few short years with the disappearance of the syndicated newspaper episodes. However, while it lasted such exploitation made quite an impression on fans.

But there were other ways to get publicity. To gain nation-wide attention for *Runaway June* (1915), Reliance announced a unique contest in March 1915. Advertisements were taken in *The Saturday Evening Post* and other leading magazines to inform the public of its opportunities to participate. Each theater that entered the competition was to have three votes per installment. One coupon was given away with each ticket sold and used by the patrons to vote for a person of their choice. By the process of voting and elimination as the episodes progressed, each state was to have a winner by September 30. The Canadian provinces also had one winner each.

In October, all fifty-five contestants were treated to a free trip from their homes to California to attend the Panama-Pacific Exposition in San Francisco and then on to the San Diego Exposition. Maids, manicurists, hair stylists and dressmakers were put at the disposal of each finalist for the duration of the trip. All expenses were taken care of by Reliance. Needless to say, the contest gave a boost at the box office to a serial that needed help. Without the interest created by this exploitation, it is rather doubtful that *Runaway June* could have been more than a mediocre success.

Pearl of the Army (1916) got away to a fast start at the box office. It had benefited greatly from the nationwide interest created by an unusual advance teaser campaign which the Pathé publicity department staged. The effect of such a campaign today would be open to conjecture, for the serial was concerned with national defense and the publicity, which appeared first in the two leading papers of the 100 largest cities in the United States, suggested that a traitor was loose in our midst. In light of the discovery of real spies among us since World War II, such a publicity stunt today would most likely draw severe criticism, provided it was even allowed to continue to its conclusion.

It went this way. Washington, D.C. was the stage and the following advertisement was released to the papers at 10:00 A.M. on Sunday, November 26, 1916.

$5000 REWARD FOR INFORMATION ! ! ! !

Regarding man of foreign appearance, military bearing, about 6′ with light hair and a double horse shoe scar on his left cheek. The man answering this description is believed to have left Washington. He was last seen taking a taxi from the New Ebbitt Hotel to Union Station. A few minutes previously, a package of vitally important papers and documents disappeared. Address Ralph Payne, Room 200, New Ebbitt Hotel, Washington, D.C.

For the next five days, the phone rang continuously, letters poured in from across the nation, representatives of other news media visited the hotel to follow the story. Thousands of leads on a non-existent man resulted. On Monday, November 27th, a variation of the first advertisement was again placed in the same papers and the uproar continued into Tuesday, when a

Frank Lackteen menaced Allene Ray in numerous Pathé serials throughout the twenties. Patrons who watched this one received free puzzles containing scenes from *Hawk of the Hills* (1927).

third variation also appeared. The interest created was maintained at a high pitch, for the pace of patriotic citizens doing their duty by mail, phone and in person did not diminish. On Wednesday, the fourth advertisement was released.

RAISE YOUR BID ! ! OTHERS WILL PAY MORE ! !

I have received this unsigned letter, delivered by an unknown messenger. I have offered all the money I have. You will serve your country if you will help me with information regarding the writer of this letter and $25,000 will be paid for the return of the package with seals unbroken which disappeared from my room at the New Ebbitt Hotel. Address Ralph Payne, Room 200, New Ebbitt Hotel, Washington, D.C.

As a result of this advertisement, the hubub rose to a new high and Pathé was satisfied that enough interest had been created. The hoax was revealed on Thursday in a nice long advertisement inviting the public to see *Pearl of the Army* and cautioning that the possibility of spies in America had not lessened. "Let every patriotic citizen beware!"

On the other hand, Universal's campaigns were rather tame at this time. To exploit *The Purple Mask* (1916) in Canada, a limerick contest was announced. Each entry had to contain the name of Cunard, Ford and *The Purple Mask*. Winners received large personally autographed photographs of the stars. Several million inch-square cubes had been handed out to theater patrons to publicize *The Black Box* and *The Broken Coin* found audiences clutching their facsimile coins as they watched Cunard and Ford in action. Interestingly enough, coin collectors have recently paid as much as $50 for one of these in good condition. *The Red Ace* (1917) used puzzles, pincushions, children's tops and pin-on buttons, all prominently featuring Marie Walcamp and the name of the serial. Thus, quite a difference existed in the approach and intensity of national advertising during this period. But by the end of the war, the serial was quite able to hold its own and drew audiences by virtue of habit, star and story.

Exploitation on the local level then became a dominant part of selling the public. It had existed from the very beginning but remained in the shadow of the national publicity generated by the releasing firms. Stepping into the limelight by the twenties, the hard-sell became part and parcel of serial merchandising. By this time, it was realized that a reasonable percentage of the people who attended the first chapter and were interested enough to return for another might miss an episode and not bother with the remainder. This was true even with the most popular chapter plays.

And this was where the releaser's publicity department entered the picture. Press books were issued, giving the exhibitor preconceived publicity items in terms of ideas, written advertisements and inserts for newspapers, handbills and the like. All kinds of banners, advertising layouts and other accessories

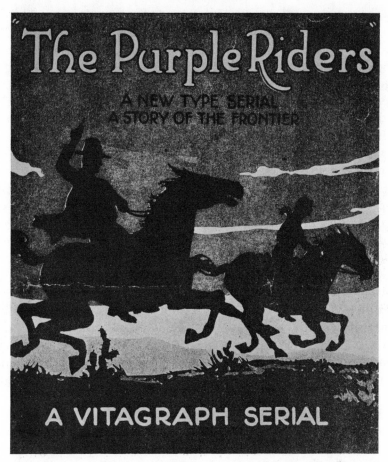

When a theater contracted to exhibit a serial, it was provided with a press book published by the serial producer to help exploit the chapter play. Although many copies of each press book were distributed, very few remain in existence today. This is the cover from a press book that accompanied the English release of a Vitagraph serial, *The Purple Riders* (1921). (Courtesy Wilfred J. Horwood)

were made available to the individual exhibitor. Naturally, the major producers pushed their product much harder than the independents who released on the state right basis. Of the major producers, Universal worked the hardest in putting their chapter plays across to the public. Each local exchange contained an exploitation expert whose job was to assist theater managers in the planning and execution of their campaigns.

The stunts and gimmicks used by exhibitors to draw attention and audiences ran the gamut from the ingenious to the mundane. One of the more novel exploitations was used by the Lyric Theater in Easley, South Carolina, in conjunction with the opening of *Bride 13* (1920). Manager Phelps Sassen considered many approaches and finally settled on a real wedding ceremony, to be performed on stage at the conclusion of the initial showing of Chapter 1. His advertising attempts to find a couple that would agree to such were not successful until two days before the event was scheduled. Hurriedly contacting several local merchants who had previously agreed to participate, he rounded up $150 worth of gifts for the couple.

On the appointed day, the house lights came on after the serial episode faded from the screen. The theater was jammed to capacity as the pianist began the wedding march. Manager Sassen and a minister, followed by the bride-to-be and an usher, marched down one side aisle, while the groom accompanied by another usher marched down the opposite aisle. As the participants took their places on stage and the strains of "Oh Promise Me" filled the theater, a voice cried out, "*Stop!*" It was the bride's mother, who was completely unaware of what was going on until she recognized her daughter about to be married. Sassen and the minister persuaded the woman to allow the ceremony to continue and giving her blessing to the daughter, the mother returned to her seat in the audience to witness the event.

Exhibitors were warned by the distributors not to leak the arrival of a serial too soon. This was done on the theory that a premature announcement might discourage patrons who would then want to see it immediately. But once a run had started, theaters were advised to place their serial advertising a day or two in advance with an ad separate from the daily announcement.

The Gem Theater in Council Bluffs, Iowa, "lapped" its serials. When the final episode of the current serial was scheduled to be shown, the manager had the opening chapter of the next serial on hand and started it the same night. Running two serials a week, the theater claimed that it built up the weak nights and that "lapping" served its purpose. Other theaters took advantage of personal-appearance tours, such as the one that Elmo Lincoln made throughout the Midwest in 1922 in conjunction with *The Adventures of Tarzan* (1921). Each night after the serial chapter had been screened, the house lights came on and Elmo stepped onto the stage where he engaged in a wrestling match with a lion cub, much to the delight of the patrons.

One exploitation angle which was worked to death across the country was the "punch-ticket." Examples of the variations on this theme, and there were more than you could count, can be found in the approaches to selling *In the Days of Daniel Boone* (1923). Phil Kahn, the exploitation specialist of the Boston Universal exchange, was called up to Lawrence, Massachusetts, to help Frank Boscketti of the Star Theater plan his campaign. A discussion led to the decision to print 2000 cards with the fifteen dates which the serial would play. If and when all fifteen were punched out, the holder of such a ticket would receive an Indian war bonnet. Within three days after the initial episode was shown, an additional 3000 were needed to accommodate those who requested them.

Louis Heiman of the Empire in Rahway, New Jersey, couldn't decide how to approach the selling angle of this serial. Joe Weil, the Universal exploitation man, decided that they would organize a Daniel Boone club. Thousands of tickets were distributed, bearing the inscription, "Coupon and 2¢ entitles bearer to admission on —— and a membership in the Daniel Boone Club." All 800 members who appeared on opening day were given a Daniel Boone button. This represented a 400 per cent increase in the Empire's serial

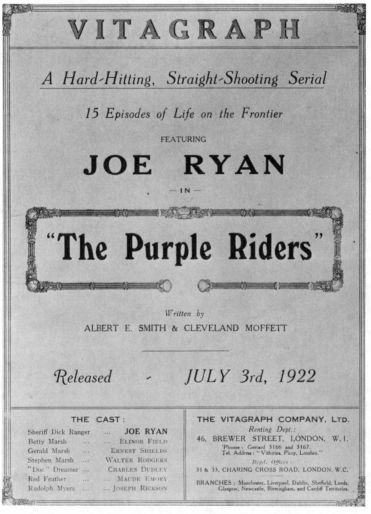

VITAGRAPH

A Hard-Hitting, Straight-Shooting Serial

15 Episodes of Life on the Frontier

FEATURING

JOE RYAN

— IN —

"The Purple Riders"

Written by
ALBERT E. SMITH & CLEVELAND MOFFETT

Released - *JULY 3rd, 1922*

THE CAST:		THE VITAGRAPH COMPANY, LTD.
Sheriff Dick Ranger	... **JOE RYAN**	*Renting Dept.:*
Betty Marsh ...	... ELINOR FIELD	46, BREWER STREET, LONDON, W. 1.
Gerald Marsh ...	ERNEST SHIELDS	'Phones : Gerrard 3166 and 3167. Tel. Address : "Vithirins, Picry, London."
Stephen Marsh ...	WALTER RODGERS	*Regd. Offices :*
"Doc" Dreamer ...	CHARLES DUDLEY	31 & 33, CHARING CROSS ROAD, LONDON, W.C.
Red Feather ...	... MAUDE EMORY	BRANCHES : Manchester, Liverpool, Dublin, Sheffield, Leeds,
Rudolph Myers ...	... JOSEPH RICKSON	Glasgow, Newcastle, Birmingham, and Cardiff Territories.

Each press book contained a title page giving necessary credits and casts . . .

business. After the initial episode had been shown, Heiman spoke briefly to his audience of children and then handed out cards to be punched for each episode attended. A completely punched card entitled the bearer to a ticket for a Daniel Boone Outing. His financial gain was small on the first chapter, but the promotion brought in many new patrons for the remaining chapters. Other theaters would admit a patron to the final episode free of charge, providing his card was punched for every previous installment.

VITAGRAPH

"The Purple Riders"
A SERIAL STORY OF THE FRONTIER
IN 15 ACTS
Featuring JOE RYAN

. . . reproductions of stills, lobby cards and posters that were made available to the exhibitor . . .

. . . as well as prepared newspaper items that the exhibitor simply filled in with his theater name and the proper dates to give the serial publicity a professional touch. (Photographs courtesy Wilfred J. Horwood)

PRESS PARS for use in your LOCAL PAPERS

CRACK SHOT, RIDER IN WESTERN FILM.

If there is a single man who can typify the best there is in the West of prairie and mountain, that man is Joe Ryan. Ryan now spends most of his time acting for the screen, but Ryan isn't a film "Westerner." Ryan merely does the things he has always done—the things he could do expertly since he could walk—and a cameraman makes a record of them.

Which explains why thousands of fans the country over rejoiced when it was announced that he would appear in "The Purple Riders," a splendid virile Vitagraph serial, with a Western setting, and a stirring, unusual plot.

The chapter play is completed, and all expectations for it have been exceeded, as Ryan's admirers will discover when the first episode is shown at the ...., theatre on .... Ryan takes the part of Sheriff Dick Ranger, a fearless, fast-riding, quick-on-the-trigger enforcer of law.

Dick's sweetheart, Betty Marsh, is the particular victim of the "Purple Rider" bandits and their leader, the mysterious Purple Shadow, and Dick thus has a double motive to run them down and land them behind bars. It is a task worthy of him, for the Riders are the pick of the Western criminals, absolute marvels and devils a-horse, shots of renown, crafty and treacherous in using the lore of woodland and forest trail.

Ryan, as Dick, actually outrides the best of the bandits, and, if he does not excel, equals their wonders of marksmanship. In addition, he is forced by them to do any number of dangerous stunts. He is dragged across the rocky trails by the horsemen at the end of a lariat trap; he is plunged, with his horse, in a raging mountain torrent; he has tons of mountainside cascaded down on him.

Ryan comes by his ability to take such a part by early training and aptitude. He was born on a ranch in Wyoming, and when he was two was hoisted on a broncho's back and allowed to ride. Shooting and swimming were soon acquired, and Ryan spent most of his life in this vigorous atmosphere. It is only in the past few years that he has had any other end in view for his ranch activities, and this came about by way of a circus engagement, a vaudeville tour, and quick recognition of his abiltiies for motion-pictures of dramatic strength and rapid action.

INNOCENT, THINKS HE IS MURDERER.

A recent case in which an innocent man believed himself guilty of murder, and was only saved from death by a witness of the crime, was a startling reversal of the usual procedure of justice.

The prisoner had spent his time in drinking and gambling, against the vehement protest of his father. The father had one enemy, in his debt, who had every reason for wanting him out of the way.

On the night of the crime, the father met his son intoxicated, stumbling down a dark street. There were hot words, then the son, stupefied, sank to the ground. The father's enemy lurked in a dark corner. As the father bent over, he raised a pistol and shot him through the heart. Then he ran to the son's side, fired a shot from his (the son's) pistol, replaced it, and fled.

The son was found, the discharged weapon still in his hand. Dazed, he thought he had shot his parent. It is an unusual situation like this, against a Western background, which lends mystery to the first episode of "The Purple Riders," the new Vitagraph serial, with Joe Ryan, which may be seen at the ....theatre......................

ACTORS DESCEND ROCKS ON HEELS.

There are mountains in the western part of the United States slippery as glass, the goals of the most persistent climbers. These formations are of solid rock, dating back millions of years to the glacial age.

Shaped and worn to the smoothness of a ballroom floor by the vast ice rivers which accompanied their beginnings, these mountains have rarely been ascended. In the first episode of "The Purple Riders," Vitagraph's fascinating new Western chapter play, not only is one of these ranges used as the setting of thrilling events, but a whole company, cameraman, actors, directors and assistants, went up its flanks to get the interesting films.

A fierce fight on the rocks between Joe Ryan as a Western sheriff, and an outlaw leader, and the crashing descent of Ryan and his leading lady, Elinor Field, into a rock pool, are gripping bits seen in the episode, to be shown at the .... theatre ....

In the course of helping the New Mission and New Fillmore theaters in San Francisco put this serial over, D. M. Vandewalker, the Universal fireball, was more creative and persuasive. A contract with the San Francisco *Call* resulted in an invitation to all children to view the first episode as guests of the newspaper. At the same time, the Anglo-California bank offered $500

in deposits as prizes for the best essay on Daniel Boone after the final installment was concluded. The result for both theaters? A full house with many
being turned away.

On a different and more ordinary level, many theaters exploited a serial
such as *The Radio King* (1922) by giving away free radio sets to a lucky
patron. Ben Fey of the Madison in Seattle, donated two sets; one on the fifth
and the other on the final chapter. The Colonial in Newark, under the
guidance of Joe Weil, went the limit by giving away a radio with the showing of each installment.

Pathé serials required less of the gimmicks usually associated with exploitation but in the twenties, it was not out of the ordinary for the firm to come
forth with something beyond the usual press book. A contract was arranged
with the Milton Bradley Company of Springfield, Massachusetts and large
quantities of "Movie Land Puzzles" were available free of any charge to exhibitors using *Hawk of the Hills* (1927). To be used as prizes, these jigsaw
puzzles depicted scenes from the serial when assembled. A bathing beauty
contest was conducted on the local level as a come-on for *Sunken Silver*
(1925), with the winner being awarded a contract good for a small role in
the following Pathé serial. Universal brought forth a novel one-sheet
(27" x 41") for *Haunted Island* (1928). This was an old pirate map, suitable for framing. It was printed in five colors and illustrated with scenes
from the chapter play in the old cartographic style, providing the viewer
with an interesting souvenir.

One of the most important exploitation aspects of any serial was its title.
This sounds a bit ridiculous at first glance, but the value of a good title was
not to be underestimated. It was the title which attracted initial attention
and created the desire to see the chapters. Sometimes the star's name alone
would draw crowds, as was the case of Pearl White and Ruth Roland, but a
good title was still important. With quite a number of the independent
chapter plays, the stars were virtually unknown to the general public, thus
the title had that much more work to do.

The choice of a title was the responsibility of the sales and/or publicity
departments. Here was where the exploitation ideas were created and therefore the reason for their involvement. If the serial came from a well-known
book, the title was ready-made, as in the case of *The Green Archer* (1925).
This allowed the chapter play to draw upon the book's popularity, for in
many cases the serial's success had been guaranteed by popular reception of
the author's work.

In cases where a title had to be created, there were three main considerations. First, the title had to possess individuality; that is, it had to avoid
repetition or a close likeness to other products in the works or recently re-

The cover reproduction from the press book distributed in England by Vitagraph to help promote *Fighting Fate* (1921). (Courtesy Wilfred J. Horwood)

leased. This was quite often difficult because of the vast amount of film turned out yearly. However, if a previous serial had been very successful, it did not hurt to identify the current one with a past effort, or so the thinking went. This was mainly done in the case of sequels, such as *The Return of the Riddle Rider* (the sequel to *The Riddle Rider*) and *The Ace of Scotland Yard* (the sequel to *Blake of Scotland Yard*).

Next, the title had to be easily remembered and the shorter it was, the better. A catchy phrase was often favored, such as *Go Get 'em Hutch*. The

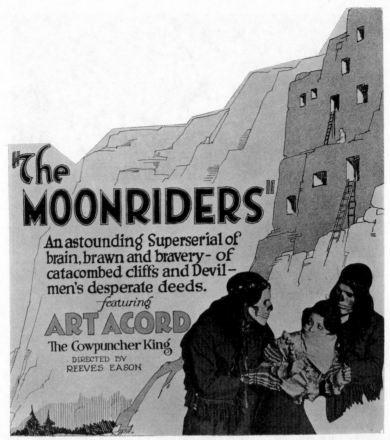

Exhibitors were subjected to weekly advertising in their trade papers, which teased them in the same manner that the cliffhanger endings teased the audiences. Strong, bizarre mystery characters could mean the difference between box-office success and failure. Universal tipped its hand to exhibitors in this *Moving Picture World* advertisement of March 13, 1920.

third consideration was that the title be as descriptive as possible of the serial's main interest. There were five main types of descriptive titles, each guaranteed to pack them in.

1. The name of the villain or mystery character. (*Moon Rider, Purple Riders, The Iron Claw, Who Is Number One?, The Lightning Raider, Hawk of the Hills*)

2. The name of the hero or heroine. (*Daredevil Jack, Elmo the Mighty, Elmo the Fearless, Ruth of the Rockies, Tarzan the Mighty, Pearl of the Army*)

3. The name of the gimmick used to create conflict. (*The Invisible Ray, $1,000,000 Reward, The Black Box, The Broken Coin, The Vanishing Dagger*)

4. A suggestion of danger. (*Perils of the Yukon, A Dangerous Adventure, Snowed In, Do or Die*)

5. The locale. (*The Lost City, Around the World in 18 Days, With Stanley in Africa, King of the Kongo*)

The value of a title can be well illustrated by the experience of Frank Leon Smith. Elmer Pearson, the vice president and general manager of Pathé, assigned Smith to do a serial concerning the lawless Idaho Territory. The idea had been conceived with a working title of *The Girl Vigilante.* To Smith, it was a fascinating challenge and he threw himself into the task with characteristic vigor. The more deeply he became involved, the higher his enthusiasm rose. Working night and day, Smith wrote detailed shooting scripts, ones he once described as being "foolproof." It was his intention to construct a story in such detail that the final footage would not deviate in the least from what he envisioned as he wrote. Inasmuch as it is possible to do so, he "directed" the serial on paper and very favorable comments were sent his way from all concerned with it. Even Robert F. Hill, who handled the actual direction, was pleased with what he had to work with.

By the time the project was in the can, Smith had conquered a longstanding fear of public speaking and chose to address the initial sales meeting. During the many weeks of hard creative effort which he had spent on the serial story, he had arrived at a definite conclusion as to the proper release title. His presentation and eloquent arguments won the resisting executives and salesmen over to his side. The sales people had wanted what they considered to be a "sales title," such as *Terror of the Hills,* but Smith's conception of it was simply *Idaho* (1925).

As the meeting broke up, one of the executives went up to him and said, "Smith, you claim you're not a salesman, but I'll give you a job anytime." Unfortunately for him and for the chapter play, the salesmen had known what he had not realized — times had changed. The adults had pretty much deserted the serial by this time, with children taking their place in the audience. The dignified, but static *Idaho* was not at all as effective as some fiercely melodramatic title such as *Dead Men's Gulch* might have been.

As the serial flashed onto the nation's theater screens, it quickly drew much praise from reviewers and critics for its atmosphere, suspense and story quality. But it was not popular with the patrons and did not bring in the expected cash receipts. Part of the blame for this box-office failure rests upon the shoulders of Pathé. Their insistance in casting Mahlon Hamilton and the non-magnetic Vivian Rich in the lead roles was a large contributing factor to its lack of popularity with the eager serial audiences. Hamilton just did not have the acting ability of Walter Miller or the audience appeal of Bruce Gordon. Although Miss Rich did a workmanlike job with her role, she was unable to establish the rapport with the audience which was so much

A Vitagraph favorite for years, Anita Stewart had been starred in *The Goddess* (1915). Bruce Gordon had been a leading man in Ruth Roland's Pathé serials. Here they are in *The Isle of Sunken Gold* (1927), a Mascot serial. (Courtesy Duke Kahanamoku)

a part of a serial heroine's popularity.

These few criticisms should not be held against the chapter play, for it was above par in quality when placed against its competition of the time. What actually hurt it the most was the lack of a flashy and teasing title — one that would have suggested conflict in a direct manner.

One of the most colorful exploitation angles were the songs, which were composed solely to plug or help sell the serial to the public. The beginning of this gimmick went all the way back to "Kathlyn," a hesitation waltz inspired by *The Adventures of Kathlyn*. The song was accompanied by a Kathlyn cocktail. By mid-1914, people were humming a tune which Charles

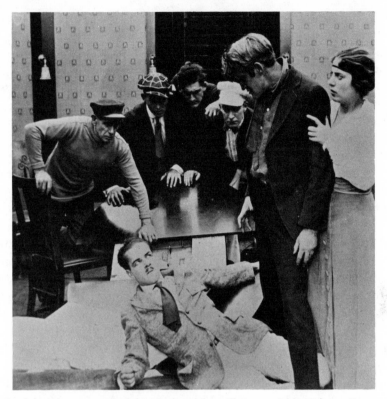

Francis Ford has just expressed his feelings for villainous Jack Holt as Grace Cunard looks on in this rare still from *The Broken Coin* (1915). (Courtesy D. Elmo Brooks)

McCarron and Ray Walker had composed, "Poor Pauline." Not directly written for the chapter play, this song satirized *The Perils of Pauline*. Its popularity could only be viewed as an asset to the Pathé release. In quick succession came title songs to add to the fortunes of *Lucille Love, Zudora* and *Runaway June*, among others. This practice continued unabated into the mid-twenties with a high degree of success. *The Adventures of Ruth* (1919) had "Romantic Ruth" and *The Fatal Fortune* (1919) had "Pretty Helen," a Hall and Sullivan song. Not even the historical westerns passed up this possibility. A foxtrot swing was written especially for Neva Gerber to accompany her Arrow release of the same title, *The Santa Fe Trail* (1923).

These title songs were used in a number of ways for maximum effect. Some theaters hired bands or street singers to carry the musical announcement of each chapter to the public. Others utilized song slides and held a community sing in the theater. A gentleman usually stood by the screen and led the audience in praising the merits of a particular serial or heroine. The most widespread practice to gain publicity was a tie-in with the sheet music publisher. Under this arrangement, the cover sheet covered a large portrait of the star with an identifying boost for the episodic thriller. Sheet music was much more common in those days and copies were found in a large number of homes across the country, each carrying the subtle message to whatever segment of the population it chanced upon. This was a golden opportunity for both publisher and producer and one which worked to mutual advantage.

How much did all of this ballyhoo cost the producer? There is no way of absolutely knowing, but the independents spent very little, compared to a company like Universal. The "Big U" sales office used a rule of thumb in allocating its publicity funds for serials. If the star was a surefire box-office draw, such as William Desmond or Eileen Sedgwick, the exploitation money was held to a minimum. The names of the cast were expected to carry the sales burden. Resultant savings were then spent on less deserving products. A serial which the sales force could only term "lousy" received an extremely heavy concentration of money — up to fifty per cent of the total production costs might be used to promote such an item. In the case of an eighteen-episode chapter play, advertising expenditures could range from practically nothing to over $90,000.

Independent firms such as Weiss Brothers Artclass, who put out the lowest-possible-quality serials, spent next to nothing in exploitation efforts. Once the rights had been sold to a distributor, these producers were finished with the film. *Perils of the Jungle* (1927), the Weiss Brothers animal chapter play, was so bad that it seems to have been purposely designed for the lowest quality houses and the rural areas, where the critical viewpoint was highly indulgent or nonexistent. Such exhibitors could be counted on to use this type of serial as often as it was made available. The rental fees were reasonable and these theaters seldom engaged in any great amount of advertising or other exploitation.

4

Gems of Jeopardy,
or
Written in Blood

Considered to be a necessary evil, serial writers were tolerated but not held in the lofty esteem which the front office reserved for its feature writers. Even though the work of feature writers might be cheap, uninspired and imitative, their lot was a choice one. All of the major companies producing serials relegated this work to a distinct and rather lowly department. As a result, serial practitioners were short on status. Two quite common remarks which were passed off the cuff and so often delivered with a sneer were: "You crazy writers" and "Oh, you're doing serials, eh?" Bearing this in mind, let's look briefly at the life and work of a serial writer. It was, to say the least, a hectic one.

Several reasons made it this. The serial was more or less a bastard medium; the best story could be dramatically told and told well in three to five episodes. The ingenuity of the scripter was therefore taxed to stretch the plot to fifteen or eighteen innings. The format of a serial really bore little resemblance to a magazine story presented in installments. Therefore, each story handed to a scenarist — and especially those to be adapted from novels — was in reality an "original" when it left his hands, providing he had done his job well. Most of the better serial writers agreed on this, although they attempted to transfer to the screen all of the vital points that the author had made in his work. There are numerous outstanding examples of this which will be discussed later.

The Lion Man (1919), one of the most unusual heroes in silent serial history. *(Motion Picture News, 1920)*

There were many originals conceived directly for the chapter-play screen but their success definitely depended, as in all other phases of screen writing, on the caliber of the writer. Although most scripters agreed that the finest kind of suspense was in the "long drawn," the easy way out was to concoct "stunty" action which was "soon over." I am indebted to Frank Leon Smith for this parallel. Because of the workload, as we shall see, a representative number of writers chose this avenue of meeting deadlines. The normal workload for a contract scenarist was one episode per week, provided he was working from a story already in hand. This varied considerably, depending upon the speed with which the director could shoot the scenes. A slow, methodical director might give the writer a break — as the script would eventually overtake the shooting schedule — but this seldom happened. It was more likely to go the other way, for time was money and thus a precious element of production.

A serial plot had to provoke dramatic interest and was therefore composed of a combination of dramatic situations. It appealed directly to the spectator by a clear presentation of conflict or conflicts. An effective emotional appeal to an audience requires that the serial writer place his characters in a series of trying situations. In this respect, the process of constructing a serial scenario was the diametric opposite of feature construction, for the chapter play was a much more complex subject. In a feature, the hero encountered numerous obstacles during the course of the story and lost every battle. In the end, circumstances were rearranged so that he emerged victorious. This pattern was reversed in the serial plot, for the hero met with success after success in each episode, only to be plunged into a violent situation from which there was no apparent escape, to remain there for a week. Picking up his adventure the following week, we discovered that he had found a last-minute method of evading disaster and was in the process of roaring triumphantly through another two reels of successes, only to find himself once more in a spot from which he apparently could not extricate himself.

To manufacture a plot by simply combining the situations was not enough, for a great deal of thought had to be given to the theme and characterization within the plot. When the spectator was given a solitary reason to doubt the reality of a character's action, the tension so vitally necessary to the success of a chapter play was lost and the dramatic effect was gone. In an attempt to create and maintain a melodramatic mood, many writers fell into a trap by using implausible situations. Such circumstances denied reality and also caused a loss of spectator involvement with the events occurring on the screen.

The simplest kind of serial plot was that in which a character was placed in a predicament, kept there as long as the suspense could be maintained and extricated in a surprising, thrilling but logical way. In addition to the bare predicament, a writer had to provide both interesting and logical reasons for his character's getting into the situation in the first place, sensible reasons for his inability to get out and understandable, but unforseen, methods of escape. The plot material had to be carefully selected so that it would not be obvious to the viewer. If the audience was not held in suspense, no dramatic effect was created. If the story could not stand the application of a reasonable degree of logic, the writer had failed in all that he set out to do.

A proper serial plot was, in theory, self-propelling. Given a certain conflict of strong forces, so many phases of that conflict could be presented as to continue the action almost indefinitely. The ever-present and inherent danger was in allowing the plot to become repetitious, tedious and/or slow in movement. Of necessity, most chapter plays were melodramatic in nature. Whereas the drama found in a feature began at a moderate tempo and ascended with growing speed to its climax, it fell away gently to the plane of repose as the final reel unwound. On the other hand, the tempo of a serial was much faster, with the first big situation coming soon after the action began, followed by several more tense and dramatic situations before the action culminated in the climax, or final installment.

The Hawk's Trail (1920), written by Nan Blair, was a fine example of the melodramatic serial. Characterized by fast action, it was filled with hair-

As *The Lion Man* (1919), Mack Wright played the mysterious creature who fought on the side of law and order. The audience, however, had no way of knowing this, and when the unveiling took place, believed it was J. Barney Sherry. Masking a hero was one way to use a double without the fans realizing that their favorite wasn't really their hero. (*Motion Picture News*, 1919)

breadth escapes and suspense-filled conflict. King Baggot portrayed Stanton Steele, a noted criminologist whose hobby was tracking down criminals. "Iron" Dugan, the master crook, was posing as the uncle of Jean and Claire Drake (Rhea Mitchell and Grace Darmond), in an effort to obtain their fortunes. Abducting Jean, he hid her in an old house. Claire was given a comfortable home because of his son, who loved her. The boy knew nothing of his father's nefarious schemes. Finally realizing that Claire was a menace to his plans, Dugan sent her to a swami's house where her abduction was to occur. Steele had been previously hired by Claire to unravel a mysterious burglary. Upon learning of the plot, he hurried to the swami's home where he impersonated him and foiled the abduction. From this point on, each

ANTONIO MORENO
in
"THE VEILED MYSTERY"
A Vitagraph Serial
EPISODE 6
"The SPAN of DEATH"

PETRIFIED WITH HORROR, THEY SEE
BRIDGE AND CAR CRASH DOWN

Smiling behind those binoculars, Henry Barrows watched Tony Moreno plunge to "certain death." As guardian of Moreno's fiancee, he was most pleased. The scriptwriter threw fans a curve with this one, for although *The Veiled Mystery* (1920) seemed to be a woman, the final chapter reveled that Barrows was the villain. (Courtesy Nan Boardman)

ANTONIO MORENO
in
'THE VEILED MYSTERY'
A Vitagraph Serial
EPISODE 9
"The SLIDE FOR LIFE"

THE VEILED MYSTERY APPEARS AT THE
HEAD OF THE CANOPY BED.

Unbeknown to Nenette de Courcy, Tony Moreno and Pauline Curley, *The Veiled Mystery*
(1920) watched their every move from behind the bed. Scenes like this used a veiled
woman to throw audiences off-guard; imagine the surprise when Miss Curley's guardian
was finally revealed as the master criminal! (Courtesy Nan Boardman)

episode contained an attempt to do away with the girl which was thwarted
by an impersonation by Steele. The serial ended, of course, with the capture
of Dugan and the freeing of Jean.

Dugan's attempt to dispose of Claire recurred in each chapter and gave a
kind of unity to the serial. Each episode ended with the heroine in the
power of the criminal and the following chapter opened with Steele effecting
her rescue, but failing to apprehend Dugan until the final denouement. Although the finished structure of such a serial appeared to be simple, it was
actually a task which required genuine technical and artistic skill.

The Lost City (1920), written by Frederic Chapin, was an example of a
melodramatic serial which incorporated several romantic elements in an

attempt to be unique. A young millionaire, Stanley Morton, and his friend, Mike Donovan, flew to Africa in search of big game. Reaching a village ruled by Gagga, a slave trader, they were captured. At this point, Princess Elyata (Juanita Hansen) was introduced. Also a prisoner of Gagga, she was the daughter of the King of Tirzah, a city in the interior which was inhabited by whites. Repulsing Gagga's advances, she was thrown into a lion pit with the two adventurers. Momba, an elephant, rescued the men, who in turn rescued Elyata with a rope thrown from their airplane. Heading for the jungle, they were hotly pursued by Gagga who realized that their plane would soon run out of gasoline. In each succeeding episode they were recaptured only to escape again. Throughout the remainder of the chapter play, wild beasts and all the other dangers of the jungle threatened them, in addition to the pursuit by Gagga.

Through the use of clever twists to the plot situations (the mysterious city of whites in the heart of black Africa, the use of an airplane in the jungle, etc.), the story served its purpose as a basis for the thrilling and unusual stunts. The success of such a serial depended more upon skillful direction and novel incidents than upon the basis of the plot itself, for this was the type of chapter play which could easily degenerate into a laugh-provoking farce, by virtue of its locale.

Relying less on melodrama and more on a strong story line, *A Woman in Grey* (1920) was a throwback to the earlier days of the serial, but quite out of step with the other productions of that year. Written by C. N. and A. M. Williamson, the scenario was done by Walter R. Hall.

The old Amory residence had remained vacant since the murder of old Mrs. Haynes, the housekeeper. Florence Haynes, an adopted daughter of the old woman, had been convicted of the crime but died in prison. Mary Edwards, the servant whose testimony had convicted Florence, then disappeared. Convinced that his father had hidden a valuable treasure on the property, Wilfred Amory took advantage of a tax sale to regain possession of his birthplace. His secretary, Tom Thurston (Henry G. Sell), was sent to look over the acquisition and found Ruth Hope (Arline Pretty), a young girl dressed in grey, inside the house. She refused to tell Thurston how she had obtained entrance to the property, but jokingly claimed that she was also inspecting.

When Amory arrived with his niece, Paula Wynne, they discovered a code paper inside an old family Bible. Unfortunately, J. Haviland Hunter, the villain, had also gained entrance via a secret passage and heard of the find. Determined to get the paper, he kidnapped Ruth but Thurston rescued her. Upon their return to the house, Amory recognized her as the author of a novel, *A Woman In Grey*. Realizing that she had a strong interest in the code and its key (contained in another document), he toyed with the idea that she might be Mary Edwards.

By this time, Tom had fallen out of love with Paula and in love with Ruth. Ruth had recovered one code and Hunter had the other. Paula's jealousy had led her to conspire with Hunter, who needed both papers. In the meantime, Ralph Gordon, the attorney for Florence Haynes at her trial, had been summoned to help clear up the mystery.

It took a full six chapters to establish the complicated plot, with little action taking place up to this point. From here on, the episodes dealt with the attempts of Hunter and Ruth to gain possession of the two codes, while

Chapter 3 was too early in the game to tell who would win, but you can bet that Paul Panzer's momentary triumph was just that. Before *The Black Book* (1929) was over, Walter Miller and Allene Ray survived several more doubtful situations. (Courtesy John Hampton)

the viewer was left to speculate on Ruth's identity. Although the plot was a strong one, the acting and photography contained in the final result of this state-right serial left much to be desired and distracted audience attention from the story.

A basic requirement which every serial writer made use of was the "dramatic triad." This meant that there were three persons or factions vieing for audience attention. It was most often expressed as (1) the hero and/or heroine; (2) the adversary; (3) the object around which conflict centered. Number three could be animate or inanimate — a person or a map, treasure or some other valuable item. It might even be a combination, as in *The Hawk's Trail*.

Temporarily sidetracked from her mission *With Stanley in Africa* (1922), Louise Lorraine was auctioned off as a slave girl. Such divergent subplots were added to the raw history by serial writers to provide the thrills that the historical account lacked. (Courtesy Louise Lorraine)

One of the most difficult factors in serial plot construction was the absolute necessity of getting the story off to a fast start in the first episode. This
held true simply because the successful chapter play required that the seeds
of all complications which were to follow later had to be planted in a swift
and interesting initial installment. A general outline to follow as the preser-
vation of a clear and definite conflict, motivated by some overwhelming
desire. Within such a framework, the writer could then carry the conflict
into all of its possible ramifications, thereby automatically advancing the
plot toward its successful conclusion. This was sometimes violated, as in
A Woman in Grey, but worked out well.

The first two chapters of *Trailed by Three* (1920) gave a good example of
a fast and exciting inception of plot. Jane Creighton (Frances Mann) was
the daughter of an island missionary. Rankin, a cruel man, had established
himself as ruler over the natives. Jane offered to help Anoto, the chief, in
his efforts to regain control of his tribe. With his cache of priceless pearls,
Anoto came to America with Jane to sell them in order to obtain the needed
cash to ransom his people.

Shortly after arriving here, the two lost possession of the jewels to Trent
and his accomplices. Tom Carewe, a friend of Jane, tried to help. He traced
the pearls to a Chinese establishment, only to be dropped into a pit for his
troubles. Anoto rescued him, but in the meantime, Jane had been duped
into visiting the same shop. Her cries for help were the signal for Tom and
Anoto to dash to her assistance. Just as the second episode ended, Tom was
about to be stabbed to death by an infuriated Chinaman.

The plot material was not novel, but in the hands of Charles T. Dazey, it
gave the serial a fast, interesting and effective sendoff. The conflict was presented, the factions identified and the central characters were then plunged
at once into an adventurous series of dangers.

There were two main methods of constructing a serial story, with numerous variations of each. The method used depended upon whether the
scenario was to be an original conceived for the screen directly or an adaptation of a popular work already in existence. A well-done original scenario
was perhaps a greater challenge, as the writer had to start from scratch. However, a proper adaptation required as much, and in some cases more, skill in
many respects.

In working out an original story, the writer first decided upon the broad
plot line within the framework of several questions.

1. What type of serial was it to be — a mystery, adventure, western or combination of these?

2. What should be the proper basis for conflict — a missing map or valuable jewel, buried treasure, control of land or property, a master criminal
seeking power, etc?

3. What type of characters should represent the forces of good and evil? Would the lead be a damsel in distress or a strong hero on whose shoulders the heroine could lean? What supporting roles would be needed to fill out the basic plot?

After deciding upon the answers to these questions, the writer had an outline which served to contain the individual chapters. It was then a matter of constructing the necessary action for each episode, making certain that continuity was maintained throughout. This was the point where many writers failed, for the chore of designing subplots to fill two reels and which could be resolved within that length, still advancing the basic story line in a logical manner, was a difficult task to say the least.

Conferences between the hero and the police were important to the silent serial. Having established the connection, viewers knew that the police would appear at the one moment when the script writer had no other way of saving the star. Here Antonio Moreno fulfills his obligation to the audience in *The Invisible Hand* (1920). (Courtesy Larry Edmunds Bookshop)

WILLIAM DUNCAN
AND
EDITH JOHNSTON
IN
"FIGHTING FATE"
A VITAGRAPH SERIAL
CHAPTER # 7
"A DEMON'S BLUFF"

THE GANG IS EXULTANTLY PLANNING A TRIP
AFTER THE HIDDEN TREASURE

This unusual looking group of crooks is typical of the weird disguises used in the silent serials. Such gatherings were photographed to convey an air of mystery, a sense of impending evil, and usually represented the "minions of the arch-criminal." This meeting of the Black Circle took place in *Fighting Fate* (1921). (Courtesy Larry Edmunds Bookshop)

Each chapter required a certain amount of action to satisfy the fans and move the plot forward. This usually involved a dangerous situation in which fast action or stunting played a major role. Many serials went overboard in this respect and packed thrill upon thrill within each episode, in an effort to bring the fans back the following week. To the less discriminating audiences, a simple or trite plot was easily overlooked in favor of the thrills and entertainment which the inclusion of many unusual feats of heroism provided. Many serial fans remember not the story but the agility of the star.

WILLIAM DUNCAN
AND
EDITH JOHNSTON
IN
"FIGHTING FATE"
A VITAGRAPH SERIAL
CHAPTER # 3
"A MODERN DANIEL"

THE KNIGHT-IN-ARMOR, MYSTIC HEAD
OF THE GANG GIVES STRANGE ORDERS

To magnify the air of mystery surrounding the master criminal and protect his identity from the audience, he was quite often dressed in a macabre costume. In *Fighting Fate*, the master criminal, known at The Iron Mask, was garbed as a knight, making it difficult for William Duncan to land a solid blow. (Courtesy Larry Edmunds Bookshop)

One action star who had a say in the production of his chapter plays and insisted on such a scenario was Eddie Polo. His fans were legion and one of the main reasons for this huge coterie was the fact that Polo's serials moved at a rapid pace from the very first episode. They never let up on action or suspense until the last few feet of the final chapter, but one had to dispense with logic and substitute the long arm of coincidence throughout. This explains why the theaters were packed with children when a Polo serial was playing.

A fine example of this was *Do Or Die* (1921). In "Buried Treasure," the eighteenth episode, Polo was bound tightly by the villains. Yet he managed to get a revolver which had been dropped by a wounded bandit, and with the weapon he shot through the ropes which held Delores, who then freed him. Meanwhile, the Mystery Woman had noticed a box of dynamite in Satan's car. Suspecting him of villainy, she buried it. Just by chance, her choice of a burial spot happened to be the place where Jack Merton (Polo) had started to dig for the buried treasure. Satisfied that she had foiled Satan, she left.

This set the stage for one of the bandit gang to locate the treasure. Starting to dig, his pick struck the hidden cache and his reward for faithfulness to his master was instant destruction as the explosion took place. In the interim, Satan had recaptured Merton and Delores for the millionth (or so it seemed) time. As he was about to do them in, help arrived in the nick of time to save our heroes and capture the villains. At this point, the Mystery Woman asked that Satan be granted mercy; revealing herself to be his daughter. However, Satan and crew were immediately incarcerated while Merton set in motion the preparations for his marriage to Delores. Not content to end the chapter play on this note, a hireling freed Satan and the entire band rushed off to the scene of the wedding.

A suspicious noise in the garden caused Merton to rush outside to investigate. Seized and held by the villains, Merton was at the mercy of Satan, who drew a revolver. Taking deliberate aim, he started to squeeze the trigger when he was killed. The Captain of the Port, alarmed at Jack's delay in returning, had also stepped outside. Seeing the danger which had overwhelmed his friend, he shot Satan. The wedding continued with the Mystery Woman professing her love for the Captain.

Anthony Coldewey did the script and although the story line was quite thin and implausible in many spots, the furious action and fast pacing took the place of logic for many viewers. The audience interest, especially with children, was thus worked up and held to a maximum with each succeeding chapter. Because of the large number of serials made in this same vein, we should note that the necessity of appealing to a wide and often indiscriminating audience placed many limits on the chapter play. For this reason, it would not be valid to judge or even attempt to measure the artistic achievement from other than the popular viewpoint.

Another form of original serial screen play which represented the best in this type of writing was found in *Snowed In* (1926), one of the Pathé Miller-Ray epics. Within the ten episodes allowed, Frank Leon Smith created one of the classic mystery serials using nothing but standard ingredients. Much of the action centered around an inaccessible area of the Sierras. Motivation was found in the form of a series of highly successful mail robberies and an innocent man wrongfully accused. The faith of a believing sister, aided by the love of a forest ranger, served as the forces of good which

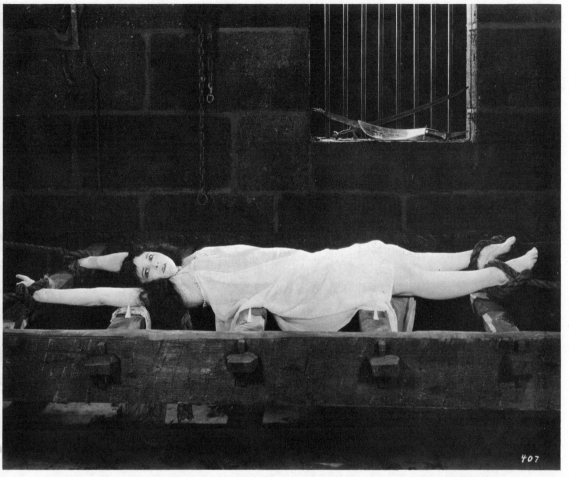

Beautiful Allene Ray is about to pay with her life for having refused marriage to the scheming Frank Lackteen in *The Fortieth Door* (1924).

met in mortal combat with evil. This was provided by a strangely attired arch-criminal, Redfield, whose identity was hinted at, but was not revealed until the final moment. Throughout the ten chapters, the finger of suspicion was pointed at those playing featured roles. This was done in a manner which served to convince the viewer that he had logically solved the mystery. The following chapter then proved how wrong his logic had been.

This interconnecting of the cast in such a way required a skilled hand — one that was adept at designating stories plotted as a complex, but workable maze. Smith was highly capable in this capacity and was able to advance the story by weaving his characterizations while maintaining a high degree of continuity.

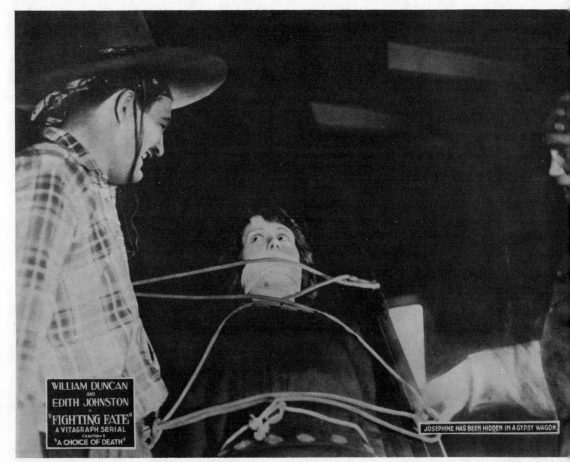

WILLIAM DUNCAN
AND
EDITH JOHNSTON
IN
"FIGHTING FATE"
A VITAGRAPH SERIAL
CHAPTER II
"A CHOICE OF DEATH"

JOSEPHINE HAS BEEN HIDDEN IN A GYPSY WAGON.

Edith Johnson is bound and gagged — a not-uncommon situation in the silent serials. From *Fighting Fate*. (Courtesy Larry Edmunds Bookshop)

Sometimes, there was an unusual tale behind an original story, such as one Ford Beebe did for Universal. Let's let him tell it: "In my late teens, I wandered around Mexico for a few years, working on railroad constructions, running eating houses and doing a little prospecting, etc. While trying to bring back an old Indian mine, we camped back in the hinterland of Sinaloa in a canyon called Sal Si Puedes (Get out if you can). As the name suggests, it was a pretty wild country and we seldom had visitors. On one occasion, a bee-hunter turned up and spent a night with the Mexicans we had working with us. He was a born story teller and regaled our boys with a lot of tales mostly of a weird variety — ghosts and the like. Listening from our campfire, there was one that struck me as worth remembering.

HELEN'S RESCUE OF TOM.

The situation is not so hopeless as it appears. Helen Holmes will save Leo Maloney in *A Lass of the Lumberlands* (1916). (Courtesy John Hampton)

Across from our camp was a range called San Pedro. The mountain ran straight up to a steep cliff on which nothing grew. The story ran something like this: A bee-hunter, looking for honey, went up a hill very much like San Pedro to the bottom of the cliff. As he wormed his way through the brush, he heard a kind of scraping, as of rocks sliding over one another. He ducked for cover and there before his eyes, the cliff started to open, until a passageway of several feet was exposed. Overawed, he fell flat and watched. Now out of the chasm came seven black mules, in single file. Each of them had black trappings and on each packsaddle, there rested a pair of black bags. Each mule had an attendant, all of whom were in black clothing. At the closest edge of the chasm, the procession turned and worked its way along the face of the cliff. Not a word was spoken and there was no sound of hoofs as the cavalcade passed him. He stared after them, then turned to investigate the passage through the bluff. To his amazement, it had closed behind them and there was no trace of its having been there. Nerving himself, he scurried after the mules but naturally never found them. He backtracked looking for the trail they should have left, but found nothing. They had passed without leaving any trace.

"That was the end of the story. I don't know why it should have occurred to me while I was trying to find a basis for *The White Horseman* (1921), but it did: a moving mountain inside which lived at one time a race of Indians who toiled their fields by day, then returned to their mountain fastness and by a feat of engineering, closed the door behind them. I suggested

The mysterious Tiger Face (Harry Moody) has some tall explaining to do if he escapes this time in *The Tiger's Trail* (1919). (Courtesy Larry Edmunds Bookshop)

Francis Ford made the phone call, but it was against his better judgment in *The Mystery of 13* (1919). An independent serial, it made use of hooded villains who plotted in secret underground chambers to rule the world. The first three episodes were good, as was the finale, but the intervening eleven chapters were short on plot and long on padding. (Courtesy Alan Brock)

it to Bill Wright, never expecting him to buy it but he did. So we wrote a story of the last two members of the Indian tribe who came back to open the mountain and who became involved in the story of the villains who found what they were after and got in their dirty work, and so on. For its day, we had quite an elaborate set for the moving mountain. To the Indian mind, Art Acord was a kind of reincarnation of a white horseman who, centuries before, had come to the aid of the tribe in defending themselves against their enemies."

1916 found Pearl White in this perilous position. Although her opponent was *The Iron Claw,* she had no reason to fear danger as long as "The Laughing Mark" (center) was behind her. Harry Fraser played the masked role with great aplomb. (Courtesy Alan Brock)

Less successful ventures in the original chapter play field were quite often found in independent serials. Many of these were excellent in conception and execution with the final results vastly entertaining, but the odds were against them. The tendency of the independent showmen was to rush in order to capitalize on the market. This hurry was evident in a number of lesser serials. One such, and an excellent example of the surprisingly crude results obtained when chapter-play production was hurried, was the unimaginative *Officer 444* (1926), the final Wilson-Gerber offering.

The plot dealt with the activities of the sinister Frog, ruler of a vast criminal empire. Determined to control a secret formula with which he could rule the world, the Frog was opposed by *Officer 444*, none other than the aging Ben Wilson. A fake doctor's office (Dr. Blakely) was used as a cover for the nefarious activities of the villains. When Gloria Grey (Neva Gerber) was kidnapped to further the ambitions of the Frog, 444 swung into action in a determined manner. The police finally picked up the trail of the master criminal, but the Frog camouflaged his hideout, which became "Cohen and O'Brien, Coveralls." Fake partitions were erected but 444 saw through the scheme and destruction of the lair followed.

The amazing lack of logic in many of these scenes gave the alert viewer the impression that shooting preceded the writing of a script, for a few chapters later, we found 444 in plain clothes, patiently stalking his quarry. Hot on the trail of the arch-fiend, 444 followed the Frog to his underground quarters. When the villain reached the depths of his stronghold, who was slouched in a corner, hat pulled down over his eyes? None other than our hero, good old 444. How did he beat the Frog to his lair? A subtitle conveniently informed us that "disguised as a workman, 444 gained entrance."

Discovered by the gang, he was thrust into the dungeon with Gloria and Dr. Blakely's victims. His escape from this predicament was as logic-free as his entrance. Chapter #8 was a prime example of the worst that the silent serial had to offer. Taking on the henchmen of the Frog singlehanded in a railroad yard, 444 was struck down and fell across the track. At this moment, reinforcements arrived in strength and carried on his fight. However, no one paid the least attention to the hero and what was coming around the bend, up the track? You guessed it — a thundering metal monster. Only Gloria was aware of 444's desperate plight and what did she do about it? Pull him off the track? No, she attempted to fend off the Vulture, a henchwoman of the Frog (capably played by Ruth Royce, an expert villainess), while trying to throw the switch which would send the train hurtling by 444, rather than do him in. The editing developed high suspense in this sequence, but the audience could not figure out why she didn't just walk over and drag him off the tracks. It would have been easier, quicker and much more sensible.

Scenes such as these, along with the unbelievable fight sequences, left the viewers laughing. An overwhelming number of thugs would back 444 into a corner behind a blind, but seconds later he emerged, while the hoodlums staggered around holding their heads. Never in serial history did so many police raids net such a huge number of prisoners. In each episode, 444 and his fellow officers rounded up dozens of followers of the Frog. What a payroll that boy had!

While the main interest centered on Wilson and Gerber, the acting honors went to Jack Mower. Cast as an Irish cop, sidekick to 444, Mower turned in a fine comic bit. Whether this was intentional or not will never be known, but he carried off his role in a manner which suggested that he was laughing at his actions all the while. The financial failure of David Distributing Division destroyed much of the release potential of *Officer 444*, but oddly enough a number of prints of this obscure serial are still around and are well worth viewing for both historical reasons and the inherent laughs.

Another example which serves as an illustration of how not to make a serial was *Days of '49* (1924), an Arrow release. The story was basically simple in terms of plot, but unduly protracted in execution. John A. Sutter (Charles Brinley) held claim to a large tract of territory in what is now

Villains of the twenties often distinguished themselves with disfigured appendages. "The Claw" (Tom London) wanted that deed held by Derelys Perdue in *The Mystery Rider* (1928).

The strange birdlike creature strangling Marie Walcamp's companion was one of the many dangers she faced as *Liberty, A Daughter of the U.S.A.* (1916). (Courtesy Alan Brock)

California, but at the beginning of the serial was still part of Mexico. Two adventurers, Arabella Ryan (Ruth Royce) and Robert Marsdon (Wilbur McGaugh), attempted to influence Sutter to revolt and establish an empire all of his own which they hoped to exploit. Although Arabella expended all of her feminine wiles on him, Sutter wavered between dreams of empire and statehood.

Cal Calhoun (Edmund Cobb), famed trail guide, led the Bear Flag Revolution in 1846 which gave California to the United States and Sutter faded out of the picture. Calhoun's friendship with Sonora Cardosa (Neva Gerber), a large land-holder, blossomed into love which lasted throughout the

The Great Gamble (1919) was filled with exciting rescues of Anne Luther engineered by Charles Hutchison. (Courtesy Alan Brock)

"ZUDORA" IN THE $20,000,000 MYSTERY   EPISODE No. 12   A BAG OF DIAMONDS

Villainy in the early serials was elemental compared to the skullduggery of the twenties. (Courtesy Sam Rubin)

Serial production stills were often taken during the action to avoid expensive and time-consuming posing. Many were thus a bit unsharp, as this scene of Joe Cuny gagging June Caprice in *The Sky Ranger* (1921). (Courtesy Tom Dino)

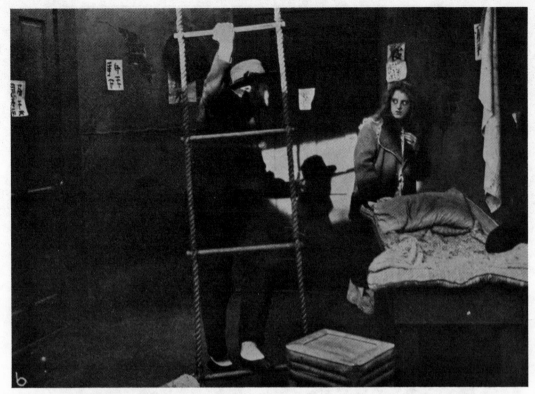

Held captive in a Chinese opium den, Ella Hall is certain that her search for *The Master Key* (1914) is over.

remainder of the serial. The settlement of the territory and the growth of San Francisco saw Marsdon try to extend his influence through the leadership of a gang of ruffians, but he met his just end in a duel with Judge Coleman (Clark Coffey), Cal's father. Peace and prosperity then settled upon California.

Sound like serial stuff? Nope. Spread over fifteen episodes, this plot was woefully weak and the acting (on the same level) was not calculated to help strengthen it. For the most part, the serial was reminiscent of a prewar state-right release, complete with the overexaggerated emotional displays and the understaged scuffles which passed vaguely for fights. There seemed to have been a dire shortage of Indians on the days that scenes of the red menace were filmed and the wagon train attacks were more ludicrous than the awkward fist fights. Ed Cobb showed that he had a great deal yet to learn and Neva Gerber vacillated between radiant displays of beauty and ugly, childish tantrums. Clearly, she did not lend herself very well to historical and costume serials. As a demure young lady, she registered extremely well but lacked that something which makes an "outdoor" girl. The portrayal of the domineering, ruthless schemer by Ruth Royce was effective and continued to mark her for "other woman" roles. Photographed by a crew of five, the technical work was passable but the direction was uninspiring to say the least. Ben Wilson and Jacques Jaccard seldom struck the bottom so hard. It was rare that such a potentially good cast turned in such a mediocre performance. The entire affair was a genuine representation of Arrow's lost interest in serial thrillers, from the story by Karl Coolidge to the results on screen.

Arrow made an attempt at editing the serial from its original 30,000 feet into a 5,444-foot feature. Considering the fact that the serial was very poor to begin with, one would think that the feature was just as bad. It was worse. Crudely constructed, the story line was altered somewhat and Neva Gerber's role became that of the daughter of Sutter. The feature version lacked the needed punch and was anti-climactic, for the welcome finale was reached with little suspense. Serials that were recut into features sometimes made the grade as good entertainment (*Hawk of the Hills* was one), but the odds were against it. It was a staggering task to cut 20,000 or 30,000 feet of film into a five- to seven-reel feature and retain the story line and characterization in a coherent manner.

Adaptations of popular novels were a challenge of sizable proportions to the writer. This type of scenario could be very well done or not, depending upon the serial scripter and his basic attitudes toward his work. A conscientious writer attempted to transfer the novel to the screen as closely as possible and still retain the native flavor of the work. Here was the difficult part: translating a work done with the written word to a visual medium and maintaining what the author had felt to be important. Few were as skilled at this as Frank Leon Smith and his achievement, reflected in *The Green Archer* (1925), taken from the Edgar Wallace novel, still ranks as the best of the silent serials.

It was left to the individual writer to examine a novel, select what he felt to be basic to his script and then proceed to fill out this framework in terms suitable for cinematic presentation. For the most part, the worst adaptations were found in the historical serials. The writers were tempted to play fast and loose with history and many succumbed. A great number of the works on which historical serials were based were unfit in one or several ways for the screen. It was nearly impossible to adapt "Robinson Crusoe" or "The Swiss Family Robinson" to the serial screen in eighteen episodes and fulfill the needs of a rousing serial. The stories by themselves simply did not have the necessary ingredients. The Universal historical westerns were average, fast-moving and in most cases, interesting plots, but as history, they left quite a bit to be desired. They required invention on the part of the scripter as well as padding to extend the story to the necessary length.

The first of these was *Winners of the West* (1921). It was an attempt by William Lord Wright to counteract the letter, if not the spirit, of the censorship movement which had marshalled its forces against the chapter play. He felt that Universal could get away with it if what they produced was *supposed* to be historical in background. Thus the title of the Art Acord serial gave the impression of something above and beyond the ordinary; a history lesson served up by a visual presentation of facts. It served the purpose, for most of the censors failed to see that it was the same old violent action with a fancy name.

Supposedly based on Fremont's expedition to California, the formula used

Even a serial which began as a Graustarkian romance eventually found its way to the old West, a change in locale favored by nearly all viewers. Here, Princess Julia (Arline Pretty) and Phil Barr, rightful King of Alania (Charles Richman, far right) exchange glances in episode 2 of *The Secret Kingdom* (1917).

by Ford Beebe in constructing the early episodes did not differ at all from previous Universal thrillers. It included an occasional historical character, but had little to do with the real Fremont journey. Since the use of his name added to its stature, no one apparently ever took the trouble to research the history of that period, as to the authenticity of the incidents portrayed, and it got by handily. Wright and Beebe had an argument as the story reached its halfway mark and Robert Dillon was brought in to finish the script in the same manner as the preceding chapters.

In this respect, serial production differed very little from feature production, as Hollywood has always been notorious for the manner in which it

A gag still from *The Green Archer*, produced in New York in 1925. Left to right, Frank Leon Smith, who wrote many successful serials for Pathé; Allene Ray, the star of the picture; Spencer G. Bennet, the director. (Courtesy of Frank Leon Smith)

Neva Gerber as she appeared in *Days of '49* (1924).

treats history. The point here is that the adaptations of history — such as
Universal made from the William F. Cody story "The Great West That
Was" — were hardly recognizable as emanating from the written work. The
adaptation was one in name only, for the great bulk of the footage came
from the brain of the scenario writer and actually amounted to an original
screenplay. Universal seldom reached the point where its serials could be
favorably compared to the Pathé products, from the standpoint of story.
Smith, Millhauser and George Arthur Gray were among the most talented
people working in the writing end of the business and it was difficult for
other writers to match their pace and output with any degree of consistency.

Even in the area of adaptations, the independent serials were in a very
unfavorable position insofar as plots were concerned. Many firms felt that
the story was an area in which economy could be safely practiced and as
a result, the entire effort suffered. With the exception of Mascot serials, few
independents were able to even compare favorably with the Universal product. At that, Mascot owed more to fast action embellished with above-average

Tom London (once known as Leonard Clapham) holds all the cards as well as the gun in *Snowed In* (1926). As the fighting forest ranger, Walter Miller protects Allene Ray. (Courtesy National Film Archive, Great Britain)

production values then it did to strong, logical plots. The independents had a smaller amount of money to spend on production, which meant a less capable cast, fewer production values and a general corner-cutting evident in nearly all respects. A strong story would have a large asset in such a situation.

One of the more knowledgeable independent writers, Robert Dillon eventually turned to directing for Rayart release in the mid-twenties. Starting at the bottom, he had worked his way up the ladder. By 1923, Dillon was chief of the serial and short subject department at Universal City and had scripted several serials. Taken as a whole, his work as it appeared on the screen was uneven and at times a bit rough, with his best coming during the early period when he was with Universal. However, Dillon understood his craft and some of his failure to present a plausible chapter play should be placed on the shoulders of those for whom he worked. It is quite difficult to stage a rousing and exciting Indian attack with only seventeen Indians.

The dean of the serial writers was found in the person of Frank Leon Smith. Although there were other fine people working in the business, none turned out such a variety of top work for so long a time as did Smith. A modest fellow who would certainly not agree, Smith possessed a style all his own and his talent was at its best when dealing with continuity. His scripts were constructed so perfectly that practically anyone with a knowledge of dramatics could direct from them without any difficulty. Spencer G. Bennet worked with many writers in his active days and looking back now, he still credits Smith as the best scripter that he ever met.

Call him foolhardy if you like, but Eddie Polo simply liked to hang from unusual places.

Another "in-the-nick-of-time" rescue performed for the serial camera by Henry G. Sell as he saves Arline Pretty from certain death in an episode of *A Woman in Grey*. (1920)

After being graduated from the Everett, Massachusetts public school system, Smith worked during the next five years as an office boy in a Boston advertising agency, assistant to the syndication manager of the Boston *Traveler, Everywoman's Magazine*, Morrison's *Chicago Weekly*, edited the *American Artisan* and then rejoined his former boss on the *Traveler* in a venture called Associated Newspapers. At this point, he found time to write short stories. The Munsey magazines and his own syndicate began buying his work and he promptly quit his job to free-lance. At first, he did well and lived in Washington Square with a fellow named George Brackett Seitz, another budding author who had turned to the movies for a living.

By 1915, Smith was looking for work with a more reliable paycheck and Seitz placed him in the title department at Pathé where he wrote subtitles,

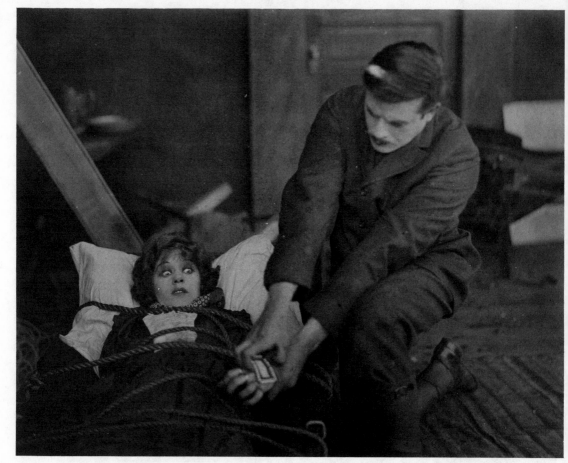

Fred Jones has Arline Pretty in his power and now tries to acquire the "weenie" (Pearl White's term for the motivating factor behind a serial). In this case, it's a bracelet securely fastened to her wrist and to each finger by a chained ring. (From *A Woman In Grey*, 1920.) (Courtesy Arline Pretty)

breaking in on the *Our Feathered Friends* series. It was at this time that he acquired an attitude toward films which he carried through life. He heartily disliked the movie business. Upon selling three of his stories, he happily left Pathé, to return to the harried life of a free-lance. Fortunately for serial history, he fell in love. Realizing that the type of life he led offered little security with which to begin married life, he again turned to Seitz, who was looking for a scenario editor at Astra. Philip Bartholomae, a Broadway playwright, had held the job at $400 weekly, but he decided to leave and Smith took over at $40.00 a week. His position at Astra demanded his location of enough material to keep two serial and four feature units moving. It also involved the hiring of writers, assignment of scripts, doing the necessary rewrites and acting as a liaison between Astra and the Pathé Film Committee to insure that his department's work was passed favorably by the latter.

After a time, he was told by Louis Gasnier, president of Astra, that a move to California was in the wind and although Smith did not desire to go, his job was on the line. Off he went at Pathé's expense, but the fare for his wife came out of his pocket! To this point, he had not concerned himself strictly with serial writing, although a friend at Astra, Bertram Millhauser, had urged him to do so. The job on the Coast involved rewrites for two Ruth Roland vehicles and several other chores with a salary of $50.00. It was at this turn in life that he was pushed into serial work. Seitz bailed him out, brought him back East and put him into a more comfortable wage bracket. The fabulous team was born.

Smith had once thought of doing an original for Douglas Fairbanks and had even committed a few pages to paper. Seitz saw it and liked it enough to encourage its finish. He then sold it to Pathé at the rate of $300 per episode. This became *Bound and Gagged* (1919), a comedy melodrama in serial form, conceived as a spoof on serials. It was also a light love story in chapter-play form and one of the few writing jobs which Smith enjoyed. Seitz also paid him for doing the scripts and this was the beginning of a period of prosperity for the author.

The story was well cast, with Marguerite Courtot as the charming heroine and Frank Redman (a Pathé prop man) as the villain. Smith had written it with Walter McGrail — an experienced and excellent young actor — in mind as the male lead. A crushing blow came when Seitz announced that he would play the role himself, but considering how much Smith owed to his friend, the concession was easily made. The serial holds a unique position in Pathé history as the only film of its kind to get an *All Good* vote from the Pathé Film Committee.

The team worked on other projects, but the high point financially came with *The Phantom Foe* (1920). This was a sketch sold to Pathé by Seitz, who then engaged Smith to do the scripts. The final story did not exist until completion of the fifteenth chapter. At that time, Pathé gave Seitz a check for $4500, which he quickly turned over to Smith. True friendship! After Seitz closed down his studio, the two worked for Pathé directly. The organization had finally grown to appreciate Smith for something well understood and taken for granted in the publishing world, but not so well known or understood in the movies — "author's integrity."

At this stage in his career, Smith took a giant leap forward. Gilson Willets, Pathé's first, last and only real serial production manager, was dying and a Ruth Roland vehicle, *Ruth of the Range* (1923), was hanging in the balance. Pathé had committed itself and too much was at stake to drop the project. Elmer Pearson sent Smith to the West Coast where he found that the Willets story had died in midstream with its creator. No one knew what the next twist in the plot was to have been; and what Smith was asked to do, in effect, was to finish a story that didn't exist. In addition, he was to do all the shooting scripts, supervise production and battle with Mike Levee, the nominal producer, in order to obtain the quality which Pathé held him responsible for. Furthermore, he was a perfectionist for detail and insisted on having his way in all areas that he felt to be important — such as location, sets, supporting cast and costumes. This was not all, however; he was also

Arline Pretty was not surprised to see villainous Fred Jones crawl out of the woodwork. It was a common feature in the serials. (From *A Woman in Grey*, 1920). (Courtesy Arline Pretty)

responsible for the preparation of *Haunted Valley* (1923), the following Ruth Roland serial.

Smith spent the next few years in this manner, always retiring to his farm in the Catskills after each job was done and remaining there until the next call came from Pathé. Those short intervals of bucolic country life helped to fortify him for a return to Hollywood, which he disliked intensely. He also spent time in the Pathé office buying various properties and weighing the possibilities of various serial propositions brought before the firm.

Seitz left Pathé after *Sunken Silver* (1925) and Smith's wife died in

Juanita Hansen, as she appeared in October, 1919, just prior to the filming of *The Lost City*.

Florida just as he and Bennet were starting *Play Ball* (1925). With his distaste for movies, there was little left for him after that. He had wished for some time to return to New York, but had qualms about leaving Bennet and the unit which they had created. Shortly, an incident occurred which made the decision quite easy. Many years before, a fellow named Joseph Storey had helped Elmer Pearson gain employment with a Midwestern railroad. As vice president and general manager of Pathé, Pearson was in a position to help his old benefactor, who soon became a fifth wheel in the New York office. His welcome worn, Storey was sent into the field and attached to Smith and Bennet. He leaned on his authority and put his brother Thomas on the payroll as an assistant cameraman. Eventually, Tom Storey was elevated to the position of co-director and associate producer, much to the disgust of most who knew him.

Smith had taken a dose of something similar. While scripting *The Green Archer* (1925), he was in poor health. Although not a sickly person by nature, he had not been feeling up to par for some time and his wife's death had only added to his illness. Recalling what a problem the death of Gilson Willets had created a few years before, the overanxious Pathé executives assigned Arch B. Heath to keep Smith company. This was done to insure that someone would be able to continue the story line, should Smith become incapacitated.

Not paying any particular attention to what was going on, Smith continued turning out the scripts, only to find that Heath was representing the finished episodes to Pathé as being his own work. Smith's ego simply wouldn't allow anyone else to doctor his writing and Heath's claims irked him to no end. To show Pathé that his poor health did not mean that he was finished, he sat down and penned *Snowed In* (1926) without confiding in or consulting with anyone. This serial met with equal success at the box office and proved his point.

Having contracted pleurisy and his fill of serials and the Storey brothers, he quit Pathé. His mother-in-law, of whom he was very fond, had passed away while he was working on properties in the New York office. His grief was compounded and ill health continued to plague him. Feeling that feature production might well offer him a challenge, he accepted a one-year contract with Paramount, which he soon broke. Having been the top man in a rather small organization, he didn't adjust very well to a reduction in stature. As he once put it, "Seventy-four writers on the payroll and only one scenario editor to screen the stuff. Finish a script for a feature and be told, 'Now do it over,' even though the script had not yet been read. Just a means of getting a writer out of the editor's hair for awhile. Nuts. Actually, I'd had my fill of movies; I'd built up a good reserve and I wanted to get back to short stories. By the time I'd finished the Biggers' story [*House With-out A Key*, 1926] and the Tunney job [*The Fighting Marine*, 1926], I'd had all the best that serials could offer me and I knew it. The fun was gone and I was too damned independent to care for Hollywood and studio fears, com-promises and politics."

Surrounded by hot lead and cold steel, Ben Wilson comes face to face with Howard Crampton, the master villain of *The Screaming Shadow* (1920). (Courtesy D. Elmo Brooks)

Actually, Smith's job at Pathé had encompassed much more than it was meant to. When he succeeded to Willets' position in the early twenties, Pearson had impressed upon him that he was only to manage writers, but good ones were scarce. In Smith's humble opinion, serial writers didn't appear to exist in quantity and the few good ones in the field were already employed. He was plagued by the question, "Who, in his right mind, would wish to learn the serial writer's craft?" Thus, he hired writers who sat around while he did their work for them. It was his feeling that this was the easiest way out, easier than trying to teach or explain. At this time, it was his firm conviction that the golden days of the silent serial were over and how right he proved to be!

The influence behind Smith's decision to write for the serial medium was Bertram Millhauser. Ranking behind Smith, to whom writing was a craft, and Seitz, who had used writing as a stepping stone to directing, Millhauser was the most valuable Pathé property in the script department. The son of

Independent serials made use of stars who no longer commanded the attention of major studios. Here Grace Darmond searches for a clue in the Kosmick Films *Hope Diamond Mystery* (1921). (Courtesy D. Elmo Brooks)

a New York City police lieutenant, he had found his way into the Pathé New York office. A kind and amiable sort of chap, he wrote titles and worked in the publicity department at the outset, but soon began to spend his spare time working on scripts and turning out some of his own. Although short in stature, his handsome features and energetic personality were contained in a muscular frame. Gregarious by nature, he soon came to know all of the staff in the office, both male and female, and was well liked by each. His contacts kept him posted on all of the office intrigues and gossip. Millhauser knew his way around.

Early Pathé villains were primitive in conception and bore no resemblance to the fascinating characters created in the twenties. This is the "Clutching Hand," from *The Exploits of Elaine* (1914). In Chapter 9, "The Death Ray," he warns Craig Kennedy, the scientific detective, of his intention to destroy innocent bystanders unless Kennedy withdraws from the case. (Courtesy D. Elmo Brooks)

Taken from an original print, these perilous scenes from *The Railroad Raiders* (1917) show how editing helped to build suspense. Intercutting closeups of Helen Holmes with long shots of the train approaching helped keep the fans on the edge of their seats. (Courtesy D. Elmo Brooks)

Circus backgrounds were popular in the early serials, providing a setting for action, adventure and romance. Grace Cunard flees from the taunting clowns in this scene from *Adventures of Peg O' The Ring* (1916). (Courtesy D. Elmo Brooks)

As he did with so many others, Seitz realized that Millhauser had great potential that was being wasted and urged him to put his creative talents to good use. To Seitz, Millhauser was a script writer of the first caliber. It did not require a great deal of urging or cajoling, as the little fellow possessed a natural taste for melodrama. If it could be said that such a thing existed as a flair for screen writing, Millhauser had it and was well equipped to make excellent use of his ability. He was one of the first writers to realize the value of a villain and to play this aspect to the limit. It was his contention that an effective villain meant a successful serial. While other writers fastened their attention upon the hero or heroine, Millhauser built his villains up very carefully. He considered this to be the pivotal point of each chapter play.

When Frank Leon Smith joined the organization, it was Millhauser who took him in tow and urged him to write. He possessed a hearty sense of humor which was ever-present and the team of Seitz, Millhauser and Smith soon became known as "The Last of the Mohicans." As individuals, as well as a team, these three men felt that it was up to them to maintain, and raise if possible, the quality of the footage which bore the famed rooster trade mark.

When Seitz found himself overburdened, Millhauser stepped into director's shoes for the two Juanita Hansen serials and both efforts were slick and clean examples of what a good chapter play should be. He wrote for such stars as Pearl White, Charles Hutchison, Mollie King and Ruth Roland. Quite possibly his best effort came in the Roland serial, *The Timber Queen* (1922). Although it is sometimes difficult to pick the best work of a highly skilled writer, this tightly constructed effort, produced by Roach and directed by Fred Jackman, contained one of the most famous, and rightly so, scenes in serial history — the runaway boxcar sequence.

After Seitz left Pathé, Millhauser went to the West Coast, where he worked for various studios, serving as an assistant to Cecil B. De Mille for a time. Like Seitz, his death was untimely but he had left a lasting impression through his years at Pathé at a time when "The House of Serials" had possessed the finest talent gathered under one roof.

5

The Inner Circle,
or
By Whose Hand

While producers were concerned with the business end of production, the techniques properly rested within the province of the director. In the early days of the film, both functions had been the responsibility of the director, but as the industry grew and maturity began to develop, the creative end was separated from and subordinated to the more mundane business of providing a finished product to be sold. The responsibility for many of the creative tasks which the early directors had performed was taken away as part and parcel of the growing unionization movement. Let's look at what made a director and how he functioned through the silent period, with special emphasis on that peculiar creature called a serial director.

The talents necessary for success as a serial director were a bit different from those required of feature directors. Directing was an art which required both ability and personality. These two merged into a sort of uncanny sixth sense which nearly all directors possessed to some degree.

Picture sense, or the ability to visualize a written scene in terms of the picture on the screen, was perhaps the most important aspect. This ability was innate and not made or gained, but it could be developed by the person who had it. In this respect, it can honestly be said that some are born directors while others just go through the motions. As he read and prepared a script, the director had to visually note the sort of sets to be used, along with properties, costumes, entrances and exits from scenes and a thousand other details.

Peering from behind a building in *Pearl of the Army* (1916) was one thing for Pearl White, but hanging by a fraying rope in *The Fatal Ring* (1917) was something different.

Lightning Bryce (Jack Hoxie) and Solvang (Paul C. Hurst) come face to face in Episode 5 of *Lightning Bryce* (1919). Hurst directed this chapter play and would continue his villainy well into the sound era. (Courtesy Don Overton)

As the emotional content of a serial was the most important property relating to its success, the best-equipped directors were men who had a wide groundwork or basis of emotional feeling. Thus, the director had to be somewhat of a student of human nature whose sympathies were not totally submerged.

Lesser attributes included not only the ability to "feel the atmosphere," but the ability to achieve it on film. A knowledge of acting allowed the director to handle his cast with diplomacy and tact, as well as to demonstrate what he desired. An understanding of tempo was most important, for the serials were rapidly paced and an uneven tempo could completely destroy the audience belief in what he had done. This understanding was related to the art of editing, as well as the actual direction. A good editor could improve upon the tempo whereas a poor or indifferent one could literally ruin it.

The triumphant meeting of Livingstone and Stanley was witnessed by Louise Lorraine and George Walsh, the coadventurers in *With Stanley in Africa*. (1922). (Courtesy Louise Lorraine)

The ways that the qualities of a serial director differed from his contemporaries in feature production were eloquently summed up by Ford Beebe, a serial writer who learned his craft in the silents and went on to direct many interesting sound serials: "To make serials, it took someone who knew the business from every angle. He had to know how to get his results the easiest possible way. He had to be able and willing to compromise between the *best* way to get them and settle for second best if the best would cost too much, if second best was adequate. He had to avail himself of standing sets to cut production costs. This might mean taking a big sequence out of a church and playing it in a livery stable by making a few quick changes in story line so the switch would be logical. In short, he had to know the film business forward and backward; know how to get 'production' by making

Louise Lorraine and Elmo Lincoln in *The Flaming Disc (1920)*. The man with the false scar was Monty Montague, Lincoln's double in long shots. (Courtesy Louise Lorraine)

use of backgrounds made for 'big' pictures at terrific cost and how to shape his story so that the action would be germane to the backgrounds, and so on and on and on, not to mention that he must know cutting and have total recall as regards stock material so he could steal a few feet out of a thousand-foot reel to fit some need he hadn't enough money to shoot. In short, he had to be a near magician and above all, he had to be a guy who loved the challenge and above even that, he had to have assembled a crew of the same caliber — guys who unconsciously forgot about their paychecks in their interest in the immediate undertaking."

The problems faced by an actor who directed his own chapter plays (as did William Duncan and Francis Ford) were multiplied many times. As the star, he had to face the camera and project the desired personality into the role. At the same time, he had to be able to visualize his own work from behind the camera in order to maintain the proper perspective of both. The tendency of such multi-faceted persons was to neglect the supervision of the production as a whole, in concentrating on their own performance.

William Bertram (left) director of *Hidden Dangers* (1920) talks over a scene with Jean Paige (center) and Joe Ryan. This was Ryan's first serial role; he had previously served as the chief "heavy" in Vitagraph's chapter plays. (Courtesy Alan Brock)

At the beginning of the serial period, the director worked closely with his story editor and scenarists in the development of a logical story, punctuated with suspense. Effective communication between these people was absolutely necessary if the correct story interpretation was to appear in the finished footage. Such communication was also essential in developing the continuity of a cinematic translation. In some cases, the director could and would improve, alter or throw away the prepared script in favor of his own ideas about how the story should progress.

He also worked closely with the cameramen in order that they might record on film the ideas which he and the writers had evolved. Until strong unionization took place, there was no director of cinematography. The director was responsible for camera placement (as well as lighting) to shoot the scenes as he wanted them. Rehearsal of the cast with a script and megaphone helped him to visualize his ideas and gave the players a close approximation of his desires. A good director was capable of demonstrating the scene to his cast. Thus, if a stunt had to be done, he had to be able to put across exactly what he wanted, even if he had to execute the action sequence himself.

Having collaborated this intimately, from conception through filming, it was only natural that the director would help edit the rough footage to final form, or at least supervise the cutting and assembly of the product. The most capable directors were able to "edit" their episodes with the camera, in effect saving the cutter much work and assuring themselves that the final footage was as they wished it to be. Of course, this held true only in the early days of the chapter play and the picture was to change considerably as time went on.

Special effect work was rare. The different techniques that are used today had not been developed or were at best imperfect in practice. Faking a scene completely, as is done now, was practically impossible in the days of the silents. The technology was not available at the time. For example, suppose that the director wished to show the heroine hanging from the roof of a building by her hands. This was to be shot from above to show the street below and to increase audience awareness of the frightful peril she was in. Today, an eight-foot reproduction on-set and a process screen would give a perfect illusion with absolutely no danger involved.

Spencer G. Bennet needed just such a scene for *Play Ball* (1925), a Miller-Ray serial. The compromise at which he arrived was to build a false roof about six feet above the real one and set it back about four feet from the edge of the building. This allowed placement of a mattress below the actress. By moving the camera back slightly, the illusion was as satisfactory as it would have been had she actually been placed in jeopardy. Good directors had just such a bag of tricks to draw from when needed, and Bennet was inventive by nature.

By the end of the war period, the industry had become too large and impersonal for one person to perform all of these creative tasks within the

This production still was taken during a break at the filming of *Elmo the Fearless* (1920).
Louise Lorraine is seen at the far right and her director, J. P. McGowan, scowls at the
camera. (Courtesy Louise Lorraine)

short time period allowed from story conference to release date. It also
varied from company to company. Within the larger firms, such as Universal, strict controls were placed on the directors. They received a script, cast,
crew, budget and time allotment. Finished footage, as assembled by the
editors, often surprised its director upon his initial screening. Pathé, as
explained in Chapter 2, often combined both the creative and business ends.
The persons charged with production hardly entered the picture in many
cases. However, within the small independent firms, the director remained
a jack-of-all-trades almost until the demise of the silents.

At the start, the personality of the director had thoroughly permeated and
colored the finished serial. As the creative functions were separated from

A production still from *The Adventures of Tarzan* (1921). The youthful heroine, Louise Lorraine, is closest to the camera. Robert F. Hill, who directed, sits behind her and orders script changes. (Courtesy Louise Lorraine)

the hands of the director, serials suddenly acquired the same assembly-line look that characterized the Universal product of the twenties. At this point, the primary concern and responsibility of the director was narrowed to bringing the chapter play in under the budget estimate established by the people in the front office. Many of these persons were quite notorious for their inability to project a realistic figure — one in line with the quality which they desired in the finished product. Creative talents were thus molded more or less rigidly in a system which placed them under superiors far less imaginative and far more conscious of merchandising a product, regardless of its merits. Few serial directors were able to transcend the artificial boundaries which this system placed them under.

Standing head and shoulders above his contemporaries, George B. Seitz was the dean of serial directors. Only his assistant, Spencer G. Bennet, came close to approaching his skill with a megaphone. For roughly ten years, Seitz led and the others followed. His talents were many and varied. As a serial writer, he ranked close to Frank Leon Smith as one of the best in the business. A shrewd businessman, he was also a first-rate leading man. The wonder of it all is that he was able to lead a happy and normal family life in addition to his work.

Born in Boston on January 3, 1888, he came from a well-to-do New England family which moved to Philadelphia soon after his birth. Swarthmore College was his objective after high school, but the family had returned to Boston and George went to work in a bank. During this time, he developed a passion for amateur theatricals. It did not take him too long to lose in-

As Bellamy, Burr McIntosh gave no quarter in *The Green Archer* (1925). (Courtesy Frank Lackteen)

terest in the bank and he moved on — to the Eric Pape Art School, where he studied magazine illustration and continued toying with the theatre. The combination of stock and a road company gave him a keen insight into the problems of playwriting, stagecraft and acting. Writing had become a driving force by this time, and at twenty-two he sold his first play, *The King's Game.* James K. Hackett starred in this Graustarkian romance, which went over quite well. This was the turning point in Seitz's life

A romantic by nature, he found himself bucking a trend toward realism in writing. Although he sold a few articles to magazines, his funds were rapidly disappearing. This posed a rather large problem, for by this time George wanted to marry a childhood sweetheart, Mary Harris. Her father quite properly demanded that George be able to show an indication of his ability to support her. This was the motivation that sent him knocking on the door of Pathé.

It was a stroke of good fortune that the firm had need of a writer with a flair for melodrama. Seitz was taken on. In a very short time, he had mastered the scenario technique and worked on the shooting script of *The Perils of Pauline* (1914). Proving that he was a worthwhile addition to the company, George managed to get himself removed from the payroll and onto a piece-work basis with bonus. Soon after this, he was so loaded down with work that he set free-lance scenarists to work on script-writing jobs. By the fall of 1914, Seitz was able to return to Philadelphia to claim his bride.

A prolific writer of the first draft variety, he turned his unsold plays and stories into scenarios and sold them to Pathé. The year 1915 found him doing originals and adaptations for five-reel features, but it was *The Exploits of Elaine.* (1914) that placed him on the track to fame. The *Elaine* cycle ran to thirty-six episodes and was followed by twenty scripts for *The Iron Claw* (1916). In 1916, he was instrumental in forming the Astra Film Corporation and took over the Pathé studio facilities. He then set about gathering a crew of helpers who were to play an important role in serial history. Bertram Millhauser came as adapter, writer and director; Edward Snyder as cameraman; Spencer G. Bennet as stuntman, second-unit director and utility man; and Frank Leon Smith.

Astra made many excellent serials for Pathé release but Seitz was not happy about the way in which the company was managed and in 1919, he decided to form his own studio. A Harlem dance hall at 134th Street and Park Avenue was renovated and he was in business. Many of his old friends and fellow workers turned up on the payroll and it was a happy venture from the very beginning. Seitz was sincerely concerned with the welfare of his group, and among other things he developed a minimum wage scale and operated a free dining room. Anyone with a good idea was able to find a

Frank Lackteen makes a perfect looking gentleman in *The Green Archer* (1925). Dorothy King and Allene Ray provide the feminine interest in one of the best of the silent serials. (Courtesy Frank Lackteen)

receptive ear and many stage hands increased their pay by playing secondary roles. Frank Redman (head props) and Tom Goodwin (costume department) were among those who regularly drew important roles.

With *Bound and Gagged* (1919), Seitz came into his own as an actor. He made several profitable serials and then wrote *Rogues and Romance* (1920), a feature in which he starred with June Caprice and Marguerite Courtot. The exteriors were done in Spain and the film was finished in the Harlem studio. A thin story line, coupled with release during a time of economic difficulties, cost Seitz his independence. It was his own money which had been invested in the film and he was unable to get it back. Pathé put him back to work on three vehicles for Charles Hutchison and Pearl White's final serial. After that, he went to the West Coast where he made the first three Allene Ray serials, returning to the East for *Galloping Hoofs* (1924) and *Into the Net* (1924). Early in 1925, he took a crew to Florida to do *Sunken*

WILLIAM DUNCAN
—IN—
"THE SILENT AVENGER"
A VITAGRAPH SERIAL
EPISODE N°10
"BLADES of HORROR"

PHIL GETS IMPORTANT INFORMATION
ON A TAPPED WIRE.

Without a doubt, this phone call means trouble for William Duncan and Edith Johnson. Who is *The Silent Avenger?* (1920). (Courtesy Larry Edmunds Bookshop)

Silver, his final serial. At the close of filming, he left Pathé for feature work at Paramount. Although Seitz continued to add to his fame in features (especially the *Andy Hardy* series) until his death in 1944, his departure had ended an era in Pathé serial history.

As a director, Seitz had many unique qualities. He knew exactly what he was after and was as proficient in shooting scenes as in writing them. A fast worker who was able to coax the best from his cast, he seemed to realize more than most serial directors that time was the most important production factor. His secret formula for success was based on skill, preparation and speed, plus an early start each day. Resourceful to the *nth* degree, Seitz never compromised his loyalty or integrity. He managed to divorce his personal life completely from his profession and remained a romantic to his death. Many who knew him say that in spite of his happy-go-lucky attitude, he had the "touch" and it never failed him. Superstition aside, there is no doubt that Seitz was able to combine all of the ingredients necessary for success. He had a feeling for what he was doing and was completely at home with his work. Few other serial directors were able to work at such a high level with any degree of consistency.

Spencer Gordon Bennet was one director who knew where he wanted to go and worked very hard to get there. Born in Brooklyn on January 5, 1893, of Anglo-French parents, he attended the Brooklyn public schools while nurturing a desire to be a part of the theatre. At the age of thirteen, he acquired a job as program boy in a Brooklyn theatre which presented some of the top attractions of the day. He even played small roles in some of the plays. Cast as a newsboy selling programs in *Brown of Harvard*, he had to play hookey from school in order to appear in the Wednesday matinee. It was only a matter of time before he was caught and as Bennet recalled: "One beautiful Saturday afternoon, I was dishing out programs when I spotted my teacher approaching and the only thing I could do was to keep my head down, hide my face, hoping that she would pass through and I would be unnoticed, but the figure remained at the program table. As I looked up, she was glancing at me askance, with that knowing look, enough to say, 'What beautiful absentee notes you have written to me for those Wednesday afternoons when you didn't show up.' However, she was a good skate and let me get away with it."

Having had enough of school, he left to spend two years in the wilds of Canada and returned to the United States in 1912 as a stunt man for the Edison studio in Fordham, New York. He quickly took a liking to movie making, for he found it not only interesting but lucrative as well. His first stunt was a leap into water from a cliff. Edison paid by the foot for such a stunt and when he was asked what he would take to do it, he insisted they measure the leap. It turned out to be 62½ feet. This amounted to $62.50 for the leap, which he agreed to do. Returning after completing the stunt, Bennet found that the director was not satisfied with other action which took place in the scene and for another $62.50, he did it all over again. Convinced that this was his future, he set out to learn all that he could about it. In 1914, he joined Pathé where he stunted and served as an assistant director. This was his great stroke of fortune. Working under George B. Seitz, Bennet proved to be a willing and able pupil. He soon acquired a finesse in his direction that brought him to the cherished role of co-director with Seitz.

By this time, the young man had definitely set his sights on becoming a

Dressed as the "Great Chief," William Duncan escaped from the bloodthirsty Indians to inform his friends that he had located the treasure tomb, the motivation for *Fighting Fate* (1921). Duncan was quite successful in directing his own serials for Vitagraph and became a favorite with fans. (Courtesy Larry Edmunds Bookshop)

full-fledged director in his own right, a position he was to achieve when Seitz finally left Pathé. There is some doubt as to whether Pathé would have realized his full potential had it not been for Frank Leon Smith. Smith had worked closely with Bennet as well as Seitz and all three men clearly appreciated each others' talents. Pathé was determined to replace Seitz with a "name" director when Smith intervened and secured the position for Bennet. Neither man had cause for regret, as Smith's shrewd assessment of his friend proved to be a correct one. Bennet's work carried on in the tradition set by Seitz.

Actually, his technique was more methodical than that of his teacher.

Working with Seitz over the years, he made it a firm practice to study the
cutting and assembling of his serials. Bennet was one of the rare directors
who could edit nearly all of his picture in the camera — saving time, effort,
film and money. His knowledge of editing meant that he very rarely over-
shot a scene, because he was able to correctly visualize just what was needed
and what angles would most effectively portray his ideas. He usually got
his scenes on the first take, which meant very few retakes. All this he learned
from Seitz, but in his hands it was put to more efficient use. He was not
involved in writing and the financial end of serial production, as was his
mentor.

Mistakes were made to learn from and he was careful not to repeat an
error. Many years of self-correction and the cutting knowledge gained by it

After a long absence from the serial screen, Grace Cunard returned to supporting roles.
In *Blake of Scotland Yard* (1927), she played the mysterious woman in white who always
managed to save Gloria Gray from "The Spider." The serial was an immense success.

made him a favorite of editors in later years. When he was restricted to directing (in the sound era), they would practically beg to be assigned to cut his pictures. The money he was able to save Pathé by his able and unique technique of directing more than paid his salary. He received a flat $500 per week, but because of his ability to turn out consistently fine material, the Pathé bonus system brought his wages to an average $750 weekly.

Other aspects of his talent served him equally well. A fine example of his ability to do the job well, quickly and inexpensively can be found by the manner in which he worked out a problem that confronted him in the production of a Charles Hutchison vehicle. The scene called for Hutch to jump a motorcycle from a dock to the deck of a departing ferry. It just happened that the only ferry available was anchored out in the water. To move the ship into the dock would have required the services of all hands plus a tugboat. This job was priced at $10,000, and it would have required quite a bit of shooting time just to properly position the ferry.

Bennet's lunch period, which served him so well on many occasions, provided the answer to this vexing problem. He hired a scow, the front of which appeared identical to a dock. The scow was towed up to the stationary ferry and the tugboat was placed behind the scow. He asked the ferry captain to start his motors to give the desired spray and as the tug towed the scow away from the ferry, Joe Bonomo, (doubling for Hutch) roared down the scow and jumped the cycle across the open water onto the ferry. On the screen, it was impossible to tell the difference. Bennet saved hours and spent only $50.00 for the entire scene. Such was the talent of the man who so admirably filled the shoes of Seitz.

Before shipping the finished episodes to New York City, Bennet held a free preview for all of the kids that he could lay his hands on in the neighborhood, along with all of their pals. It was his belief that the reactions which he received would serve as a key to tell him whether or not he was on the right track. He never had any difficulty in filling the house. The idea worked out well for him but he did receive quite a shock at the outset. As the first episode ended, he met with dead silence. Puzzled, he quickly assessed the chapter as a real lemon. A short investigation gave him the reason for the unnatural and unwarranted behavior — the mothers had warned their children that they would not be allowed to attend future screenings unless they behaved and acted as ladies and gentlemen.

With this knowledge, Bennet told the kids that he wanted to know how they liked the chapter and to make all the noise that they wanted to. They did just that and the roof nearly came off. The kids wound up with ice cream and cake and he had the reaction he had waited for. Actually, there was nothing new or novel about the idea of pretesting. It amounted to a sneak

The Master Mystery (1919), Houdini's only serial, had very good production values for an independent serial, but audiences weren't able to accept the ridiculous-looking "Automaton" as a serious villain. (Courtesy John Hampton)

preview but Bennet paid faithful attention to it, and over the years it paid off handsomely for him.

The most effective combination of his talents was found in *The Green Archer* (1925), the best serial that Bennet ever made, silent or sound. In fact, it stands out today as probably the finest of the silent serials. Bennet has always felt that had it been made in Pathécolor,[1] the added value could have easily doubled its gross receipts. Of course, no practical color process was available at the time.

Frank Leon Smith had leaped at an opportunity to purchase the movie rights from the author, Edgar Wallace. As Smith recalled the transaction, a sum of $1500 was involved. The story had a British locale, but Smith transposed everything to America. The necessary castles were found in the

[1] A semi-mechanical process of hand coloring each frame by the use of stencils.

Hudson River Valley of New York, not too far from where the remainder of production facilities were located. For Scotland Yard, he substituted the New York State Police. This transposition was explained by having the villain transfer an English castle to a site on the Hudson, stone by stone. The ghost of the castle supposedly went with it. Beyond these liberties, Smith remained faithful to the flavor of the original story.

One problem which did present itself was in showing the mystery character on screen in full view without giving his identity away. Smith later attributed what followed to good luck and proper timing. It seems that Benda masks were the rage at the moment. An artist, Benda's reputation came from his *papier-mâché* masks. Here was the answer. For the sum of

The Florida everglades served as a location for Allene Ray and Walter Miller in *Sunken Silver* (1925). (Courtesy John Hampton)

$100, a mask was obtained. The face was out of true just a bit, but symmetrical in line from the forehead down through the nose, mouth and chin. This added to Wallace's vivid depiction of his mystery man and solved the problem.

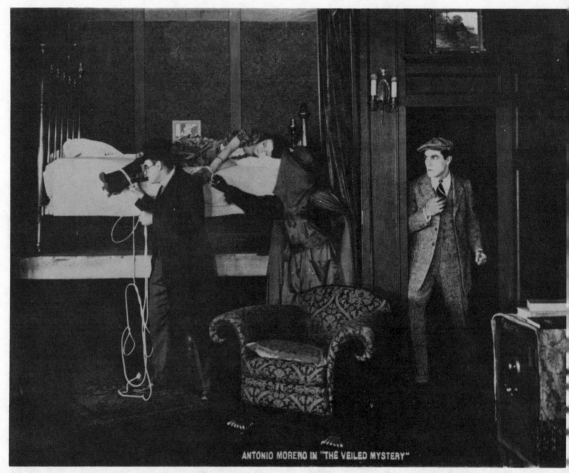

ANTONIO MORENO IN "THE VEILED MYSTERY"

Rescue in the nick of time! *The Veiled Mystery* (1920) and his mad doctor were about to dispose of Nenette de Courcy in a trick bed as Tony Moreno stumbled onto their hiding place. (Courtesy Nan Boardman)

A partial replica of the castle, including its entrance, was constructed in the Pathé Long Island studio and some location scenes were done in Nyack. It was there, on a high bluff overlooking the Hudson, that Bennet had a crenelated tower built. The cameras were placed on this structure and when they photographed the scenes, the crenelated edges of the tower in the background with the river far below gave just the right atmosphere. The illusion was perfect. Other location scenes were done on an estate in Kingston, New York.

The estate grounds had been carefully kept up and appeared as flawless as a fine golf-course green. Several scenes called for the State Troopers to enter and exit on horse back. Informed that the horses would not damage the beautiful lawn, Bennet allowed them to short-cut across the lawn to the castle entrance for dramatic effect. Luckily, he did not have a weak heart or ulcers. The agony he felt when he discovered the results of the short-cuts would have made either an unbearable state. Never told how much the damage cost, he was not overly anxious to find out. However, he was certain that it cost Pathé plenty and doubts to this day if any other film company ever received permission to use that location again. Fortunately, the shots were exciting touches which added to the suspense of the serial chapters.

Bennet's ability to handle his cast was tested to the limit in this chapter play. Burr McIntosh was admirably cast as Bellamy, the owner of the castle and villain of the piece, who kept his wife in a dungeon in the cellar. McIntosh had a radio program of his own which was broadcast five nights weekly and he came into the houses of millions of Americans as *The Cheerful Philosopher*. Actually, he was one of the crabbiest old actors that one could ever hope to come across and fitted the role of Bellamy perfectly. The slightest provocation would send his temper flying and the unit crew usually worked him over, all in good humor. One evening, Bennet asked him to stay over for a closeup, lying on the floor. McIntosh waited around for nearly three hours, growing more impatient and bitter as the minutes passed.

During this time, Bennet came to the realization that he really didn't need that shot after all, but how to explain it to the highly disgusted villain? He seriously believed that McIntosh would never have finished the picture had he known the truth, so with the aid of his cameraman, he went ahead and filmed the scene with an empty camera. McIntosh never knew the difference and Bennet was prepared to explain that the scene had wound up on the cutting room floor.

Directors working at Universal had several handicaps to overcome, not the least being average or below-average stories to work with. The reluctance of the company to spend money for quality also hindered them. Company policy was to squeeze the most from the least, a trick at which a few directors became quite proficient. The most talented of a long line of serial directors who worked for Universal was Robert F. Hill, a product of Port Rohen, Ontario. An early interest in the stage eventually brought him, as it did so

Lowering himself from the roof by rope, Tony Moreno sought to free Nenette de Courcy from *The Veiled Mystery* (1920). (Courtesy Nan Boardman)

many others, to the motion picture. Before he reached the world of make-believe, Hill had served a long stage apprenticeship, beginning with a nine-year engagement in stock with Vaughn Glaser. This was followed by three more seasons in the legitimate theater; one in *The Bridge*, one in *St. Elmo* and one as stage director and producer of *College Widow*, in which he played a role.

A lean, ascetic fellow, Bob Hill entered the movies in 1914 with an independent company operating in Michigan and made one of the first two pictures shot in that state. He found this work a new challenge and decided to stay in films. During the next two years, he ranged East and West playing heavies for Edison and working for various units of Carl Laemmle's Universal. He directed heavy drama starring Mary Fuller and also did light comedy for the Victor brand. A better offer came from Triangle in 1917 and Hill

ANTONIO MORENO
in
'THE VEILED MYSTERY'
A Vitagraph Serial
EPISODE 10
"A DEMONS DEVICE"

RALPH, ETHEL AND TOM FASTENED TO WALL
IRONS IN THE SUBTERRANEAN VAULT.

George Cooper and friend are about to leave Tony Moreno and Nenette de Courcy imprisoned in an underground vault. As the episode ended, water would fill the chamber — how could they escape? (Courtesy Nan Boardman)

made the switch, also moving from directing to writing. By this time he had written fifty-six original stories, all of which were sold as film scripts. His talents did not go unnoticed, and in September 1918 he became assistant story editor to Daniel Carson Goodman, head of Triangle's scenario department. Unfortunately, Triangle was in the process of decay and shortly went out of existence. Hill returned to Universal as a writer-director and in 1919, he began his career as a serial director with *The Great Radium Mystery*.

Throughout the silent period, Hill constantly turned in the best serials to bear the Universal trade mark. An extremely nervous and high strung individual, he was very generous and well-liked by those who worked with him but was a stern taskmaster who demanded the best from his people. Basically a good chap to work for, Hill learned early in the game that protection is the best insurance. While shooting scenes for *The Adventures of Tarzan* (1921), he had a run-in with the star, Elmo Lincoln. Louise Lorraine's costume had been pinned on her and Elmo made a wild grab to pick her up. In the process of doing so, he pricked his finger on a pin, dropped Louise and screamed to high heaven. The crew thought this very funny and broke out in gales of hilarity. Elmo, a sensitive person for his size, immediately took offense and walked off the set. He refused to return until what he felt to be proper apologies were made.

This was a serious matter, for even though Lincoln seldom carried through on his many threats, Hill realized that just this once he might mean it. While the proper attempts to cajole Lincoln into returning were made, the director concocted a scheme which he felt certain would frighten Elmo into backing down. Elmo's double was a small fellow who couldn't be used in medium or close shots, but whose shape closely followed the star's when seen in a long shot. Taking cameraman Jerry Ash aside, Hill told him to "yes" him on everything he was about to say. In front of Monty Montague, the double and a close friend of Lincoln's, Hill announced to the cast that he would finish the serial without the services of his temperamental star.

With much emotion, Hill explained that he planned on inserting a scene by the jungle river, with the witch doctor on one side and Tarzan (the double in a long shot) on the other. The witch doctor would place a curse on Tarzan, who would walk into the river and emerge on the other side as a nine-year-old boy. Hearing this and listening to Ash figure out the camera angles, Montague slipped quietly away and informed Elmo of the plot to take him out of the lead. Lincoln returned to the set the next day, meek as a lamb and more than willing to do whatever Hill asked of him. The really amusing thing was that Laemmle heard of Hill's thoughts on the serial and decided that it would make a terrific twist. He insisted that it be incorporated and shooting was held up several more days while Hill talked him out of the idea.

In 1924, Hill was assigned to direct *The Jack O'Clubs*, a Red Feather ("B") Feature with Herbert Rawlinson as star. The picture was rehearsed and shot in eleven days, two ahead of the schedule. When the editing was completed, Hill arranged for Laemmle to view it alone. Laemmle was in the habit of taking his advisors into the projection room to watch the finished product. This was the time for company politicking and many people had their throats slashed in this manner. The politicians would begin to mutter about various errors and Laemmle, an impressionable person, would be easily swayed this way. Alone with Hill, Laemmle enjoyed the film greatly. When it was released, both men watched the "Scoreboard" in *The*

Moving Picture World. This was a rating service in a trade paper and any-thing above 64 per cent was considered to be of "A" picture quality. *The Jack O'Clubs* received 89 per cent over a nine-month average. Hill felt that it was time to ask for a raise from $325 weekly to $500. It was turned down.

Hill left Universal soon after this event and joined C. W. Patton, an in-dependent producer who had a pair of Pathé serials ready to go before the camera. After they were finished, Universal approached him in November 1925 and he rejoined the organization, mostly as a personal favor to Carl Laemmle. Universal wanted to establish a studio in Japan and Laemmle decided that Hill was the man for the job. He was given a budget of $350,000 to set up a working arrangement and took his wife, a cameraman and one lab man with him.

Every serial had at least one good brawl or donnybrook. Here are three typical ones. (1) Pearl White fights for her life in *Plunder* (1923).

THE WINKING IDOL
CHAPTER 1
THE EYE OF EVIL

(2) William Desmond prepares to clean house in *The Winking Idol* (1926).

Although still a Canadian, Hill made friends with a young American consul once he arrived in Japan. The consul was helpful and informed him of
the local method of doing business. It seemed that others had tried to open
studios, only to build up the area and then be threatened by an uprising of
the local populace, who usually put on a good show. The frightened foreign-
ers could expect no help from the local police and the end result was an
abandoned studio which was then taken over by the Japanese and put into
operation.

After many consultations with his new acquaintance, Hill made several
trips into the interior and assured himself that this was indeed the truth. He
then decided against spending the money in such a wasteful manner. Wiring

(3) Wiliam Desmond (minus his disguise) and Eileen Sedgwick dispose of those who would destroy free speech and the local paper which served as Desmond's cover in *The Riddle Rider* (1924). (All 3 courtesy of John Hampton)

the New York office of his decision, Hill received a reply, warning him that failure to erect the studio meant a willful breaking of his new five-year contract. Determined, Bob made arrangements to reenter the United States. He had no reentry permit and was granted such only after a friendly doctor in California signed a paper to the effect that Mrs. Hill was in need of medical care obtainable only in the United States.

Returning to Universal, he found himself in disfavor. Jay Marchant was sent over to do the same job and the outcome was exactly as Hill had predicted. Fearing for his life, Marchant abandoned the studio after its completion. This turn of events reinstated Hill in Laemmle's eye and one day at lunch, the studio head was bemoaning the quality of Universal serials. Bob had been doing mostly features, but put forth an idea that brought Laemmle to life.

Calling William Lord Wright (head of serial production) into his office, Laemmle announced that Hill was going back to serials. Wright was informed that he would have no control whatsoever over Hill's project; Bob was to report directly to Laemmle. Hill presided over the construction of a serial script that did not rely on explosions, wrecks and disasters for its thrills. Given a budget of $125,000 by Laemmle, Bob brought *Blake of Scotland Yard* in for $97,000. The serial was booked for $900,000 of business even before it was released and eventually grossed over $3,500,000 on a world-wide basis.

Hill had proven his point and went on into the sound period as one of Universal's most successful directors. In 1940, he was involuntarily retired from active directing. This resulted from a head injury suffered when a bullet ricocheted during the filming of a sequence. He lived quietly in his Hollywood home and reminisced willingly about the old days until his death in 1966.

Of the fast-action, low budget directors associated with serials during the twenties, one of the better was a young man officially known as Woodbridge Strong Van Dyke II, nicknamed "Woody" or Van. W. S. Van Dyke was born in March 1889 to Laura Winston and Woodbridge Van Dyke in San Diego, California. His father, a promising young lawyer in the process of establishing a practice, died the day following his son's birth. This left the mother, a former concert pianist, with no source of support and she was forced to return to her former calling for a living. A move to San Francisco in 1892 found concert engagements scarce for Laura Winston Van Dyke. Taking her maiden name, the young widow entered the theater as a member of the Morosco Stock Company. Young Woody made his stage debut at an early age as the son of Damon in *Damon and Pythias*. For the next few years, Laura and her son were on the road, traveling across the United States with various stock companies.

In 1903, finances were firm enough for the formation of the Laura Winston Players and Woody left for Seattle to live with his grandmother while attending business school. A husky lad for his age, Van Dyke held all kinds of odd jobs while completing his schooling and then went into a lumbering camp to work for a season. While in Seattle, he met and married Zina Ashform. Rejoining his mother and her repertory company, Woody and his wife went on the road. He played leading man to his mother.

It was during this time that they met with an old theater acquaintance, Walter Long. Long was ultimately responsible for Van Dyke's debut in

Charles Hutchison was doubled quite often during the latter part of his serial career, but this scene from *Lightning Hutch* (1926) was very real. Hutch could climb up or down buildings in this manner. (Courtesy John Hampton)

motion pictures. Woody, like so many other legitimate actors, had only contempt for the "flickers," but Long changed that feeling into one of curiosity. He had been working with Griffith in *The Birth of a Nation* (1915) and brought a few members of the cast to a party in Los Angeles which was attended by Van and his mother. Surprised that the actors were *not* the dregs of the stage, Woody listened condescendingly at first, but soon the enthusiasm of the picture players caught his ear and he began to wonder if the movies might be worth investigating after all. Long promised him a job with Griffith and so Van Dyke found himself an extra in *Intolerance* (1916).

Serials were not all made on the back lot in Hollywood. Spencer G. Bennet took his crew to McCall, Idaho, to film one of Frank Leon Smith's finest chapter plays, *Snowed In* (1926). Allene Ray is the girl in danger. (Courtesy John Hampton)

Spending much of his free time watching Griffith direct, Woody decided that his future was in that branch of the film business. After *Intolerance* was finished, he joined the Lasky Feature Play Company as an assistant to James Young, a top director of the period. Here he learned, practiced and improvised under the guidance of Young. When an offer to join Essanay appeared, they both took advantage of it and moved to Chicago. Shortly, Van Dyke was sent to California to open and operate a Culver City studio for Essanay. It was during this short adventure that he learned to operate fast and efficiently with limited funds and help, for Essanay was rapidly dying. He wrote, directed and cut a few pictures in 1917 before the studio was closed down and he was drafted.

Returning from Army life, Van Dyke found himself a forgotten man in the land of make-believe. The picture business had changed a good deal and he was able to find only "quickie" jobs with the various independents that were springing up like wildfire. In the meantime, Woody wrote stories and sold one to Fox, where he caught the eye of Sol Wurtzel, a man who was later to be a great help to him.

Pathé had acquired the services of Jack Dempsey, the reigning ring favorite. Dempsey had only three months before leaving to tour the sawdust trail with a circus to which he was committed. Robert G. Brunton, the independent producer who was to bring in *Daredevil Jack* (1920) for Pathé release, offered Van the serial to direct. A bonus for each episode finished within a week was established and Woody met a Pathé representative at the railroad station. The man had scripts for two chapters in hand and Van Dyke called for shooting to begin at 6:00 A.M. the next day. He had developed a penchant for practical jokes to which Dempsey was not fond, but the two got along famously otherwise and the chapter play came in under the wire. Van Dyke even coaxed a passable acting performance from the pugilist. He made a financial killing, Pathé was satisfied and Dempsey's popularity increased measurably. But Van Dyke and Zina had decided to go their separate ways.

Louis Burston, whose low-budget producing company had turned out some fine action serials with Francis Ford, was in need of a "quickie" director and Van Dyke was hired to do *The Hawk's Trail* (1920), a step down the ladder for the aging favorite, King Baggot. It was a step up for Woody, who remained at Burston to do features. Characterized by this time as an action and serial director, he chaffed at the thought of such a future and looked forward anxiously to a contract which Burston had negotiated with Louis B. Mayer for eight pictures. On the day set for the celebration of the contract, Burston was killed in an automobile accident as he was returning from a horse stable in Pomona.

The contract was quickly cancelled, as the financial backers would not release the money to a dead producer. Although greatly grieved at Burston's passing, Van Dyke was beginning to wonder if he would ever be able to direct the king of pictures he wanted to. The answer was a temporary NO, which came in the form of an offer to direct the debut of Pathé's new action king, Charles Hutchison. The two did not hit it off too well and after *The Fortieth Door* was cancelled, Woody accepted Brunton's proposition that he work on a Ruth Roland serial, *The Avenging Arrow* (1921). He did the action sequences while William Bowman handled the story proper.

His next job of note was *White Eagle* (1922), another Ruth Roland serial which Hal Roach produced. Close in story line to her earlier success, *Hands*

Up (1918), it was not quite so violent in tone. By this time Van Dyke had managed to earn Ruth's undying enmity, for his production techniques were ruthless in one sense. He asked for and received performances from the stunt doubles that should never have been risked. They responded with gusto and came back to regard him with the fond eyes of faithful though abused puppies.

A good example of this was a stunt which Woody bungled in *Ruth of the Range* (1923). He had been hired by Mike Levee to put some action into

Exteriors for *Hawk of the Hills* (1927) were shot in Newhall, California. The Indian village and the Hawk's headquarters appear to be a miniature set in this clever still, but director Spencer G. Bennet and Eddie Snyder (behind the cameras) were inserted by double printing in the darkroom to give this unusual effect. Notice the two cameras. One was used to film the serial, the other to shoot scenes for the five-reel feature version that was also released. (Courtesy Spencer G. Bennet)

the otherwise lifeless footage which Ernest C. Warde was turning in. Ruth absolutely refused to work with Van Dyke under any circumstances. By this time, her distaste for him was as great as she ever held for anyone. Thus, he had to function once more as a second unit director using Robert Rose in the stunt sequences. This particular one revolved around a "boiling, poisonous pool." Bruce Gordon as the hero was to swing across the pool to rescue Rose, who posed as Ruth.

Usually, such a sequence was worked up by placing sulphur smoke pots to burn and bubble under the water. This created the illusion of hot, steam-

On the roof of the Algonquin Hotel, New York City. Spencer Bennet (in straw hat) directs a scene before the invention of process photography. The prop roof man was a replica of the one just out of view in the lower right hand corner. Horace G. Plympton was shooting down Broadway showing the traffic and making Allene Ray appear to be in a very precarious position in this scene from *Play Ball* (1925). (Courtesy Spencer G. Bennet)

ing water. Woody insisted on doing it his own way and had the pool heated by using steam from an old fire engine. This was a needless substitution, for on film one way was as effective as the other. The sulphur smoke pots provided the safest method in case of an accident. An accident was exactly what happened. Gordon swung across the pool, and in the process both he and Rose fell into the scalding water. Emerging with bad burns, they were told to change into dry clothes. Van Dyke made them continue with bandages over their burns.

What made Van Dyke this way? Although he was completely at home and at ease with his contemporaries, it is doubtful if anyone over penetrated the man sufficiently to really understand him. His first wife was unable to and his biographer certainly didn't, presenting him as a two-dimensional figure.[2] To those who knew him, he possessed a strange form of personal magnetism; a terrific driving force which was cold. He was the sort of man who had command everywhere – that rare sort of person who gave the feeling to those around him that he was on top of the situation at all times. He seemed to know instinctively just the right move to make next and the ability to project this feeling to others resulted in their placing complete confidence in him. He regarded himself as the LAW on-set and the personnel assigned to work for him were expected to respond accordingly.

In many other ways, Woody was a kind, generous sort of fellow. He was utterly loyal to those who had worked with and for him. At his bungalow, there were always out-of-luck people living free on Van. They weren't freeloaders in any sense of the word; just friends who knew that they could count on him. For many years after Edward Hearn lost his place in the limelight, Van befriended him and gave him work. With tears in their eyes, old-time stage actors spoke of Van Dyke as though he belonged with the Deity.

In retrospect, the man had perhaps the strangest personality in the motion picture business. He was difficult to understand but very easy to accept. Once you accepted this man, you became a Van Dyke fan for life, through thick and thin. He refused to play studio politics and in so doing, set himself apart from the general breed so abundant in the film capital.

His work became his life and he turned in ample footage of high quality to rank among the best of the action directors. It was when he tried to depart from the written blueprint which had been provided by the best brains in the Pathé writing department that his footage lost its flavor and became filled with the familiar old clichés that he had used so often. These departures from the script were few and far between, for every foot of film

[2] Robert C. Cannon, *Van Dyke and the Mythical City* (Culver City, 1948)

George B. Seitz, Frank Redman and a youthful Spencer G. Bennet in *The Sky Ranger* (1921). (Courtesy Spencer G. Bennet)

William Duncan and Carol Holloway, the stars of *The Fighting Trail* (1917). Duncan became Vitagraph's most popular serial hero and his western serials thrilled audiences the world over from 1917 to 1924. (Courtesy New York Public Library Theatre Collection)

was carefully checked by the Pathé committees for deviations from the authorized version. Pathé's contracts with producers spelled out clearly that the finished product was to conform exactly to the script. The only changes that could be justified in view of the contract stipulations were those which might be deemed necessary in unforseen circumstances on location and these had to be for the better of the film or the committee's eyebrows lifted and someone had a lot of explaining to do.

Van was known to resent his reputation as a serial and action director

A young Spencer Bennet feigns horror as Allene Ray, Frank Leon Smith and George B. Seitz attempt to upset his houseboat during the filming of *Sunken Silver*. Every serial furnished photographers with ample opportunities for such gag shots. (Courtesy Spencer G. Bennet)

and held serials in contempt, staging stunts as the easy way out. It is not surprising that when taken as a whole, his work left no legacy of distinctiveness or original approach. He was expert, reliable and equal to all occasions — he delivered. A fast worker who knew what he wanted and felt that he was the best judge of how to get it with no nonsense, he earned the nickname "One-Take Woody." A director who directed, he could not be accused of being one of the press-agented boy wonders, no matter what his other faults might be. Even with the heavy emphasis on his work, Van Dyke found time to enjoy himself socially and was always welcomed wherever he went. He became well-known for the Hollywood parties he hosted.

Van Dyke went on to make many pictures with Buck Jones at Fox (courtesy of Sol Wurtzel) and did a fine series with Tim McCoy at MGM before recognition of his abilities came in the early days of sound with the classic *Trader Horn.*

Another of the early serial action directors, Francis O'Ferna was born of Irish parents in Portland, Maine. Educated at Portland High School in the 1890's, he changed his name to Francis Ford and traveled with both stock companies and road shows, eventually working up to the legitimate stage. Fords' motion-picture experience began with an acting job for Edison in 1907 and the next four years saw him progress to Vitagraph, Méliès Star Films and the 101 Bison brand of the New York Motion Picture Company.

Ford had directed for both Méliès and Thomas Ince but his serial debut came with Universal's first, *Lucille Love, Girl of Mystery* (1914). Teamed with Grace Cunard, the young man made a great hit with chapter-play fans. Cunard and Ford became prolific actors, writers and directors and their four chapter plays as a team will always remain high on the list of the good early serials. Ford was to direct eleven episodic thrillers during his career in the silents, as well as playing in a number of the exciting adventure stories. As a director, he was quite skilled in the fast-action, rough and tumble play with which he filled his episodes. Not bothering to dwell upon the artistry involved. Ford delivered entertainment, and while at times it might not have been too logical it was exciting and interesting.

He was also an accomplished actor, with a rather distinguished appearance of which he was extremely proud. His ability allowed him to play both heroic and villainous roles with ease and sincerity. Ford appeared to be fascinated by the use of double exposure, for many of his serials contained dual roles which he portrayed using this technique. A face-to-face confrontation of the characterizations seldom took place for he preferred to use less difficult arrangements. For example, in Episode #11 of *The Mystery of* 13 (1919), he sat in a chair staring at a mirror to one side which contained his reflection, presumably the face which belonged to the pair of hands resting upon his shoulders.

Ford's major failure was one very common to many of the early serial producers and directors. As pointed out in an earlier chapter, the first three episodes of a serial were used as "sales episodes" and much care and attention was lavished on this initial group to make the presentation as palatable as possible. Once the serial was sold, those concerned with its production would then begin to "cheat" on the quality of the following episodes, first just a little, then more and more as the chapter play continued toward completion. In this way, the resulting profit was larger. It is quite possible that Ford's downfall came as a result of the peculiar version of integrity, for he was seldom active during the latter twenties and by 1930, had lost all status as a star. Throughout the sound period until his death in 1953, Ford relied upon his brother John for character roles to carry him over.

Not so skillful as Robert F. Hill but better known to the public, Henry McRae was a Canadian by birth. A native of Toronto, McRae had studied medicine as a young man but soon abandoned it for a tour of duty with the Royal Canadian Mounted Police. An interest in the stage led him to

GEORGE B. SEITZ
in
"VELVET FINGERS"
with
MARGUERITE COURTOT
EPISODE Nº 10
"SHOTS IN THE DARK"

"COME ALONG QUIETLY – OR I KNOW A WAY TO MAKE YOU!"

A Jack-of-all-trades, George B. Seitz wrote, directed and even starred in serials. A man of many talents, Seitz mastered all aspects of the serial and stands out as one who helped to make Pathé the "House of Serials," Here he is in a scene from *Velvet Fingers* (1920). (Courtesy Larry Edmunds Bookshop)

to take an active role in amateur dramatics, and after leaving the RCMP he gradually came to enjoy the status of a regular performer at the Princess Theater, one of Toronto's most popular houses of the day. When he entered motion pictures in the fall of 1912, McRae was a veteran of many years of stage and stock, having traveled extensively throughout Canada and the United States. In the course of this time, he had grasped a thorough knowledge of theater techniques and stagecraft. He was also quite adept at the application of this knowledge.

Translating his experience to the screen, McRae spent a few months writing and directing for Selig before moving to Universal in February 1913. His replacement in the Selig ranks was E. A. Martin, who also tried his hands at serials in later years. At Universal, McRae was given the 101 Bison

GEORGE B. SEITZ
in
"VELVET FINGERS"
with
MARGUERITE COURTOT
EPISODE N° 10
"SHOTS IN THE DARK"

VELVET'S COURAGE IS REVIVED
AT THE SIGHT OF MICKEY.

George B. Seitz managed to get into the same type of problems that he wrote for other actors. Fortunately, there's help close at hand in ·Velvet Fingers (1920). (Courtesy Larry Edmunds Bookshop)

Francis Ford's penchant for dual roles seldom took the form of face-to-face confrontations. In *The Mystery of 13* (1919), the viewer identified the hands with the reflection in the mirror.

brand to direct. Carl Laemmle was having money problems at this time and McRae helped out with the needed loan in addition to financing a trip to the Orient in March 1914. He took a troupe to Hawaii, China and Japan for the purpose of making films and shooting stock footage.

While McRae was gone, Laemmle had trouble with a silent partner and ousted the manager who had been appointed by the partner. Upon his return from abroad, McRae found the studio operating without a production head and assumed the position of Director-General in October 1915. This was the first of three times in his career that McRae held the position as head of the studio. A born politician, he was in with the front office regardless of which way the wind blew, and at various intervals he acted as director, production supervisor of serials and director-general in overall charge of the Universal product.

McRae's contribution to the silent serial was not really a large one. Between 1914 and 1920, he directed only two and co-directed two others. From

Francis Ford wrote, directed and starred in many serials. Here, he passes along a few words of advice in *Adventures of Peg O' The Ring* (1916). (Courtesy D. Elmo Brooks)

1921 to 1929, he directed five more of the company's chapter plays. His main concern was with the production of two-reel western shorts, with over-all responsibility for the serial production program at times, a task he often delegated to the individual director. The serials which he personally directed were for the most part undistinguished and reflected his concept of the two-reel short. They lacked the polish and inventiveness shown in the serials of Robert F. Hill and the output of the Pathé directors. His touch was heavy at all times and although the serials *moved*, the intervals between the movement were static and interrupted the flow or continuity of the finished footage. The fact that he was responsible for Universal's serial program may help to explain why other Universal serials were of an average caliber.

On the other hand, McRae had few equals as a production supervisor. He was better equipped to function along this line than as a creative director.

With that faraway gaze in his eyes, Jack Mulhall survived seven episodes of *Wild West* (1925), but from the look on Helen Ferguson's face, she really wondered how he did it. Robert F. Hill directed from a script by J. F. Natteford.

Perhaps his greatest contribution to the serial genre was to bring in the first outdoor western serial, *The Indians Are Coming,* proving that the technical difficulties presented by sound at the time did not need to destroy the concept that serials should move rapidly.

Although he held important positions at Universal during the thirties, the picture business passed him by. He had become married to the way in which he had always produced pictures and didn't seem to comprehend that passing time had brought with it new techniques of story telling. In the end, Universal officials decided that he had better be retired and put him out to pasture at full salary. Pointedly reassured that he had earned his "vacation," McRae's severance from the company was a body blow to the old-timer's vanity. One of those unfortunate men who have nothing other than their work to live for, he passed away in October 1944, a few months after being retired.

   Of the many men who directed serials, only a handful stood out from the crowd. Most were mediocre, for any number of reasons, and their work showed it. Now and then, one came along whose work was so bad that history should not pass him by unnoticed. Such was the case with Arch B. Heath. The son of a New York harbor pilot, he was born in Brooklyn in 1891. As a young lad, he had a natural affinity for caricature and aspired

Arch Heath's first serial struck out on all counts. *On Guard* (1927) starred Cullen Landis and Muriel Kingston in a story of the U. S. Army and national security. In this scene, Landis rescues the heroine from the clutches of the villain's underlings.

Duke Kahanamoku (left) and Anita Stewart (center) in a production scene from Mascot's *Isle of Sunken Gold* (1927). An Hawaiian athlete much in demand for independent work in the twenties, the Duke made surfing history and continued to be a very popular figure in the Islands until his recent death. (Courtesy Duke Kahanamoku)

to become an artist. Taking up drawing, he discovered an abundance of creative talent and soon put it to good use. He became a political cartoonist on the staff of the Associated Newspaper Syndicate, which placed his work in leading papers across the country. From this beginning, he went on to become an animator for a commercial film producer in New York City and it was here that Heath was discovered by Spencer G. Bennet.

Dr. Lee DeForest, who had perfected the audion tube, owned the company and hired Bennet to make a five-reel commercial feature, *From the Woods to the Wall*, for a wallpaper firm. This brought Bennet into contact with Heath and the two men struck up an acquaintance. Bennet secured a position for his new friend as an assistant director at Pathé. Heath soon became known around the lot as "Honest Abe," for his physical resemblance to Abraham Lincoln was uncanny. Heath and Bennet worked together on a number of assignments, and in the fall of 1926 Pathé handed him his first picture as a director in his own right, *On Guard* (1927). Paul Fairfax Fuller was given the task of preparing the scenario from a story by Robert Glassburn.

As Fuller was not much of a writer (he was closely related to a top Pathé executive), the serial was not too successful. In all fairness to Heath, it is doubtful that any other director could have done much better with the story. Fuller and Heath followed up with a second effort, *The Crimson Flash* (1927), which turned out better. Heath's other two serials, *The Masked Menace* (1927) and *The Mark of the Frog* (1928) were woeful. This group of four chapter plays compared favorably with the duds turned out by Jimmie Fulton and were among the poorest serials ever released by Pathé. Heath's final chapter play was guilty of nearly every sin in the book (and some that weren't) — illogical story, lack of continuity and artificial acting by the entire cast, among other things. This marked his finish behind the serial megaphone; he left Pathé to direct comedies for Hal Roach at MGM.

In reality, Heath was as creative as his co-workers maintained he was, but the man needed more experience and a firm shoulder to lean on. As an assistant director, his work had been satisfactory; as a director, the responsibility was just too much. He did not have the confidence in himself that comes only from the confidence of others. There are many bridges in a career that a man must cross in order to be a success and Heath (as with so many others) simply couldn't make it over this hurdle.

6

The Daredevils . . .

Charles Hutchison, the leading male serial star at Pathé, was born in Allegheny, Pennsylvania, and attended Western University. After graduation, he entered the employ of Marshall Field in Chicago for a short time before moving to New York City. An interest in theatrical life took him onto the stage at eighteen in *My Friend From Indiana*. His salary was the handsome sum of $25.00 weekly. After the show closed, he worked for the Murray Hill Stock Company and then spent three years in vaudeville. It was only a short step to employment with the Triumph Film Company and years of obscurity as a featured player and leading man in numerous long-forgotten celluloid dramas.[1]

While working for Crystal as a leading man and part-time director, he met his future wife. Edith Thornton had bluffed her way into the studio and approached Joseph A. Golden for a job. Although unconvinced that she had been in front of a camera before as she claimed, Golden gave her a chance to make good. She was cast at once in light comedies with Chester Barnett and Hutchison directed them. Edith was the youngest member of the unit and thus became the butt of many practical jokes. One day late in the morning, she was tied to a tree for a scene. As soon as she was securely bound, Hutchison called lunch and everyone went off to eat leaving her tied up and ready for the afternoon shots. Hutchison wouldn't let her loose until she promised to marry him.

In 1918, Golden contracted with Pathé for a serial and signed Leah Baird as the female lead and star. Sheldon Lewis was given the role of villain and

---

[1] He also worked for Crystal, Brenon, Solax, Vitagraph and Superba.

If they get the silver scarf away from *Hurricane Hutch* (1921), it'll be over his dead body and that may be just what Warner Oland is thinking. (Courtesy Larry Edmunds Book-shop)

Hutchison portrayed the hero. Lewis was a well-known and effective minor villain whose menacing leer was appreciated by the serial audiences. In addition to his tall and athletic appearance, Hutchison possessed a winsome, engaging smile which registered well on camera and his first serial appearance was *Wolves of Kultur*. This preparedness chapter play went over well with the public. Billed beneath the other leading players in the cast, Hutchison stole the show and received so much fan mail that Golden used him in two more, *The Great Gamble.* (1919) and *The Whirlwind* (1920). Pathé handled the former, which was photographed on location at Ausable Chasm in upper New York State where many other Hutchison serials were to be made.

By this time, Pathé publicity machine had sold the actor to exhibitors and public alike as "Hutch," billing him as "The Thrill-A-Minute Stunt King." Joe Golden took one look at the business which the releasing house had done with the first two Hutch serials and decided to "cash in" by selling his third on the state-right market. *The Whirlwind* was an exploitation item designed to show off Hutch's athletic ability and motorcycle skill. Marketed by the Allgood Picture Corporation through the Republic Exchanges, it was filled with exciting moments.

In the first episode, Hutch took his motorcycle and co-star Edith Thornton (whom he had married in 1918) over the side of a road and down the embankment. As a result of the rough landing one side of Miss Thornton's face was temporarily paralyzed. As she recalls it, she played the remainder of the serial photographed from only one side. Every member of the cast received at least one injury during the filming. Hutch was quite a fearless performer in those days. Portions of *The Whirlwind* were also filmed at Ausable Chasm and one scene for the fourth episode called upon the two stars to escape from their pursuers by crossing the chasm on an old log. Miss Thornton refused to do it, but Hutch told her, "If you'll go, I'll carry you across and there'll be nothing to worry about." She agreed and they started across. Reaching the middle of the log, Hutch began to sway from side to side, thoroughly frightening his lovely wife. "What are you doing? It's a 150 foot drop to the bottom!"

"Quiet," came the reply, "It's o.k. I have to make it look difficult for the camera. Can't disappoint the fans."

As a result of *The Whirlwind*, Hutch was signed by Pathé. Impressed by his personality and possibilities, the New York office sent him into the field to star in *Double Adventure* (1921). His wife was scheduled to costar but her face had not responded fully to treatment and she was forced to bow out, replaced by Josie Sedgwick. Two broken wrists during the production of this cliffhanger gave Hutch cause to think things over. However, Pathé started production at once on his next starring serial, *The Fortieth Door*. The very first episode shelved the project for several years and finished the working relationship which Woody Van Dyke and Hutch had enjoyed.

The sequence which closed down production called for Hutch to leap from a balcony onto the chandelier and swing across the room. Hutch leaped, caught the chandelier and both plunged to the floor with a terrific crash. Hurriedly extricated from the wreckage, he was in terrible pain and it was thought at first that his wrists had been broken again. The damage turned out to be a backward dislocation of his elbow and it was many months before he was able to return to work.

This accident, following so closely to the previous one, made Hutch reconsider his situation. He was the first stunt star to make the big time. His health was his prime asset, and as such it had to be protected. Basically a good businessman, he realized that even though he was a screen personality whose name meant something on a theater marquee, the years of big money couldn't continue forever. During this convalescence he arrived at a shrewd program for the future.

His decision involved a determination to be cautious in all of his action sequences once he returned to work. Hutch decided that his good friend Frank Hagney would appear in all of his future films. He and Hagney

CHARLES HUTCHISON
in
"DOUBLE ADVENTURE"
EPISODE No 4
"THE GUN RUNNERS"

CAUGHT IN THE ACT!

Hutch managed to fracture both wrists in this episodic thriller, *Double Adventure* (1921). (Courtesy Larry Edmunds Bookshop)

CHARLES HUTCHISON
"DOUBLE ADVENTURE"
EPISODE Nº 4
"THE GUN RUNNERS"

BOB OVERHEARS THE KIDNAPPING
PLANS FOR MARTHA.

Charles Hutchison won't allow this abduction of Josie Sedgwick to proceed much further. From *Double Adventure* (1921). (Courtesy Larry Edmunds Bookshop)

worked very well together, and understanding one another's moves as they did the two men could put on good fights. Pathé also exhibited concern and insisted that in the future, the extremely hazardous things would be done by a stunt double.

While recovering, Hutch worked on a script for his next serial and when he returned to work, *Hurricane Hutch*, a low-budget cliffhanger went into production at Ausable Chasm. Warner Oland, the best and most expensive villain in the business, was assigned to menace Hutch and Lucy Fox. George B. Seitz directed and the unit was in shape. Spencer Bennet and others doubled for him in an effort to get the serial in the can. Hutch didn't care for the icy water at Ausable Chasm and refused to swim the rapids until later in the season, as his elbow had not fully recovered its strength. At this point, Seitz put on the hero's garb and went through the rapids twice to avoid halting production.

An unusual publicity still conceived by Charles Hutchison in 1926 for release with *Lightning Hutch* and showing the former Pathé favorite recalling his many harrowing experiences. (Courtesy Edith Hutchison)

During the planning stages for a stunt, Hutch would outline exactly how he had decided to execute the spectacular action.[2] If his motorcycle was to carry him over a 30-foot chasm, Hutch figured out the necessary speed and incline for a takeoff. Very easy. All that he had to do was steer straight and hang on, hoping that the motor didn't miss. A few rehearsals made certain that the action would be properly photographed.

Joe Cuny often doubled for him and earned $5.00 for each stunt. Cuny

---

[2] They did not always work out as planned. In June 1918, Hutch had to make a 70-foot dive from the window of a cliff house into the water below. As he hurled himself through the window, the tip of his toe caught on the sill, causing him to turn a complete somersault in mid-air. He hit the water on his back and was out cold for 20 minutes.

Short and dark, Eddie Polo's daring adventures across the serial screen won him legions of admirers after World War I.

enjoyed this type of work and he also appreciated the extra money. Hutch would gather a group around him and say, "I'm going to jump from this roof to that one." Aside, he'd continue, "Let Joe get the five. Then I'm going to slide down that drainpipe (let Joe get the five) and leap onto the balcony (let Joe get the five)."

Hutch's coordination had suffered as a result of his accidents. In one scene for *Go Get 'em Hutch* (1922), shot near Saranac Lake, N. Y., Bennet wanted him to ski about 40 feet toward the camera for an opening shot. Hutch tried time after time, but failed to complete the action satisfactorily. Finally, Bennet called lunch and discussed the situation with Eddie Snyder, his cameraman. The two of them decided that such a request was not unreasonable and shouldn't be too difficult to accomplish. After lunch, both men tried the scene and within ten minutes they had both mastered the ski sequence perfectly. Bennet doubled for his star and shooting resumed. Because of Hutch's faulty coordination, many scenes were done slowly and the camera was undersped to give the appearance of natural motion.

A super-salesman when it came to describing his own abilities, Hutch managed to keep the Pathé front office smiling. His fans continued to clamor for more, and as long as the box office jangled Pathé was pleased. So pleased, in fact, that his contract specified that he was to be given two afternoons a week off. This was so arranged to allow Hutch to work out in a gymnasium in order to keep him in shape for the stunts he was not allowed to do.

In addition to this, Pathé paid him $1000 weekly for his histrionics. Between his salary and sometime overexuberant ego, Hutch was often a difficult person to work with. At the close of the final episode of one thriller, Bennet had only a few short scenes left to shoot. The entire crew was eager to leave Ausable Chasm for New York City. Bennet approached the star and explained that if they could shoot the few scenes on the next day (Sunday), they could all wrap up and go home. Hutch's reply was simple, "I just get paid a salary." This kept everyone on location for two additional days and endeared him to no one.

Speed, the seventh Hutch serial, ended his Pathé career in the fall of 1922. From this point on, he dropped from public view and worked as a director of independent features. In early 1926, as director and star of the Hurricane Film Corporation, he attempted a comeback with the ten-chapter *Lightning Hutch*, written by J. F. Natteford. Time had not treated him well. He had gained a good deal around the waistline and his features showed considerable age and abuse. His attempts to lead the fast life of the film colony had taken a heavy toll.

The pace of *Lightning Hutch* was rapid, but Hutch did few of the action sequences himself. As for his direction of the chapter play, it can best be summed up by saying that directing is an art and Hutch was no artist. The finished product could not begin to compare with his Pathé cliffhangers but it really didn't matter. He had gathered many of his old co-workers, including his wife, around him for this production and they all sank with the ship.

Arrow had contracted for distribution but went into receivership just after the serial was released. Hutch lost a great deal of his own money in this venture but found work directing a series of William Fairbanks westerns for California Studios in the summer of 1926. He returned the following year with several five-reel features for Pathé release, playing a secret service hero in such items as *Pirates of the Sky*, *The Trunk Mystery* and *Hidden Aces*; but the spark was no longer there. Thus did the "Thrill-A-Minute Stunt

There's no doubt about it — the villains have angered Eddie Polo and it's action ahead for serial fans.

Eddie Polo and Peggy O'Dare on board the S. S. *Magantic* as it prepared to leave for Liverpool. They had finished scenes for *The Broken Idol* — a working title later changed to *The Thirteenth Hour* — a serial which never materialized. (Museum of Modern Art Film Library)

King," whose athletic exploits had brought him fame and fortune, pass from the serial scene.

In many respects, the life of Eddie Polo is as obscure as the life of Pearl White. Many different stories and legends abound about the early days. For example, some say that he was born of American parents in Italy; others, including Polo himself, claim that he was born on the desert in Northern California. His studio biography gave his birthplace as San Francisco. Whatever the truth may be, his birth occurred sometime between 1875 and 1880. One of six children, Eddie and his parents were circus people and they toured Europe in a family act. Business wasn't too good and young Polo was apparently apprenticed at age six to Henry Wolf, a European circus star. While

It's a tense moment for Eddie Polo and Magda Lane in Chapter 7 of *Do or Die,* 1921). (Courtesy D. Elmo Brooks)

with Wolf, Eddie learned the required arts of a circus performer — contortion, wire-walking, trap work, horseback stunts, tumbling and aerial acrobatics.

Five years passed and Eddie, now eleven, ran away from Wolf and went to work in various shows on the Continent. He eventually landed in England, where he stowed away in the hold of a cattle ship bound for the United States. Soon after arriving, he went to work for Walter Mains and then joined Forepaugh and Sells. A seventeen-year stint with Barnum and Bailey and the Ringling Brothers circuses followed until, tiring of life under the big top, he went into vaudeville at the Olympic Theater in New York. By this time, he

William Duncan and Edith Johnson couldn't even escape villainy in the frozen North. Joe Bonomo is the third scoundrel from the left. A scene from *Wolves of the North* (1924). (Courtesy Joe Bonomo)

had acquired a wife (Pearl Grant, one-time circus performer) and a daughter (Malveen, who later played a few small roles in silent pictures) and security was uppermost in his mind.

Approaching Essanay about work in movies, he was given a part in the "Slippery Slim" series and joined Universal in 1914, where he spent his time doing stunt work in comedies. Injuring himself, he was given odd jobs by Grace Cunard and Francis Ford, a team then preparing *The Broken Coin* (1915) for filming. As he was an old circus performer and a *good* acrobat, a part was written into the serial for him and Eddie was on his way.

Highly egotistical, Polo was certain that he had the answers to whatever questions arose and soon made his presence known on the Universal lot. Playing a character role in *The Broken Coin*, he appeared in makeup until the fan mail began to arrive. Once the letters started to come in, Eddie decided that he no longer needed to play the game by the rules and soon appeared on-set minus his makeup. When asked about it, he informed Miss Cunard that he was tired of "looking that way" and was going to change his role. It goes without saying that this sort of behavior was not tolerated; he continued to appear in character makeup until he could be written out of the story. This performance was to be repeated the following year when he was once again cast by Cunard and Ford in *The Adventures of Peg O' the Ring* (1916).

This time, Eddie actively instigated a disagreement which caused Cunard and Ford to halt production. The two stars conferred with Carl Laemmle in New York, and although the trade papers were stating that Polo and Ruth Stonehouse would finish the serial in the leading roles, a settlement was reached. Laemmle allowed Cunard and Ford to resume shooting and both supporting players were written out.

Between these two serials, Eddie had done a small role in one chapter of *Graft* (1915) and then went off to the Panama-California Exposition in San Diego. While there, he leaped from an airplane by parachute for a 4280-foot descent to prove to Army fliers that it could be done. After *Peg O' the Ring*, he turned up in *Liberty, a Daughter of the USA* (1916) with a small role which he managed to hold onto, and 1917 found him as Marco, supporting Priscilla Dean in *The Gray Ghost*.

After finishing supporting roles in a few Red Feather features while the front office decided what to do with him, Eddie was starred in *Bull's Eye* (1918) with Vivian Reed. His fan mail had continued to grow and the feeling of self-importance was finally accepted by the studio. It had been a long, hard uphill struggle for Eddie, for he had felt perfectly capable of assuming a leading role long before this. With a complicated plot in eighteen episodes, the western background of this chapter play gave Polo ample opportunity to

A most unusual pet shop, as William Duncan will soon find out in *The Silent Avenger* (1920). (Courtesy Larry Edmunds Bookshop)

show off his stuff. In later years, he always claimed that he was never doubled, but Jean Perkins performed many of the dangerous sequences in his place.

By this time, Polo had reached a position in life which was never to change. People who knew him and/or worked with him either liked or disliked him intensely. Many claim that his head became swelled with his own vanity, although he was basically a decent fellow. His convictions were many and held strongly. Disagreement or reasoning with him would not budge or alter his ideas.

Polo went into *The Lure of the Circus* (1918) and turned out eighteen more chapters of action on a thin plot line. The next year, he made a group of double-reel westerns, the Cyclone Smith series. Other than serials, these

William Desmond and Ethlyne Clair, co-stars of Universal's 1928 release, *The Vanishing Rider.* (Courtesy Howard Nelson)

were the only starring products which he made for Universal. The return to chapter plays came in 1919 when he took a crew to Europe to film scenes for a serial to be entitled *The Broken Idol*. This working title became *The 13th Hour* and within a few weeks, the entire unit sailed for home. This thriller was released as *The Vanishing Dagger* (1920) and some of its footage was used for stock purposes. *King of the Circus* (1920) followed and Eddie took a vacation before returning to work in *Do or Die* (1921), another fast-action story. The relationship between Polo and Universal came to a crashing halt at the close of *The Secret Four* (1920), his final Universal serial which came onto the market in December.

He had been announced as the star of the forthcoming *Adventures of Robinson Crusoe* (1922) but a change in management took place at Universal and Julius Stern[3] was given the job of studio manager when Irving Thalberg left for MGM. Polo had been manageable under Henry McRae and Thalberg, but with Stern it was a different question. Eddie just had no use for him, so he quit at the close of the year. His next move was not only typical Polo, it was typical Hollywood.

[3] A nephew of Carl Laemmle. Polo and Laemmle did not get along either, dating from the controversy over *Peg O' the Ring*.

William Desmond fought with his feet as well as his fists in *Beast of Paradise* (1923). The scoundrel caught in the pincer lock? Joe Bonomo. (Courtesy Joe Bonomo)

Thumbing his nose at Carl Laemmle, he announced plans for the Star Serial Corporation, his own independent production firm. Joe Brandt was made president and the Peerless Studio in Fort Lee, New Jersey, was rented. Eddie signed J. P. McGowan, his director on three previous serials and an action expert in his own right. The handful of Universal serials had made Polo a wealthy man. His chapter plays were extremely popular with fans, but during his starring days with Universal, the studio had a tiger by the tail and Laemmle secretly breathed a sigh of relief, even though he had lost one of his top serial attractions.

To make certain that Eddie's firm did as little harm as possible, Laemmle announced via the trade papers that Polo intended to produce a Robinson Crusoe serial on his own and that Universal's version would be far superior. Of course, this only added fuel to the fire and Polo suddenly decided to make a serial based on Captain Kidd.

William Desmond, Eileen Sedgwick and Joe Bonomo in a scene from *Beasts of Paradise* (1923). Although a bit stocky, Desmond made an excellent hero and could stare down any villains he couldn't lick. (Courtesy Joe Bonomo)

The Star Serial Corporation had planned to produce six independent serials, with Polo as the star of each. Reputedly expending over $350,000 in the production of *Captain Kidd* (1922), Polo quit and his firm dissolved. *Captain Kidd* had gone out on a state-right basis and one can only suppose that it was a combination of factors that brought about his rather abrupt end. Production costs, the independent release and a pretty poor serial combined to do him in.

Eddie left the United States for Europe, where his popularity had even exceeded his American fame. Several years were spent abroad in near obscurity as far as the United States and his fans were concerned. A return to this country from the European circus circuit came as the silent period drew

Eileen Sedgwick and William Desmond in *The Riddle Rider* (1924), one of the best of the Universal serials and long coveted by collectors.

to a close and Eddie had great plans for a comeback, one which never materialized. A forgotten man as far as Hollywood was concerned, he wished to
produce another film and tramped the woods looking for a backer but none
appeared. Disgusted, disgruntled and mumbling about a conspiracy, he let it
be known that he was dropping out of the motion picture business for good
in 1930, but showed up now and then playing bit roles in westerns and
serials.

Little was heard of Eddie until his death on June 14, 1961, in a Hollywood
restaurant. He had spent the intervening thirty years far from the limelight
he loved so well. Right up to his death, Polo continued to talk to anyone
who would listen to his plans for a picture. About his only mention in the
press during these years came when a European acrobat who billed himself

as Eddie Polo was killed during a performance. Out came the obituaries and a chuckling Polo grandly stepped forth to prove that he was still alive. In a typical manner, Eddie announced that the trapeze artist had stolen his name to cash in on his fame, but that he had never interfered with the billing and suggested that the poor fellow probably could not have made a living otherwise.

Polo was somewhat of a paradox in the history of motion pictures. During his career at Universal, he worked in very few features and none of importance. His entire output of box-office importance was in two-reel western and serial format, although he did star in obscure independent features for Johnnie Walker after his return from Europe. His films were relatively limited in number but Eddie's popularity was unexcelled while he was active and it is remarkable that a large number of people today still fondly recall him.

William Duncan was a native of Scotland who had arrived in the United States at the age of ten. His early career included management and later ownership of a physical culture school, but an interest in acting brought him to the point of giving up the school to join the Forepaugh Stock Company of Philadelphia. He then went to the Coast in Ella Wheeler Wilcox's play *Mizpah*, which played at the Burbank Theater; after it closed, Duncan embarked on a foreign tour.

July 1912 found him with the Colorado unit of the Selig Polyscope Company, which was under the management and direction of Marshall Stedman. Here Duncan became well-versed in acting, writing and directing the outdoor dramas so popular with Selig at the time. A rugged, virile appearing chap with dark brown hair, he quickly found favor with theater patrons and didn't disappoint them in his screen appearances.

Duncan had many of the exciting experiences which the early picture people encountered in their work. On one occasion, in August 1912, he was making a film on location at the Colorado State Penitentiary. In the picture, he portrayed a prison convict, and was garbed accordingly for the role. During a break in shooting, Duncan pulled out a pipe and packed it with tobacco. Lighting the pipe, he casually strolled across the front yard. A tower guard shouted to him to put the pipe away, for smoking was prohibited on the prison grounds.

Duncan paid no attention to the warning; it didn't register that the tower guard was referring to him. Once again the warning was shouted but Duncan still failed to heed it. The guard then opened fire and suddenly Bill realized that he was in danger. Hitting the ground, he dispensed with the pipe and the guard ceased firing. Duncan's pipe stayed in his pocket for the remainder of the day.

Joe Bonomo teamed up with the Mystery Man (Slim Cole) to solve *The Great Circus Mystery* (1925). (Courtesy Joe Bonomo)

Duncan was popular with audiences but Selig was hardly a showcase for his talents. His stay with the company served to introduce him to all facets of motion picture production. Signing with Vitagraph was a step forward, for Vitagraph was a more progressive and active firm than Selig. Vitagraph had released *The Goddess* in 1915, which had started off well at the outset but floundered in midstream. Not the artistic success that Albert E. Smith had hoped it would be, it was not so financially rewarding as he had expected; and after studying the serials of his competitors, he decided that an action star and outdoor stories would turn the trick. Duncan's popularity, his physical build and athletic ability all added up to a box-office attraction and Smith went to work.

He closed a deal with Jack London for the picture rights to a story called *Hearts of Three* and sent Duncan and a unit off to the mountains in March

4256
Ep.4-33

Margaret Quimby and Joe Bonomo faced the *Perils of the Wild* (1925). (Courtesy Joe Bonomo)

1916 to begin filming. Several chapters had been made when it was suddenly discovered that Vitagraph did not have clear story rights. London had made several other deals involving commitments for the same story prior to the Vitagraph contract.[4] The company had no choice other than to discontinue production in April 1916. Duncan brought the crew back and the completed footage was junked.

His serial debut did not come until the following year. This time, Vitagraph took no chances and Edward J. Montagne and Garfield Thompson were put to work preparing an original story for the Duncan serial entry.

[4]Hearst's Cosmopolitan Productions had commissioned it for the sum of $25,000 and owned the rights.

The Fighting Trail (1917) brought Duncan and Carol Holloway together in a story of the outdoors, complete with rare minerals, a torn map and agents of the Central Powers.[5] Well received by the public, which accepted Duncan immediately into the top rank of male serial performers, filming began at once on *Vengeance and the Woman* (1917), another Montagne-Thompson collaboration.

For his third Vitagraph serial, Duncan acquired the services of Edith Johnson as his female lead and one of the most popular of serial teams was born.

[5] America had entered the war shortly before production began.

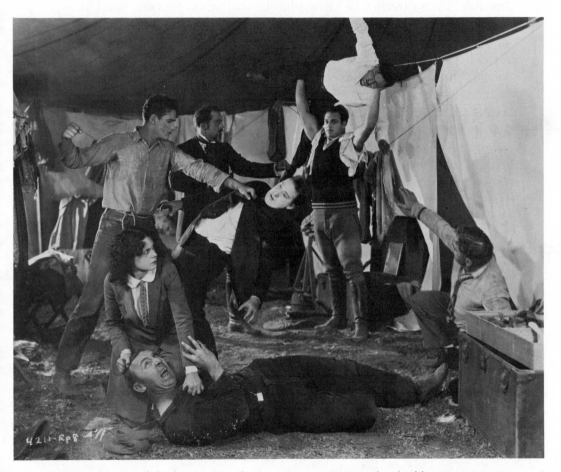

Louise Lorraine used the feminine touch as Joe Bonomo prepared to hurl his opponent out of the Universal lot in *The Great Circus Mystery* (1925). Notice carefully how Joe held the stunt extra before executing a half-whirl and letting go. Such acrobatics were done so quickly and smoothly that audiences believed Joe had a total disregard for life and limb. (Courtesy Joe Bonomo)

Miss Johnson, a native of Rochester, New York, had also entered pictures with Selig and was delighted to work with Duncan. In April 1921, the two were married and remained inseparable until his death in 1961. Together, they created eight more adventure chapter plays before retiring in 1925: five for Vitagraph and the final three for Universal.

Those who recall working with William Duncan have only good words for him. Most of his serials were made on location in the mountains, and Duncan was always kind, considerate and patient with his fellow workers. Doubles were anathema to him and his athletic ability, supported by a fine sense of timing, carried him through his scenes, regardless of the difficulties involved. As a director, he knew what he wanted on film and went after it with a vigor that carried over to the remainder of the cast. Sadly, very little of his work remains in existence today, but the memory of this handsome serial hero who thrilled millions of fans still remains vivid to those who remember his daring screen exploits.[6]

Brought to the United States at the age of one, William Desmond had been born in Dublin, Ireland, in 1878. His education took place in the New York school system and during his school years, he became interested in acting. After completing his schooling, young Desmond was determined to become an actor and went into stock. His stage career can be said to have really gained momentum when he joined the Oliver Morosco Stock Company in Burbank. The year was 1904. He had worked for numerous other companies and had held many and varied positions in the theatrical world but it was the time spent with Morosco that made the difference. As with so many other performers who were associated with this group, his progress was steady and he soon rose to a position of minor prominence in the world of the legitimate theater. His salary in 1913 was a tidy $100 weekly, pretty fair money for a young actor. But Desmond was getting older every day and the dreams of fame that he had pursued so long seemed to be forever evading his grasp.

The formation of Triangle in 1915 was based upon a heavy influx of stage stars and the thirty-seven-year old Desmond leaped at the opportunity to enter pictures. Signed by Triangle, he was to work with Leonore Ulrich in a film to be called *As the Years Go By*. It was never made, for Miss Ulrich signed with Knickerbocker Star Features. As a result, his first screen appearance was with Billie Burke in *Peggy* (1916). He then starred with Jane

---

[6] A measure of Duncan's popularity was a new Vitagraph contract in 1919. Albert E. Smith tore up the old one after *Smashing Barriers* and wrote a new pact for a three-year period. It called for six serials of fifteen episodes each. Vitagraph agreed to commit $1,500,000 for this contract, assuring Duncan an average salary of $10,000 weekly for directing and appearing in two serials per year. The firm's Hollywood studios were doubled in capacity to handle this production.

Joe Bonomo and Louise Lorraine, co-stars of *The Great Circus Mystery* (1925). (Courtesy Joe Bonomo)

Grey in *Waifs* (1916). Tall and lean, the young man possessed a heavy-set face and bushy dark eyebrows which added to his virile appearance.

Although many of Triangle's actors were virtually unknown to motion-picture audiences, Desmond was determined to make himself popular and set about creating a name for himself. While with Triangle, a great number of his roles were in society dramas, which he handled with skill. He even played opposite Gloria Swanson in one of her early Triangle features. When the firm ceased production, Desmond moved over to different companies where he was able to land outdoor roles. His broad shoulders and rugged physique made him a natural for such action and adventure pictures. However, by the time he reached Universal and began a rapid ascent into the hearts of serial fans, Bill was forty-four and putting on weight. The bloom of youth was failing.

Desmond began his serial work by doing his own stunt and dangerous

Joe Bonomo's portrayal in *The Iron Man* (1924) brought him from obscurity as a stunt man and featured villain to the hero's role in his next serial. (Courtesy Joe Bonomo)

sequences, but in his very first appearance, *Perils of the Yukon* (1922), he was quite badly injured while doing a fifty-foot dive into an icy river and began to rely on stunt doubles for the more exacting scenes. George Fiske, an excellent stuntman whose specialty was jumping a horse from a cliff into the water, doubled Desmond in many of his western adventure serials and severely hurt himself while doing scenes for *The Riddle Rider* (1924). Joe Bonomo, an upcoming stuntman, also doubled for the star.

Bill found his forte in serials and made eleven in seven years, some of the best ever put out by Universal. Between chapter plays, Desmond and his wife

The earliest of serial villains, Paul Panzer never became an important one.

Mary MacIvor toured the vaudeville circuits with a variety act which helped to increase his popularity. By 1925, he was the top serial star at Universal. His closest competitor in the big U lineup was Jack Daugherty, who couldn't hold a candle to Desmond when it came to acting but who possessed a youthful appearance which helped to cover his lack of ability.

One seldom-violated axiom of the silent movies can be simply stated: stuntmen do not become stars. Joe Bonomo successfully crossed this unwritten line. As the son of a prosperous Coney Island candy maker, young Bonomo's struggle in life was not for necessities, but with himself and school. As a small boy, he was displeased with his thin and underdeveloped body and decided to make himself a prime example of physical fitness. A program of hard exercises paid off. By the time Joe had reached high school, he was an excellent athlete with a finely developed physique. This was offset by his poor memory, a failing which plagued him for many years. As a result, his grades were constantly a worry and he was always in danger of losing his position on the school football team.

By 1921, Bonomo had topped many other young men in New York's "Modern Apollo" contest and won $1000 along with a ten-week movie contract. He spent this time doubling the cast of *A Light in the Dark,* which starred Hope Hampton. When the contract expired, Joe received a call from Nathan Hirsch, a prospective producer. Hirsch wanted to star Bonomo in pictures and the two men made a reel of test footage but the proposition did not work out and they parted.

Fascinated with films, Joe decided to stay in the business and went from studio to studio in New York City, looking for work. A visit to George B. Seitz paid off and Bonomo became a double for Charles Hutchison in *Hurricane Hutch* (1921). After the Pathé serial was finished, Joe went west and signed with Universal. He soon began receiving fan mail for his supporting (and often villainous) roles in *The Eagle's Talons* (1923), *Beasts of Paradise* (1923) and *Wolves of the North* (1924).

Lucien Albertini, a European strong man, was cast in *The Iron Man* (1925) as Paul Breen, a Paris reporter who sought to solve the mysterious disappearance of Arlene Graham (Margaret Morris). Her uncle was in Paris to take her back to the United States to claim her inheritance, but the villainous Jean DeBriac (ably assisted by Bonomo) kidnapped Arlene and a look-alike, Mimi (Lola Todd) passed as the long-lost niece. Paul finally located Arlene and the two followed her uncle and the imposter to America, where they encountered many dangers before the truth was made known.

Joe's already large fan mail doubled as a result of his fine performances in this serial and Universal decided that 1925 would be *his* year and the answer to his fans. His first starring serial, *The Great Circus Mystery,* was turned over to Jay Marchant, an action director, and Bonomo was cast as Welles "Red" Landow in a story of Hindu agents seeking to regain a stolen sacred ruby. Louise Lorraine played the female lead, Trixie Tremaine. Al Prisco, Slim Cole and Sam Polo (brother to Eddie) were all experienced serial hands and cast in support. The serial was a tremendous success and was

As Pearl White's lawyer in *The Exploits of Elaine* (1914), Sheldon Lewis discovered that "The Clutching Hand" had kept his word to kill her father. (Courtesy Alan Brock)

quickly followed by *Perils of the Wild*, an adaptation of *The Swiss Family Robinson*. Serial veteran Francis Ford directed this story of a family which had set sail for Australia with a cargo of gunpowder only to lose the ship and land on an island infested with pirates.

By this time, Bonomo was really enjoying himself and today refers to it as his period of retirement. Working thirty-six weeks per year for Universal, he drew a salary of $39,000 yearly and spent the remainder of the year in vaudeville. Extremely popular in Europe, his serials were big money-makers in the foreign market. Busy acting in features during 1926–27, Joe found time to play the villain in two serials for Mascot, *The Golden Stallion* (1927) and *Heroes of the Wild* (1927). Both chapter plays made extensive use of animals. In the former, the quest centered on a clue to hidden

A battered Henry G. Sell is freed from the clutches of Wu Fang (Warner Oland) by the Wasp (William Burt) and Lightning Raider (Pearl White). (Courtesy Manuel Weltman)

treasure. Part of the clue was located on an Indian belt, the remainder was branded around the neck of a wild horse. The latter serial was set in Argentina, and once again centered on clues to a secret ore lode. They were divided between a diary and a silver chain around the hoof of a wild white stallion.

Cast as Tarzan in a Universal serial in 1928, Joe broke his leg and was replaced by Frank Merrill. At liberty after his leg mended, Joe was approached by Trem Carr to star in an independent serial for Syndicate Pictures, *The Chinatown Mystery*. Bonomo agreed to do it for 25 per cent of the net receipts, a sum he never received. Various factions were involved in Syndicate Pictures and an audit of its books was a task never accomplished. Carr hired Francis Ford to write the story and J. P. McGowan as director. The story was developed chapter by chapter using major studio sets which

A Swede by birth, Warner Oland's Oriental portrayals were cherished by fans.

were available for use at $500 each. McGowan took advantage of them to add production values to a low-budget serial.

The story concerned a piece of jade with the formula for the manufacture of artificial diamonds inscribed upon it — a formula sought by the Mysterious Thirteen, led by Ford, who wrote himself in as the chief villain. This final Bonomo silent serial was fast in action and pacing, containing stunt after stunt by Joe. One of his most popular action sequences, which found its way into nearly every chapter, was the one-handed elevation of a villain above his head. Giving the body a slight twirl, he would throw the man across the room, into a crowd or against the wall. To do the stunt properly, Joe always used a trained tumbler. Catching the man's waist with his left arm, Joe would press his right hand into the small of the fellow's back and raise him high into the air with one arm. A slight backward motion of his arm was followed by a forward heave of his body and the tumbler went sailing across the room. It never failed to bring the house down and always helped to even the on-screen odds.

Bonomo did some work in pictures after sound, but his poor memory finally forced him out of the business. He spent hour after hour at night memorizing lines for the next day, only to have difficulty with them when the cameras rolled. Deciding that he had no future in sound pictures, Joe

Frank Lackteen's classic features were shown to good advantage in *The House Without a Key* (1926). Notice the facial bone structure and penetrating eyes. His full-face closeups frightened millions of children in the late twenties. (Courtesy Frank Lackteen)

As Dr. Sandro in *The Tiger's Shadow* (1928), Frank Lackteen was on screen as much as the hero, an unusual circumstance. (Courtesy Frank Lackteen)

left Hollywood to devote his full attention to the family candy business and his expanding physical culture program. This move paid off handsomely for today he is head of Joe Bonomo Associates, a financial complex of twenty-four corporations.

As a pivotal figure in the silent serial, the practice of villainy was an art, but actually had very few real practitioners. A majority of the chapter-play scoundrels were character actors who were equally at home on either side of the law and who became accepted in this respect by the fans. Joe Ryan, a cowboy who broke into movies with the Colorado Motion Picture Company in 1914, played the heavy in three of William Duncan's serials. He was

Howard Crampton (left), head of the Eternal Life Syndicate, had Ben Wilson in his clutches and Frances Terry was not at all sympathetic with his plight. From *The Screaming Shadow* (1920). (Courtesy D. Elmo Brooks)

successfully cast as a hero and leading man in two other Vitagraph western thrillers. Harry Carter, who had so successfully menaced Ella Hall in *The Master Key* (1914), was another hero-heavy in the early days, as was Jack Mower in the twenties. Duke R. Lee, who had done such a fine job as the criminal mastermind in *Vanishing Trails* (1920), became typecast in the Universal historical western serials of the twenties, playing Buffalo Bill and Marcus Whitman among other roles, with very little to do on screen. Joseph Girard started his sinister activities with Universal but ended in the independent serials, which really didn't give him a chance to show his ability.

When mention is made today of the serial villains, only four come quickly to mind and only two of these were outstanding. Strangely enough, they all made their name at Pathé. The first in time and perhaps the best-remembered of all was Paul Panzer. His fame stems from his role as Raymond Owen in *The Perils of Pauline* (1914). Although Panzer worked in other chapter plays, he would be virtually forgotten today had he not been featured in the first of the Pearl White serials. A lovable villain, his acting was broad, and whenever he was scheming it almost seemed as if he were letting the audience in on his plans with a great deal of glee. In his attempts to do away with Pearl, he was ruthless, crafty and cunning but he also gloated and gesticulated in a manner similar to Ford Sterling's comic villains for Keystone. Panzer never once succeeded in frightening anyone as did his later counterparts. Nor did his villainous portrayals ever progress much beyond this embryonic stage, for even as late as 1927 he was still overplaying his role. Sadly, the most famous serial villain never became an important one.

Panzer was followed by a tall, slim menace named Sheldon Lewis. Pearl White was threatened by him twice, in *The Exploits of Elaine* (1914) and *The Iron Claw* (1916). His acting was on a more subtle level and made his evil much more believable but he never caught the audiences' imagination. His most famous performance, *Dr. Jekyll and Mr. Hyde*, was released in 1920 by Metro, but greatly overshadowed by the John Barrymore version that came out at the same time, it was a financial failure.

Next in progression and the first really popular villain of the chapter plays was Johan Warner Oland, born in 1880 in Umea, Vesterbotten, Sweden (near the Gulf of Bothnia). Oland came to the United States with his parents in 1893 and was graduated from a Boston public school. The theater had caught his imagination and enrollment in Curry's Dramatic School for voice training came next. This was followed by a good deal of stage experience, and when he was thirty-five Oland entered pictures. He soon appeared on the nation's screens as Baron Huroki, the Oriental villain of *Patria* (1917). Well-received in this role, Oland's big opportunity came when he was hired to menace Pearl White in *The Fatal Ring* (1917). As Carslake, he did his best to finish off Pearl and Henry G. Sell in an effort to reclaim a precious jewel, the motivation for the action.

As Wu Fang, he made his second appearance as an Oriental villain in *The Lightning Raider* (1919), when he once again matched wits with Miss White and naturally lost. Oland was to become famed for his Oriental portrayals, even though he was far from being one himself. After the arrival of sound, he played Fu Manchu and then hit his stride as the greatest of the four actors who made Earl Derr Biggers' Charlie Chan a box-office attraction. So great was the public acceptance of his Oriental characterization that during a trip to China in the thirties he found to his surprise that the Chinese refused to believe that he was really an Occidental.

Oland made only four more chapter plays (all for Pathé) before he went on to gather new fans as a result of his appearances in various features of the latter twenties. An excellent actor, he was also a very crafty one who became an accomplished scene stealer. While threatening Miss White with his back to the camera, audience attention should have gone to Pearl. Instead, with his arms folded neatly behind him, Oland's fingers were involved in just enough nefarious activity to effectively keep most eyes focused on him.

A career which had started with identification with Pearl White ended just three days after Miss White passed away in France. On a visit to his native Sweden, Oland came down with penumonia and was hospitalized in Stockholm, where he died on August 6, 1938.

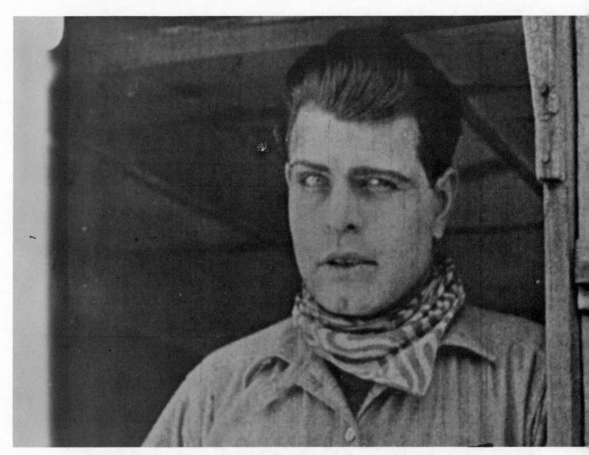

A pleasant looking hero, Jack Hoxie was a favorite of children of all ages, except when he attempted to act. Here he portrays *Lightning Bryce* (1919). (Courtesy Don Overton)

Of all the serial villains of the twenties, none were more convincing or menacing than a versatile screen scoundrel named Frank Lackteen. Born in 1894 in Kubber-Ilias, a city about thirty miles from Damascus (in what is now Lebanon), Lackteen had emigrated to the United States to live, but traveled to Canada where he soon found work in motion pictures. Joseph A. Golden was shooting an independent production there and Frank became a part of it. Returning to New York City, he decided to stay in the movie business and went to work for Ben Wilson in a Universal picture.

Shortly after his arrival in New York, Lackteen went down to the same studio where Pearl White had once worked. Here he found William Steiner producing *The Yellow Menace* (1916), with William Kennedy directing. Edwin Stevens, who had once portrayed the devil on the stage, was perfectly cast as the Oriental star (who was also the heavy of the chapter play). With no agents to worry about in those days, actors often received jobs by walking on-set and asking for work. This is just what Frank did and Kennedy hired

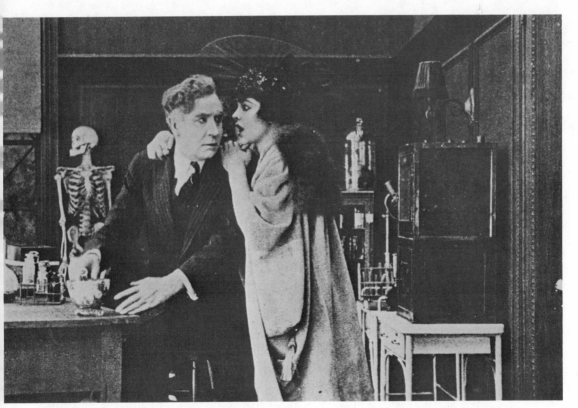

Thomas J. McGrane and Olga Olanova proved a villainous pair in *The Crimson Stain Mystery* (1916). (Courtesy Alan Brock)

Silent serial villains varied from the mundane to the exotic. This is the Wolf-Devil from *Queen of the Northwoods* (1929).

him for a Chinese role, a part which kept him busy for three weeks. It was his first taste of serial work and sort of prophetic of his later villainy.

After the filming of his role was completed, Lackteen went on to the World Film Corporation, where he worked in a number of the Robert Warwick features directed by Maurice Tourneur. These were followed by a short turn with Solax and 1918 again found him working for Tourneur in *Woman*, a seven-reel feature which has been likened to Griffith's *Intolerance* (1916) but on a smaller scale. The film consisted of five stories, each designed to show a different side of the title and Frank was put to work in the second episode, which dealt with the Emperor Claudius and his wife Messalina.

Early in his career, Lackteen had taken careful stock of himself and his talents and decided against an attempt to become a leading man. This was a

The Wolf-Devil prepares to spirit Ethlyne Clair away to his lair in a scene from *Queen of the Northwoods.*

clever move, as he was not the "type" and although leading men come and go, the character actor stays around and works consistently. Frank did some roles at Paramount and eventually turned up in California at the Vitagraph studio on Prospect Street. Here he worked for William J. Bowman in the Antonio Moreno serials. When Bowman and Moreno finally parted during *The Veiled Mystery* (1920), Lackteen went on to the Brunton studio with Bowman, who had signed to do a Ruth Roland chapter play for Pathé release.

Frank was given the role of Pablo in *The Avenging Arrow* (1921). He worked in the other two Roland serials which Woody Van Dyke directed and then suffered an eclipse for over a year. During this time, he kept busy with roles in various "B" features. His return to serial thrillers came in a

With the unconscious Ella Hall in the arms of Harry Carter, Jean Hathaway decides to search for *The Master Key* (1914).

big way when George B. Seitz tapped him for the role of Briarthorn, the Indian heavy in *Leatherstocking* (1924). Warner Oland had departed from Pathé employ in 1921 and the front office was still searching for an effective villain to replace their best arch-fiend. When the early episodes of *Leatherstocking* were unreeled in New York, Paul Fairfax Fuller pointed out to the Pathé executives that here was their man. They agreed heartily — Lackteen filled the bill.

With his unique facial structure, Frank Lackteen could play any type of villain. Here he menaces Ruth Roland in *White Eagle* (1922). (Courtesy Frank Lackteen)

Pearl White, Queen of the Serials.

After the chapter play was completed, Seitz asked Lackteen to accompany him to New York to do publicity on the serial, and once there cast him in *Into the Net* (1924) . During the following four years, the face of Frank Lackteen leered from the serial screen weekly and was automatically associated with the deepest and direst villainy that Frank Leon Smith could possibly devise. He became one of the greatest assets that the Pathé cliffhangers possessed and no one who ever saw his performance in such thriller as *Hawk of the Hills* (1927) could doubt that here was the personification of evil. In this respect his face was his fortune, for the hollow cheeks, swarthy complexion and unique structure of his facial bones heightened the villainy which he was able to project so well that children looked over their shoulders on the way home from the theater, just to make certain that he was not following them.

His method of acting was straight forward and simple — he read the script and tried to do his role exactly as he imagined it would appear in real life. His pantomime was subdued and quite restrained, giving an audience the feeling that he wasn't really acting at all but that the evil which seemed to exude from his pores was indeed very natural. Frank received a good deal of attention from the camera and was the subject of many closeups, not only because he was an effective actor. The actual projection of his villainy came mainly from his facial expressions.

Lackteen felt that the simplicity of his action and reaction was a basic part of his success. Becoming nervous and confused if he tried to do too much at one time, he simply concentrated on a few of the fundamentals which served to well establish his role within a scene. Although Frank was box-office material for Pathé, his salary reached its peak with the filming of *The Green Archer* (1925) at $350 weekly. Considering the fact that Allene Ray was only drawing $500, there is a reasonable comparison. The days of big money at Pathé had long passed. After Pearl White, Pathé deliberately kept salaries as low as possible.

Frank carried his villainy over into the sound period with serials at Universal and Republic, along with work in numerous features. Proving the wisdom of his decision made so long ago, he is in semi-retirement today but occasionally plays character roles which interest him.

7

... And Their Ladies

The life of Pearl Fay White, greatest of the serial heroines, has been sadly neglected by film historians, most of whom feel that neither she nor her serials merit attention. The problem of reconstructing her past with some degree of accuracy has been made extremely difficult. Pearl was the source of many conflicting stories about her early life and seemed to enjoy the fact that no two stories ever agreed. She even went so far as to perpetuate certain of these myths in an autobiography, *Just Me,* published by Doran in 1919.

It is certain that she came from humble beginnings in Missouri, but little else can be stated with certainty until around 1910, when she entered pictures with the Powers Company. Her salary was $30.00 weekly, a far cry from the $3000 per week that Pathé would pay her five years later. She moved to Lubin in 1911 and to Pathé in 1912. Little is known of her early activities with these film companies, but it can be supposed that she enacted a variety of roles, as did most players of the time.

In October 1912, the Crystal Film Company signed her and felt pleased enough with their new acquisition to announce to the trade papers that she would henceforth appear exclusively in their comedies. She was also the feature attraction on the 1913 calendar that Crystal used to advertise its product. At Crystal, Pearl proved to be competent as a comedienne and many of her early split-reel comedies with Chester Barnett received good notices. These films were popular enough to merit an increase in length the following year and Pearl worked hard in the production of single-reel comedies until July of 1913.

In the first chapter of *The Exploits of Elaine* (1914), Broadway favorite Arnold Daly, as Craig Kennedy (scientific detective), explains how "The Clutching Hand" killed Pearl White's father. (Courtesy Alan Brock)

At that time, she decided to take a vacation and left New York City to spend some time on the Continent. Her announced reason for the trip was to study European methods of acting and production, but in reality she was bored with work and bound for a long rest. Hard work and thrift had brought Pearl a healthy savings account of about $6000 and she was determined to enjoy herself.

A charming girl, Pearl was real and unpretentious with simple tastes. By sharing an apartment with a girlfrend and using good sense in money matters, she was easily able to provide for herself. This frugality was a trait which she carried throughout her active career and one which allowed her to retire when she wished. She was never bound to the business by a need or desire to accumulate more money.

Pearl was rescued from a burning house in Episode 7 of *The Perils of Pauline*, much to the amazement of Francis Carlyle and Paul Panzer, who had not counted on Crane Wilbur's discovery of her whereabouts.

Upon her return from abroad after seven months of sheer enjoyment, Pearl went back to work at Crystal and happened to meet an old acquaintance, Theodore Wharton. His recent association with Pathé led her to a new position. Wharton introduced her to Louis Gasnier, who was preparing *The Perils of Pauline* (1914) and Pearl was offered the leading role at $250 weekly. This proposition was also accompanied by the promise of much publicity and it proved to be the break which she had sought for so long. The Eclectic Film Company went into production and Pearl White made screen history.

The Perils of Pauline carried her to world fame and remains today as the one serial of which everyone has heard. Primitive in execution, it was simple in concept. Pearl's role was that of a young girl who wanted to be a successful writer. Harry Marvin (Crane Wilbur) wished to marry her but

Pearl White as Pearl Standish in *The Fatal Ring* (1917). (Courtesy Alan Brock)

she refused to consider his proposal until after she had spent a year pursuing her dream. Her foster father was disposed of in the first episode. Her father's secretary Owen (Paul Panzer) [1] had been left one-half of the old man's

[1] In the original release version, the villain was named Owen. When the 28mm Pathéscope Library prints were released a few years later, Owen had been altered to read Koerner, a reflection of the World War I practice of identifying villains as Germans. The surviving prints available today are the 28mm reissues and as such, have caused much confusion among historians and collectors. The original release prints contained *no* chapter titles, nor were they numbered in sequence. When Pathé executives made the decision to release 28mm prints, they selected certain chapters, arbitrarily assigning titles and sequential numbers. For example, the closing episode of the original release is available today bearing the chapter title of *"The Floating Coffin"* and carrying Chapter #9 on its main title frame. This misleads the uninitiated into believing that they actually have the 9th chapter, but in reality, it was the 20th episode of the original release.

estate; the other half was willed to Pearl. Owen hoped to get his hands upon the entire inheritance by discrediting Harry and doing away with Pearl. The will provided that upon her death the fortune would go to him unless she had married Harry. And so it went for twenty episodes, with Pearl involved in an airship race, balloon ascension, Indians, gypsies, pirates, racing cars and everything else that Charles W. Goddard and George B. Seitz could dream up.

Her fame established with one serial, Pearl went on to become the largest money-maker that Pathé ever had in the serial field. No one topped her in popularity with the audiences. She made nine more chapter plays for Pathé between 1914–19 before leaving to enter features with Fox. Each serial had

This mirror reflection from *The Fatal Ring* (1917) gives the answer to an oft-asked question of today. "What did audiences see in Pearl White?" (Courtesy D. Elmo Brooks)

proven to be a huge box-office attraction but Pearl felt she could become a greater success in dramatic roles. This was a sad mistake, for drama wasn't really her forte and the Fox features were financial failures for the most part. After a trip abroad and semi-retirement, she returned once more to Pathé and *Plunder* (1923), her last, and some feel her least memorable, serial.

The production of *Plunder* resulted in the death of John Stevenson, who had offered to double her in a dangerous scene. She would not have allowed it, but for a combination of factors. Her eyesight was not good, her timing was off and an old back injury incurred during the filming of her first serial was acting up once more. After Stevenson's unfortunate death, the se-

Pearl White played rough in *Plunder* (1923), her final serial . . .

. . . So did the villains.

rial was rushed to completion and Pearl returned to France where she made her home until death overtook her in 1938.

Pearl White had rarely employed a double. When she did so, it was not because of the hazard involved but rather because Pearl lacked the necessary physical strength or athletic ability to carry out the assignment. Over the years, many writers have given the impression that Miss White was hired, dramatized and exploited as a "stunt girl." In the eyes of the Pathé people, Pearl was a competent and serious dramatic actress who was reacting to the evil machinations of the villain. They did not desire to present her to the public as a circus queen or daredevil acrobat, nor did Pathé wish to use Pearl in so-called stunt situations. Their idea was simply to present her in thrilling, hazardous and dangerous situations and the entire Pathé policy regarding this was implicit in Louis Gasnier's simple directive to his writers:

With Warren Krech unconscious, has Pearl White lost her only hope of salvation from "The Swamp of Lost Souls"? See the next episode of *Plunder* (1923) at this theater for the answer.

"Put the girl in danger." Danger was the key word. This is also the key to the slow, methodical pacing of the Pearl White chapter plays.

As anyone who remembers Miss White's serials or has recently seen some of her work knows, she received a lot of rough handling. Tied up, hung up, thrown around and involved in many royal fights with the henchmen of the "mastermind," she was not often doubled. According to competent eyewitnesses, her first five serials contained only three scenes where a double was used. Interestingly enough, she did not like to be doubled. For aesthetic reasons, her producers did not like to use a substitute for her. The doubling business was still very clumsy at that stage of movie development. Eddie

Kelly and other small men were on hand to be used if necessary, but it was done in extreme long shots or the substitution became obvious and ludicrous.

This is where the factor of time entered the picture. Time, not safety or any other combination, was the prime concern in the early days. It took time to dress a double, place him properly and match mannerisms. This was a waste which held up speedy production and if there ever was an actress who believed in "keeping the show going," it was Pearl White.

An interesting sidelight is the fact that Ruth Roland, Pathé's second serial queen was just the opposite. She was doubled in every situation which involved risk or hardship. Robert Rose, a slight, small-boned ex-cowboy, was

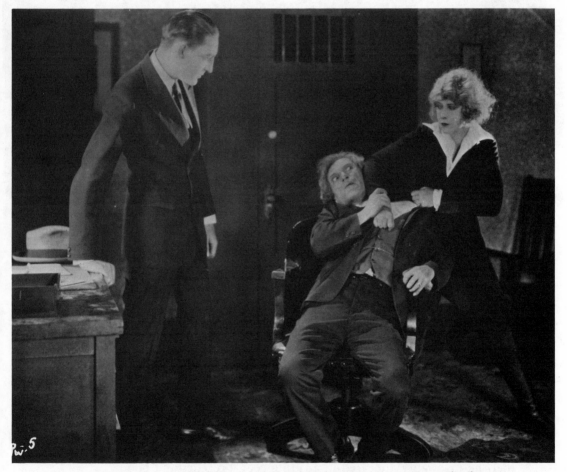

Warren Krech let Pearl use her own method of obtaining information in *Plunder*.

RUTH ROLAND
IN
"THE TIGER'S TRAIL"
EPISODE NO. 2
"THE GLOWING EYES"

A BREATHLESS MOMENT—AS HER PURSUER
THUNDERED AT THE DOOR!

Ruth Roland's penchant for many closeups such as this was one reason directors found her difficult to work with. From *The Tiger's Trail* (1919). (Courtesy Larry Edmunds Bookshop)

a perfect substitute for Miss Roland. Dressed in a wig and riding breeches, he could and did pass for her even when moving close by the camera. Her last serials contained almost as many scenes of Rose impersonating her as they did scenes in which she actually appeared. This was due in part to her inability to get along with her directors.

As a performer in her own right, Ruth was adequate in handling the type of roles which she portrayed. During the early twenties, she was without equal among serial actresses in her ability to put across a strong emotional effect in the midst of exciting situations. Seemingly fearless and athletic, she managed at the same time to hold her feminine appeal regardless of the fact that she invariably appeared in a riding coat, breeches and boots.

In a popularity contest sponsored by *Motion Picture Classic* in 1919–20,

Allene Ray, Pathé's Pearl White of the twenties and one of the most beautiful of the Serial Queens.

Ruth placed thirteenth with 3121 votes. (Pearl White received 26,558). As she was second only to Miss White in serial popularity, a few interesting comparisons can be made. Whereas Pearl was warm and gregarious on and off set, Ruth was aloof and cautious — a keen businesswoman out to make money, an objective of which she never lost sight. While Pearl was without pretensions and enjoyed a reputation for give-and-take with the unit crew, Ruth wrapped herself in a carefully developed air of superiority. Feeling that she had worked her way to the top, she seemed happy only with those inferior in social status — persons she could dominate. It was not unusual for her to go weeks without speaking to her male lead and she even made one entire serial without speaking to her director.

In a surprising reversal of form (and a good example of Hollywood publicity), she was quoted by Inez and Helen Klumph in their 1922 volume, *Screen Acting,* as placing the ability to make audiences like the star as a requirement more pertinent for serial success than talent. Her advice for would-be serial actresses: develop a capacity for making friends in real life!

The closest competition offered to Pearl White and Ruth Roland came

A prisoner of love, Allene Ray patiently awaits her fate. Perhaps dashing Bruce Gordon will arrive before she disappears behind *The Fortieth Door* (1924).

from a daring young Indiana girl, Helen Holmes. Miss Holmes gained initial
fame at Kalem as the star of the long-running series, *The Hazards of Helen,*
by capitalizing on her athletic ability and the great American romance with
railroading. After filming forty-eight chapters of *The Hazards,* Helen and
her director-husband, J. P. McGowan, left Kalem for Universal where she
spent only a few weeks before succumbing to the blandishments of Samuel
S. Hutchison of Mutual, who formed the Signal Film Corporation to exploit
her in chapter plays.

The Girl and the Game, her first Signal serial of 1915, was a smashing
success, earning over $2,250,000 while in release. She followed with *Lass of*

Allene Ray knew the fate ahead if the villain's henchmen succeeded in mummifying her.
The result is just to her lower left. But viewers knew that Bruce Gordon was about to
arrive . . .

. . . in the guise of a native. Bruce rescues Allene and searches for a means of escape . . .

the Lumberlands, The Lost Express and *The Railroad Raiders,* each a western railroad story and each more popular than the one preceding it. But as Helen's star rose, Mutual's waxed and waned. Hard times had befallen the releasing organization after Harry Aitken was forced out in 1915. By 1919, Mutual was nearly out of existence and Helen moved into the independent field with several series of five-reel features.

She reappeared in the serial fold with *The Fatal Fortune, The Tiger Band* and *Battling Brewster* sandwiched in between various series of independent features, but failed to recapture the audiences which had sat spellbound week after week as she chased villains across the top of a moving train, leaped from horseback onto the side of a runaway boxcar and engaged desperate criminals in hand-to-hand combat.

. . . which lies beyond the secret passage. (*The Fortieth Door,* 1924.)

Written by Frank Spearman or Frederic Bennett, her serials featured strong story lines and were polished productions. As directed by J. P. McGowan, the plots moved rapidly and were filled with exciting moments. But Mutual's diminishing importance as it slipped from a position of strength in the industry could not give Helen the exposure she needed to compete with Pearl, Ruth and Pathé's far-flung distribution empire. Her move into independent films meant a steady income but removed her from real competition with the Pathé and Universal serial stars.

The latter twenties found Helen reduced to supporting roles as a villainess in Universal and independent serials. The public's fascination with railroads had reached its peak during World War I and was gradually replaced by other interests. Repeated comeback attempts failed to gain her steady employment and Helen retired to the San Fernando Valley where she operated a small antique shop until her death in 1950.

It's all up to Allene Ray now. Can she fend off Noble Johnson long enough to throw the switch and save the express? Or will the villains gain possession of *The Yellow Cameo* (1928)? (Courtesy John Hampton)

Ethlyne Clair holds a minion of the Wolf-Devil at bay as Walter Miller tries to find out the identity of the master criminal in *Queen of the Northwoods* (1929). (Courtesy John Hampton)

George Walsh and Louise Lorraine encountered unknown dangers *With Stanley in Africa* (1922). (Courtesy Louise Lorraine)

In the latter twenties, the Pathé serial program rested squarely upon the lovely shoulders of Allene Ray. Standing 5'3" and fair of figure, her beautiful blue eyes stood out under a cap of luscious honey-blond hair. As a featured player in independent pictures, her success had been only modest but once *Way of a Man* (1924) was released, she was on her way up.

Prompt on the set and extremely serious about her work, she was actually very much an introvert. Although she was well-liked by all who knew and worked with her, Miss Ray did not encourage familiarity and kept to herself. The fact that she was a perfect lady in all respects was not lost on the unit crew which worked with her. In the silent days, profanity on the set was a casual part of film making and accepted as such. This language was taboo in

Louise Lorraine reaffirmed her faith in detective Hayden Stevenson in this scene from *The Diamond Master* (1929). Stevenson's efforts to retrieve the machine, which created diamonds from dust, required only ten chapters.

her presence, for the unit members held the highest respect for her. However they did enjoy teasing her. She blushed easily and the scarlet coloring would quickly show through her makeup.

Allene's greatest drawback was without a doubt her reserve. Lacking emotion and the natural ability to project it, her quiet nature made it difficult to register fear when placed in a hazardous situation. This was a grave liability for a serial queen, but Seitz was an understanding and patient director. The task of seeing that she reacted as expected fell on Spencer Bennet, who was always able to rise to the occasion. In an effort to obtain the

Was it true? Did beautiful Priscilla Dean know the secret of *The Gray Ghost* (1917)? (Courtesy Priscilla Dean)

proper tense and excited reactions. Bennet would resort to underhanded and sneaky tactics. Crew members were placed in out-of-the-way locations on set and armed with guns and other noise-creating devices. On a given signal, pandemonium broke loose giving bystanders the impression that the studio was being destroyed by an earthquake. Fortunately for Bennet's sake, as well as her own, the ruse never failed to frighten Allene half to death and the scene usually turned out as envisioned.

A fine athlete, her cooperative attitude made her game for every stunt that came along. She never refused to do a scene that was physically difficult or dangerous. None of her co-workers ever recall the use of a double, even though she was a major asset to Pathé.

Allene had the misfortune to "arrive" near the end of the silent period. The early days of sound were quite unkind to her. After Pathé went under, Miss Ray moved to Universal where she had the signal honor of starring in the final silent serial (which was also the first sound chapter play), *The Indians Are Coming.* Her thin, high voice did not register in a satisfactory manner, for the primitive electronic equipment was unable to modulate sound for highs and lows. Intelligent enough to see the handwriting on the wall, she disappeared completely from view after a few low-grade features.

Ethlyne Clair was an exact opposite to Allene Ray. A happy extrovert who loved people and social standing, she had the drive and ambition necessary

Years after the accident that brought her to Africa, Elinor Field was regarded by the natives as *The Jungle Goddess* (1922) and treated her as such.

Neva Gerber's long serial association with Ben Wilson was temporarily broken as she took time out to co-star with Jack Perrin in a western adventure story of Kit Carson and *The Santa Fe Trail (1923).* (Courtesy Don Overton)

to forge ahead in the dog-eat-dog world of motion pictures, but she never really made it. It was also her misfortune to "arrive" just as the silent film was being dealt its death blow.

Born Ethlyne Williamson, she won a beauty contest in Atlanta, Georgia, the year prior to attending the National Academy of Fine and Applied Arts in Washington, D.C. At the end of her stay in Washington, she went to New York City to visit a brother, who introduced her to an agent. Her first contract was with Walter Kane Productions, an independent unit shooting pictures at the old Marion Davies studios on 125th Street. This amounted to a few small roles but nothing spectacular appeared to be in the future. One night, while attending a theatrical social function at the Astor Hotel, she met Julius Stern who offered her a Hollywood contract. She was to play the

When audiences saw what Eugenia Gilbert had just seen in *King of the Kongo* (1929), their eyes and mouths opened too.

Ethel Grandin as Florence Montrose, heroine of *The Crimson Stain Mystery* (1916). (Courtesy Alan Brock)

role of Mrs. Newlywed in a comedy series to be released by Universal. A release from Walter Kane allowed her to sign with the Stern Brothers at $100 weekly.

After a two-year contract with Universal expired, she went to Pathé on a free-lance basis. Her first serial had been done for Universal, *The Vanishing Rider* (1928), one of the best of the William Desmond chapter plays. At Pathé, she was teamed with Walter Miller, their most virile male lead. The result was the best Pathé cliffhanger of 1929, *Queen of the Northwoods*. Full of action and high suspense, this well-constructed thriller utilized one of the most mysterious villains to hit the serial screen in the twenties. A man of many disguises, he most often appeared in the role of the Wolf-Devil. Wielding a strong and almost supernatural power over the wolf packs, he terrorized the entire Northwest. Ethlyne's role was generous and although doubles performed her more strenuous scenes, she turned in a fine performance. Unfortunately, this was the spring of 1929 and Pathé was in the process of abandoning serial production. There was no more work for the determined heroine of the chapter play screen.

Moving back to features, she played the feminine lead with Monte Blue in *From Headquarters*, a part-talkie. A few short subjects followed, but the industry was in such a state of flux that nothing came of her efforts. Marriage to Ernie Westmore, the makeup artist whom she had met at Warners while doing the picture with Blue, meant graceful retirement from the hectic life of an aspiring starlet. The marriage brought a daughter but did not last, for although her career was ended, Ethlyne was restless. Divorce was followed by a lasting marriage to Art Frost, who was not connected with the film industry.

Born in New York City in 1898, Mollie King was the youngest member of a well-known theatre family. Show business was her destiny. Her brother Charles was teamed with Elizabeth Brice in one of the more popular acts of the day. Only eight months old when she made her first stage appearance, Mollie continued to play child roles while attending school. Of necessity, she attended many different schools, but was finally graduated from Wadleigh High School. During this time, she had played several important roles on the stage. Mollie's most valuable contribution was in support of Maxine Elliot in *Her Own Way*, but she received excellent notices for her appearance in *The Royal Family* and *The Little Princess*. She also appeared with Denham Thompson in the vaudeville sketch, *Joshua Whitcomb*.

After finishing school at the age of fifteen, she understudied for Miss Brice in a musical comedy, *The Winsome Widow*. This led to a supporting role with Sam Bernard in *The Bell of Bond Street* and an engagement at the

Serial heroines had to be equally adept at handling locomotives, trolley cars, automobiles, motorcycles and horses. Here is Helen Holmes, in *The Hazards of Helen*, the Kalem railroad series that rocketed her to fame as one of the foremost of the Serial Queens.

fabulous Winter Garden. Her featured appearance there was followed by a two-year tour of the Orpheum circuit where she and her sister Nellie did an act which was very popular with the vaudeville audiences. This led directly to motion pictures and a contract with the World Film Corporation.

World Film was in trouble. Organized in 1915 by Arthur Spiegel, the mail order house magnate, it was financed by Laddenberg Thalman and Company and numbered William A. Brady, a legitimate showman, and Lewis J. Selznick among its top executives. The only important pictures which World released were the series made with Clara Kimball Young, who was acquired from Vitagraph by the ambitious Selznick. A disagreement between Selznick

One of the earliest and most popular of the Serial Queens, Helen Holmes took time out for this picture at the Signal studios in 1917. (Courtesy Manuel Weltman)

and the directors of World Film led to his dismissal but when he left he took the services of Miss Young with him.

This placed World Film in a precarious position and Brady attempted to salvage what was left. Turning to the stage for players, Mollie was among those he approached. Her first starring role, *A Woman's Power* was released in 1916 and she went on to make several features for World. Opportunity knocked a second time and she joined Pathé where she continued making celluloid dramas. With the departure of Pearl White eminent, Pathé was searching for a successor and had a dream of turning Mollie into another "Lady Daredevil of the Fillums" but that was not to be.

Fair of complexion, the long-limbed beauty was a natural for serials. Her reddish-blonde hair effectively framed large hazel eyes which registered ter-

Popular serial heroines were not the demure types found in romantic dramas of the day. As daughter of the fire commissioner in *The Flame Fighter* (1925), Brenda Lane answered the "Silent Alarm" with the department.

ror or love equally well. But after completing two serials for Pathé which were both well received, she left the film world to return to the stage. Romance had entered her life and she married a wealthy socialite. Headlining at the Century Grove in January 1919, she then joined a New York musical comedy, *Good Morning Judge*. While appearing in this role, she signed a contract with the American Cinema Corporation in May and did a group of features, disappearing from sight until 1922 when her last screen roles were done under the banner of Associated Exhibitors. One of the most talented young actresses to appear in serials, Mollie stood a very good chance of becoming a top attraction in the twenties had she chosen to remain in chapter plays.

The earlier mention of the *Motion Picture Classic* contest helps to explain why few of the Universal serial actresses were regarded as top attractions. The wide disparity between the first and second cliffhanger heroine is something to ponder but then consider that no other members of this breed even placed on the popularity list. Universal directed its attention mainly to the male stars and plodded along turning out its yearly quota of serials.

Universal's most durable serial attraction at the box office during the early twenties, Louise Lorraine, almost failed to get into pictures. A native of Los Angeles, Louise was one of five children. Her father had met with an early death and the family struggled along as best it could. When she was in her early teens, a door-to-door salesman proved to be the deciding element in her

Ann Little, the petite and popular heroine in *Nan of the North* (1922). (Courtesy John Hampton)

life. When young Louise answered the door, the salesman was so struck by her beauty that he uttered the classic and time-worn comment, "You ought to be in pictures."

But this man truly meant it and he sent around a friend who also happened to be a representative of Thomas Ince. The friend also believed that she had a future in front of the camera and offered to sign Louise to a contract on the spot. At this point, mother stepped in and said no. She had definite ideas about Hollywood and its people. The Ince representative made three attempts to sign Louise but each to no avail.

In the meantime, Louise thought over the suggestion that she work in pictures and decided it would be an ideal manner in which to earn money for the family. Pleading with her mother, Louise finally broke down the resistance. Accompanied by her mother, Louise made the rounds of the local studios. Work as an extra came first and she appeared in the Clara Kimball Young features then in production by the famous star. Miss Young had formed a company to produce her own pictures and Louise was picked out of a crowd scene by the star. The aspiring young actress was chosen to emote in a scene with Miss Young, an honor she still cherishes.

A contract at Century followed the extra work. Century belonged to the Stern brothers and produced comedies which were released under the Universal banner. Her weekly salary of $50.00 was a great help and the Sterns were so impressed with her work that they quickly tore up her contract. It was replaced by one which doubled her salary, and with this income Louise did not even complain when they billed her as Louise Fortune in the two-reel Century Comedies.

Louise received her big boost as well as another new name in *Elmo the Fearless*, an eighteen-episode serial produced by the Great Western Photoplay Company (also owned by the Sterns) for Universal release. After completing *Elmo the Mighty*, Grace Cunard had been scheduled for the role opposite Elmo Lincoln but was unable to do the serial because of poor health. Louise's success in this role led to a contract at Universal as a serial heroine and she also appeared in many of the two-reel Universal westerns then coming off the Laemmle assembly line. In *Elmo the Fearless*, Louise Fortune had become Louise Lorraine and Universal continued to bill her that way.

Rising to a salary of $500 weekly, Louise costarred in five serials before leaving Universal in June 1922. She left on the advice of her manager and free-lanced in an attempt to avoid serials and comedies. Two additional serials at Universal followed, along with feature roles and more comedies before she was given an option at MGM in August 1926 with a salary of $400 weekly. Her stay at MGM did not work out and Louise soon found herself back at Universal but with a lower salary, courtesy of her manager's poor advice.

Under the influence of a mystical Indian drug, Ann Little is prepared to do as she is told. But rescue by *Lightning Bryce* was imminent. (Courtesy Don Overton)

Her manager was only one of the many hindrances to her career. Louise was always (or so it seemed to her) just behind the big break. Her work as a light comedienne at Century had qualified her for a job with Harold Lloyd, who was searching desperately for someone to replace Bebe Daniels. Louise tried out for the role and could have had it, but she was signed in the meantime for a serial by her manager and Universal would not release her from the contract. She worked steadily throughout the silent period with many of the top names at Universal, starring opposite Joe Bonomo, George Walsh, Elmo Lincoln, Lane Chandler, Roy Stewart and Art Acord. A quiet, demure and willing star, she did much of her own stunt work without ever incurring a serious injury.

As a real trouper, Louise hesitated to let someone else take the risks, preferring to do the scenes herself. Several close calls came her way, but the only time a serious accident took place was in a sequence that her director

Henry G. Sell pleads with Arline Pretty to join forces against the machinations of the unscrupulous Haviland-Hunter in *A Woman in Grey* (1920). (Courtesy Arline Pretty)

insisted should be done by a stunt double. A simple car skid scene, it took place in *The Great Circus Mystery*. Jay Marchant refused to let her do it and while the cameras rolled, the automobile overturned, killing all of the occupants. From that point on, Louise accepted the judgment of her director without question.

She did many difficult stunts and looking back today, wonders how she came through those years with no real mishaps. For example, in *Elmo the Fearless* she climbed a rope ladder hanging over a precipice. The script called for the ladder to break and the heroine to drop out of camera range. The next scene would show her crumpled body on the ledge below. To accomplish this, a man stood below the ladder (well out of camera range) and as she dropped, he caught her.

Although she enjoyed working around wild animals, one scene in *The Great Circus Mystery* finally cured her of any affection she might have had for lions. She was supposed to faint and allow a lion to sniff her limp body. For some unknown reason, the big cat refused to leave her once the sequence was in the camera. Jay Marchant realized the danger and called out warning her to remain lifeless while prop men teased, begged and cajoled the lion to move. He refused to obey and finally a tamer had to go into the cage, drawing the cat's attention away while Louise made her exit. By this time, every nerve in her body felt as if the breaking point were near. The rescue was made without incident but a somewhat wiser young lady emerged from the cage.

Her marriage to Art Acord did not survive, but Louise made a second and

Serial actresses were often called upon to do their own dangerous stunts, especially in the low-budget independents. Here's Arline Pretty in Serico's *A Woman in Grey* (1920).

Jean Sothern, star of the *Mysteries of Myra* (1916), one of the early serials based on occult phenomena. (Courtesy Alan Brock)

happier union which led to her exit from the movies. Although her voice was highly acceptable in the talkies, Louise retired five months after the birth of her first child. She had just learned that she was to have another. A widow with two grown-up children today, Louise Lorraine is amazed to find out that she is still thought of by fans. Youthful in appearance and thought,

Someone broke into Lola Todd's safe in *The Scarlet Streak* (1926) and Jack Daugherty vowed he'd find the person responsible.

she is grateful for the career she once had but entertains no regrets that she gave it up for a family.

Of the other Universal actresses, Eileen Sedgwick was the best known. A member of the popular theatrical family billed as the Five Sedgwicks, she worked on vaudeville stages across the country with her parents, brother Edward and sister Josie. Ed Sedgwick was the first to enter motion pictures, working as a comic. Ed was a fairly good-sized fellow and there was always room for a fat comic on any lot in the early days. He didn't enjoy taking pratfalls for a living and rejoined the family on stage. He would later become a serial director for Universal.

Ed Sedgwick reentered pictures with Lubin in 1914 while passing through Galveston, Texas, on tour and within a short time the family act was broken up for good. Eileen and Josie both appeared on the lot at Universal City and went to work in two-reel western and adventure shorts. Eileen's big chance came in 1918 when she replaced Molly Malone in *The Lure of the Circus*, Eddie Polo's second starring serial. Miss Malone had undergone surgery for appendicitis and her recovery was very slow. The story line was altered by William Wing and Eileen became the leading woman. It was her first of twelve serials and she soon became the leading heroine on the Uni-

Kathlyn Williams can't believe her ears. The villainous Charles Clary has just misinterpreted a letter from her father in this first episode of *The Adventures of Kathlvn* (1913).

versal lot, replacing Marie Walcamp who retired in 1920 after marrying her leading man.

Miss Sedgwick kept busy during the next twelve years, for she appeared in countless short westerns between her serial stints. An accomplished horse-woman, she was on a par with Ruth Roland insofar as acting was concerned but Universal had no intention of making her a star of the same caliber. She was also a victim of the Universal production methods and even her best appearances (such as the classic *The Riddle Rider*) were not given the meticulous touch with which Pathé's young team of Seitz, Bennet and Smith bestowed on their chapter plays.

With this, we have come to the end of a long road. The serials, their directors, stars and stories are of the past. While they were in existence, these weekly installments of thrills and adventures thrilled millions of fans, young and old alike. Their memory is still strong in the minds of many. Those who do not remember are a bit poorer for their loss.

8

Epilogue, or the End of the Trail

To what sources can a person interested in viewing silent serials turn? Very few, I am afraid. None of the major film archives in the United States have accumulated any footage from the chapter plays. The bulk of what remains today rests in the hands of individual collectors. On occasion material presumed lost forever turns up but by and large it is nearly all gone. Many of the Pathé master negatives were destroyed in a laboratory fire in the thirties. Universal did next to nothing to prevent deterioration in its vaults. Vitagraph turned over the footage it had not destroyed to the Warner Brothers who have made little effort to preserve it. Surprisingly enough, much of the serial remains which are available today are from the independent field. How they fell into the hands of collectors is quite interesting.

In the early days of sound, many of the independent exchanges shuttered their doors and sold their silent footage for a paltry sum per reel in order to salvage some financial gain from their bankruptcy. This placed 35mm nitrate release prints on the market. Throughout the twenties, the film rental libraries which existed circulated first 28mm and then 16mm prints among organizations and individuals. These libraries also cleaned house and a representative amount of material fell into the hands of collectors. Over the years, duplicates have been struck and circulated among a growing hard core of enthusiasts.

John Hampton, who operates the Silent Movie Treater in Los Angeles, periodically exhibits scattered episodes of *The Perils of Pauline*, complete prints of *The Power God, King of the Kongo, The Flame Fighter, Sunken Silver, The Tiger's Shadow, Lightning Bryce, Lightning Hutch, Thunderbolt Jack* and *The Master Mystery*, plus fourteen and a half chapters of

Ben Wilson in his final chapter play, *Officer 444* (1926). Wilson's career began with the Edison Company almost at the dawn of movies and although he and Neva Gerber formed a popular serial team, few illustrations and fewer feet of their films have survived the ravages of time.

William Desmond holds the hand of Eileen Sedgwick, his blushing bride, as the final reel of *Strings of Steel* (1926) unfolds.

Happiness is just over the ridge for the stars of The Fighting Marine (1926), Gene Tunney and Marjorie Gay. (Courtesy Spencer G. Bennet)

Walter Miller and Allene Ray, the All-American serial duo of the twenties, are well represented in that serial footage which has survived. The interested fan who wishes to study their career can start with Sunken Silver (1925), occasionally shown at John and Dorothy Hampton's Silent Movie Theater in Hollywood. (Courtesy John Hampton)

Art Acord, a popular western hero, Mildred Moore and Tote DuCrow in a scene from *The Moon Riders* (1920). This serial has lived in the lore of collector's as one of the most desirable to acquire and many hope that a print will eventually be located. One of those western actors who was really a cowpoke, Acord's screen adventures were followed by a legion of fans. His career came to a tragic end in Mexico after sound finished his film career. (Courtesy John Hampton)

Plunder. Missing is the second reel of a chapter, stolen from a theater in New York City where it was being shown in the late forties. He has also worked hard to save about half of *The Jungle Goddess* from a decomposing 35mm print. By a process of re-fixing and re-washing, he salvaged close to seven chapters; the remainder had turned to jelly and powder, the eventual end of all nitrate film.

Charles Tarbox of Film Classic Exchange in Los Angeles went through an experience some years back that might be termed typical. His organization was rushed with work when a print of *The Mystery of 13* came in. A duplicate 16mm negative was struck without a complete examination of the positive and it received little attention. Tarbox had no idea of the actual condition of the print until the work was finished, the bill paid and he viewed the completed 16mm prints. He was horrified at what he saw. A great deal of hypo deterioration had set in on the positive. Whole sections were cut out as unprintable. The work that came from the lab consisted of "all they could print" from the original thirty-one reels. Some episodes were almost entirely good. Others had one complete or almost complete reel plus another reel in which there were long jumps in the action. Remaining chapters did not total over a few hundred feet of film from both reels.

ANTONIO MORENO
in
"THE VEILED MYSTERY"
A Vitagraph Serial
EPISODE 10
"A DEMONS DEVICE"

IMPRISONED IN THE TOP OF THE BURNING WATERTOWER.

About to make his bid for freedom from the burning water tower, Tony Moreno reassured Nenette de Courcy that everything would be all right — they would all escape from the clutches of *The Veiled Mystery* (1920). (Courtesy Nan Boardman)

Nenette de Courcy, Antonio Moreno and Pauline Curley have solved *The Veiled Mystery*.
(Courtesy Nan Boardman)

Allene Ray has taken just about all she can stand from Frank Lackteen. Now it's her turn in *The Fortieth Door* (1924).

The map tells Eileen Sedgwick and William Desmond that they've located what they were searching for in *Beasts of Paradise* (1923). A bandaged Joe Bonomo follows their gaze. (Courtesy Joe Bonomo)

Happy endings closed out the final reel of all serials. Joe Bonomo and Margaret Quimby can face the future confidently now that the *Perils of the Wild* (1925) have been conquered. (Courtesy Joe Bonomo)

WILLIAM DUNCAN
AND
EDITH JOHNSTON
IN
"FIGHTING FATE"
A VITAGRAPH SERIAL
CHAPTER 12
"CLEANING THE BLOT"

KERN AND JOSEPHINE CERTAIN THAT THEIR FUTURE LIFE WILL BE SERENE AND UN- TROUBLED.

Another happy ending. William Duncan and Edith Johnson successfully met all the challenges posed in *Fighting Fate* (1921) and were ready to start another cliffhanger. (Courtesy Larry Edmunds Bookshop)

For a long time after the delivery of the finished prints, he kept them to look at, hoping to edit the footage and arrive at nine, seven or even five chapters which would be reasonably coherent. Finally he gave up and the serial has just collected dust, representing a tremendous amount of money and time invested with no results. As Francis Ford had a considerable impact on serial history, this situation is sad indeed.

Other equally frustrating cases are periodically brought to light. The location of the original 35mm negative of *Pearl of the Army* is known and its condition when this writer learned of it was good. For some unknown reason, all of the American titles have been removed and the negative itself is in completely disconnected order. To this point, no one has attempted to

Antonio Moreno and Carol Holloway in a tender embrace under the watchful eye of Jack Waltemeyer, who felt certain that the *Perils of Thunder Mountain* (1919) would dispose of our stalwarts. (Courtesy Larry Edmunds Bookshop)

That Ruth Hope (Arline Pretty) was also the *Woman in Grey* was a well-kept secret from Wilfred Amory (James Heenan).

Hugh Allan and Gladys McConnell came together as the silent era ended, missing the opportunity to win fame as a serial team. *The Tiger's Shadow* (1928) pitted the two against the machinations of veteran villain Frank Lackteen.

research and reassemble this rare Pearl White chapter play and so it waits for the inevitable deterioration to set in. A re-cut version of this Astra production was marketed in the twenties and the tenth and final chapter of the re-cut version is available to the collector in 8mm but this leaves a great deal to be desired.

At one time not too long ago, Hollywood Film Enterprises in Los Angeles placed *The Adventures of Tarzan* and *Officer 444* on the home-movie market in one-reel chapters, but these are no longer available except for a few reels from the Tarzan serial. Probably the best work has been done by Black-hawk Films of Davenport, Iowa, which has cooperated with collectors and placed some chapters of *The Perils of Pauline, The Trail of the Octopus,*

No serial fan who saw *Officer 444* (1926) could understand how the arch-villain known as *The Frog* could laboriously move about the streets at will, when Ben Wilson and every policeman in the city were searching for him. This serial was filled with such peculiar lapses but its fast pace tended to blur the poor scripting.

Eddie Polo is about to make Inez McDonald his bride as *Do or Die* (1921) draws to a close. (Courtesy D. Elmo Brooks)

Princess Istra (Marguerite Courtot) rescues Archy Barlow (George B. Seitz) from the clutches of evil Barcelona Ben. Joe Cuny overplayed the villain nicely in this satire of melodramatic serials written by the dean of serial scripters, Frank Leon Smith. (Courtesy Joe Cuny)

The Woman in Grey, The Exploits of Elaine, The Hazards of Helen and
The Iron Claw on the market. Others are scheduled to come but the trend
is toward compilation of episode thrills rather than complete chapters.

A surprising aspect of this picture is the fact that much more serial footage
remains in the hands of collectors in England and Europe than exists here
in the United States. For some unknown reason, more seems to have been
preserved overseas. Scouting around the British Commonwealth, it is possible to locate the complete *Exploits of Elaine*. The whereabouts of one
chapter of Charles Hutchison's first serial (*Wolves of Kultur*) is known to
the author. Holland has contributed a feature version of Eddie Polo's *Lure
of the Circus*. This is an important find, as Polo's work is rarely seen by
serial fans today. Along with the thrillers of Art Acord, William Duncan and
Charles Hutchison, it is most scarce. Thus through the neglect and short-
sightedness of the film industry itself, a part of Hollywood's fabulous heritage
of entertainment has been all but lost forever.

Warner Oland tried to force the truth from villainous Joe Cuny, who maintained his
captor was *The Phantom Foe*. Obviously, his story was not believed by Wallace
McCutcheon, Tom Goodwin, Juanita Hansen and William N. Bailey. (Courtesy Joe Cuny)

Appendix

Prints of the serials are scarce indeed, but rarer yet are the original scripts used. Reproduced herein exactly as it was written by Frank Leon Smith is the first chapter of the 1920 Pathé serial, *Pirate Gold*. This particular script is an example of the better writing to be found in the serial genre, as Smith's ability to use words for description allows the reader to conjure up a fairly accurate mental image of what the final footage looked like on screen.

1st Episode

"PIRATE GOLD"

Chapter One: In Which Hoey Buys a Map.

501—Subtitle . . . .
  Treasure.

Scene 1. (A tropical beach location studded with a few palms.)

———

Open diaphragm on a foreground of a pirates' treasure chest setting on the sands. It is hump-backed, iron-strapped and aged.
Dissolve into:
Scene 2. (A hole in the sands.)

———

Sixty dirty picturesque pirates at work eye-deep excavating with picks and shovels. As they work two of them look up obiquely and mutter timid curses as at someone above.
Scene 3. (Outside hole on sand.)

———

As close as possible a shot of the full figure of devilish pirate chief watching

men work. A sinister figure and set expressionless stare.
Scene 4.
Wide view: If possible get something of the sea into this picture. The six men are coming up out of the hole with their tools of excavation. When they get up, the chief orders them, with a word and a gesture to throw their tools down, and to take up chest. They answer with sullen alacrity by going toward chest. The chief watches.
Scene 5.
Foreground hiding place nearby, probably a large boulder. Hoey's face gazes off at action out of scene from behind boulder. Get the proper expression of excited awe.
Scene 6.
Close foreground by treasure chest as the middle parts of men's bodies and their hands come into picture and lay hold of handles. They try to lift it. It is so heavy they can just budge it.
Scene 7.
Head and shoulders foreground of Hoey who swallows hard at the proximity of treasure so heavy that six men can just about manage it.
Scene 8.
As close a foreground as possible showing the figures of the six men lugging chest laboriously out of foreground.
Scene 9.
Foreground of pirate chief. He just watches, hard faced.
Scene 10.
As close as possible a shot showing edge of hole in ground and chief in picture. The six pirates slowly lug the chest in. One or two of them glance fearfully over his or their shoulders at the sinister motionless figure of the chief.
Scene 11.
Foreground Hoey gazing from behind hiding place, eyes popping.
Scene 12.
Shot taking in the hole, the chief, pirates and chest. The men lug the chest to the edge of the hole and then look to the chief for an order. He orders three down. They leap into the hole. At another order, the three on top start easing chest over edge of hole to three below.
Scene 13.
Shot into hole, showing the three men easing chest down from above.
Scene 14.
Foreground chief. He gives an order to men out of picture.
Scene 15.
Foreground by hole. The three men have lowered the chest so that just one edge of it is up in picture. At chief's order, they leap down into hole.
Scene 16.
Shot into hole showing the three men from above leaping in, and helping the other three to ease it down.

Scene 17.
Foreground chief whose eyes flash a sinister gleam as he draws two large guns from his waist and steps out of foreground.
Scene 18.
Medium foreground by hole. Chief comes in stealthily, looks down into hole and shoots twice, once with each gun.

Chapter 2 of *Pirate Gold* found Gabrielle (Marguerite Courtot) and Ivanhoe Tuttle (George B. Seitz), menaced by Kaidy (Joe Cuny) and Siebert (Harry Semels). (Courtesy Joe Cuny)

Scene 19.
Shot into hole. Two pirates drop dead. Others cringe back, then start up out of hole in panic.
Scene 20.
Foreground by hole. The pirate chief draws his cutlass. As the first man comes up, he swings cutlass, cuts off the man's head and man and head fall back into hole.

Scene 21.

Shot into hole. Do not show the body of man whose head is cut off. Just show a foreground of the remaining pirate taken from the rear as he starts to scramble madly up opposite side of hole.

Scene 22.

Top of hole — Pirate chief with cutlass leaps down into hole.

Scene 23.

Foreground of Hoey pop-eyed.

Scene 24.

Medium foreground by hole as pirate chief comes up out of hole, breathing hard. He stands at rest and wipes his cutlass on the sash of his waist.

Scene 25.

Foreground Hoey whose dress we now see entirely for the first time. He carries a short midshipman's sword. For exact description of his dress see Mr. Smith. Unable any longer to contain himself, he rushes madly from behind boulder, his sword tightly gripped.

Scene 26.

A shot with chief in foreground and showing Hoey rushing from his hiding place at him. When Hoey is within a few yards of the chief, the latter turns quickly meets his rush and a furious duel sets in.

Scenes 27–28–
29–30.

Four scenes of the duel with camera placements at director's discretion. If the thought that Hoey's sword might be broken and that he might pick up one of the dead pirate's tools as a weapon should appeal to the director, he may use it. At any rate, Hoey finally kills the chief in foreground.

Scene 31.

Wide view: showing chief falling and Hoey staggering back. He's pretty well blowed, but not all in from his exertions. He staggers forward again in offensive and looks at the chief as if expecting a ruse. He might spare himself a step, however, for the chief is dead. Hoey turns now and goes to the treasure hole and leaps in, first throwing his sword on the sand.

Scene 32.

A masked shot into hole showing Hoey leaping in at side of treasure chest. The shot is masked to keep objectionable view of dead bodies out of picture. Just the leg of one dead pirate is in scene. Hoey lays hold of chest and tries to lift it. He can't do it. Again he lays hold of chest. This time with a mighty effort he manages to lift it with both hands and hoists it up out of picture.

Scene 33.

Top of hole — chest is shoved into picture and Hoey comes up after it. He is rather exhausted with exertion but stoops nevertheless and picks up his broken or unbroken midshipman's sword. Now he glares around truculently as one who would have the world come on if it's coming. It would seem, however, that the world declines, for Hoey sinks down by the side of the chest, resting his sword elbow on it and rests quite tired and breathing hard. Hold this a moment and then

Dissolve into:

Scene 34. (Tuttle Pharmacy.)

———

A foreground by cash register on counter. Hoey in the garb of a small city suburb's young man, stands asleep leaning one elbow on the cash register and holding a large pair of scissors in his hand in the identical pose of the midshipman with his sword and the treasure chest. For description of this pair of scissors see Mr. Millhauser. There is a 'No Sale' tab up on the cash register. Hold this scene long enough for the symbolism etc. to get over. Then the fingers holding the scissors relax and the scissors falls with a clatter to the counter. The noise of this awakens Hoey whose eyes open but who nevertheless is in that state between dreaming and waking, wherein the dream is still a reality. There is treasure in his eyes. Slowly and subtly the vision fades and Hoey becomes aware — sorrowfully aware — of his surroundings. He becomes conscious of his conventional citrate of magnesia personality and the embarrassment of a possible audience causes him to slowly turn and look around.

Scene 35.

A wide view of Tuttle's Pharmacy showing Hoey looking cautiously around. Never mind, Hoey, the store is empty. Hoey's eyes travel back to the cash register before him. He glares at it as though it were a living thing and the frustrator of his life.

Scene 36.

A foreground shot sidewise behind the counter to register the following: Hoey is glaring at the cash register as though it were his nemesis. His anger mounts. He hauls off and hits the keys a wallop. As he does so, the drawer flies out and socks him in the stomach and ten cents rings up. Hoey is foolishly mad, and his expression shows how futile he knows his anger to be. He still looking at the cash register.

Scene 37.

Closeup top of cash register showing a ten cent tab up.

Scene 38.

Foreground as per 36. Only shot from the other side. Hoey sorrowfully notes the ten cent tab and takes a dime out of his pocket, looks at it and puts it into the drawer which he closes. Austin Tuttle appears for a moment and looks out from behind prescription department, and then disappears again.

502—Subtitle . . . .

> What a dream for a dime! Yet Ivanhoe, Greenwood Tuttle — Hoey for short — scorned dreams even as barbers scorn safety razors . . . What merit the close shave without the risk of a cut?"

Scene 39.

Another foreground of Hoey as he leans discouraged on counter.

503—Subtitle . . . .

> It was always that way with Hoey. Had he not enlisted in the army to *fight?*; and had they not set him to filling capsules and inspecting hot water bags? . . They had.

Scene 40.

A wide view showing Hoey leaning discouraged on counter as before. A customer comes in and Hoey has to wait on him.

504—Subtitle . . . .

   The Senior Tuttle . . . Austin Tuttle.

Scene 41. (Prescription compounding department with counter behind store.)

———

Austin Tuttle works intently cooking something in a retort and consulting a large book nearby. (Foreground)

Scene 42.

A wider view: Austin goes on with his work as Hoey appears, a cap in his hand. Austin guiltily closes and stands before book, still, however, retaining parental dignity. It seems as though Hoey and his cap are going out for a walk. Hoey's father nods and Hoey exits. He opens book and continues his work. He seems a bit excited as he takes a certain bottle and adds a drop to the retort. The result pleases him for he takes another bottle and adds another drop. Immediately there is an explosion which singes his eye-brows. When it is over, he looks at the mess sorrowfully and then his hand goes to his eye-brows and feels the singed part. He turns and goes to a small mirror to look at his eyes.

Scene 43.

Closeup the open book lying bespattered on counter. The prominent title line at the top of the page reads:

   DEXTER'S THEORY FOR EXTRACTING GOLD FROM SEAWATER.

   (Hold it long enough to get it over.)

505—Subtitle . . . .

———

All of which makes Mrs. Tuttle's remark about her two men understandable . . . "Two boys" she always said, "only Hoey is a little more grown up."

Scene 44.

Wide view: Austin Tuttle before the mirror as before has a little box of salve in his hand which he applies to his eyebrows. He sighs and turns back to clean up the mess.

Scene 45. (A suburban street lined with trees which cast black shadows on the ground. Moonlight effect.)

———

Hoey comes walking on toward the camera from mid-distance, his head high in the manner of an energetic dreamer.

506—Subtitle . . . .

Imagination, with Hoey, was a serious affair . . . He took it out for a walk every night as the city man takes out his dog; and once free from possible objectors, he let it run wild . . .

Scene 46. (Another suburban street location lined with trees as before. Moonlight.)

———

Shot about a quarter of a block away from corner around which Hoey comes, his head high as before. And now around corner that Hoey came, come the wraith

figures of two yelling Indians riding bareback. At an interval there follow, riding booted and spurred and masked, the wraith figures of three western bandits. A Spanish Cavalier wearing a plumed hat, high boots, a cape, and a very long thin sword trailing at his side steps out from the shadows and walks beside Hoey, as the riders pass and come toward camera. A knight in full armor riding a heavy palfrey and with penant-tipped lance set ready for the joust comes from behind camera and rides away toward corner. As this happens, a half dozen black barbarous South Sea Islanders with rings through their noses, fuzzy hair, huge shields and lances come in from all sides, and Lief Ericson, huge and thick, wing-helmeted, strap-saddled, and carrying a battle axe, strides mightily around the corner where Hoey came. All these, of course, are wraith figures and Hoey's imagination peoples the street with them. They come and go while Hoey is still walking toward the camera, and none notes him. Even Hoey sees nothing so palpable as a wraith figure. They are in his mind. As Hoey passes the camera, the figure disappears and we
Fade out:
Scene 47. (Tuttle pharmacy as per 34.)

————

Wide view: Mrs. Tuttle carrying a plate covered with a napkin comes into store and advances to cash register. She sets plate down and starts to lift up the little brass plate at side of register which shows the amount of the day's sales.
Scene 48.
Foreground by cash register showing Mrs. Tuttle lifting up the brass plate to add the amount of the day's sales. She takes up plate and exits foreground.
Scene 49. (Prescription department as per 41.)

————

Austin at work rolling pills. Mrs. Tuttle enters with plate and is delighted to see her. He comes forward and looks at the plate, smiling and happy-eyed. "You don't mean to say," he says, "you've brought me something to eat!" She just smiles at him. He bends to take the plate. She shakes her head no. "Guess what it is," she says. He makes a guess. No. He leans down and smells through the napkin, then he raises his head and says, "I know! Liver and onions!" She shakes her head no. This sets him back a moment, then he looks shrewdly at her, then at the plate. Then he says "I know, a chop!" She shakes her head no. Now he runs his fingers over the top of the napkin as if feeling the contour of the stuff underneath. Now he has her "Sausages!" No. "Meat balls, then!" "Yes!" "Hurray!" And he does a little jig and kisses her. She tells him to stop his nonsense and sets the plate down which he uncovers and draws a chair up to as we
Fade out.
Scene 50.
Fade up.
(A dock or pier on the ocean. Ocean meets horizon. Moonlight effect.)

————

A shot taken from behind Hoey, whose arched back as he sits on a spile, rises black against the ocean and sky. We are shooting into the sun. We see the figure express a sigh. The sheer beauty of this scene and the poignant quality of the lonely figure in it are its only reason for being.

507—Subtitle . . . .

Out there, somewhere — somewhere — lay Romance, and Life, and Love . . .

Scene 51.

Foreground Hoey seated on spile as before and gazing past camera. He thinks — but does not speak — the following:

508—Spoken title . . .

"Guess I'll get out of all this and go away . . ."

Continuing foreground, Hoey thinks on:

509—Spoken title . . .

"Guess I'll go to Persia and dig rubies . . ."

Continuing foreground, Hoey thinks on:

510—Spoken title . . .

"Guess I'll go to Africa and hunt tusks . . ."

Continuing foreground, Hoey thinks on:

511—Spoken title . . .

"Guess I'll go to Burma and mine sapphires . . ."

Continuing foreground, Hoey thinks on.

Scene 52.

Shot of a church steeple against moon cloudy sky. The clock registers ten, and the bell tolls.

Scene 53. (Dock as per 50. Moonlight effect.)

————

Foreground Hoey as per 51. He turns his head slightly over his shoulder as in recognition of that bell which is his present moment cash register, and says:

512—Spoken title . . .

"Guess I'll go home and help Pa close up the pill palace."

Scene 54.

Wide view shooting toward land as Hoey slumps off spile and wearily, heavy-footed, hands in pockets, starts up the dock or pier back to camera.

Fade out.

Fade in:

Scene 55. (Suburban street location as per 46. Moonlight effect.)

————

Hoey comes on toward camera in the manner of Scene 54.

(Street corner of street as per 46 and 55. Moonlight effect.)

Tanner comes around corner. After he has walked a few paces toward camera, Kaidy, a black chunk of swift body, comes sailing out of shadows and attacks him.

Scene 57. (Location as per 55. Moonlight effect.)

————

Hoey comes into foreground, sees something off, and stops, startled.

Scene 58. (Location as per 56. Moonlight effect.)

————

A long shot from where Hoey stands of the two struggling figures. Faces don't matter in this.

Scene 59. (Location as per 46. Moonlight effect.)

Foreground Hoey gazing all a tremble. Short scene.

Scene 60. (Location as per 56. Moonlight effect.)

Long shot as per 58. In this shot we see Tanner fall as result of blow with black-jack or some other instrument and Kaidy bending over him.

Scene 61. (Location as per 46. Moonlight effect.)
Hoey shouts and runs past camera, toward figures.

Scene 62. (Location as per 58, Moonlight effect.)

A long shot taken from behind Hoey showing him racing toward the two figures. When he gets half way to them, Kaidy, who is bending over Tanner, turns, sees him and, rising quickly, exits around corner. Hoey reaches Tanner and starts to bend down over him.

Scene 63.
Foreground by prostrate Tanner as Hoey bends over him. Tanner is not "out" but seems in a bad way. Hoey runs his fingers over Tanner's head feeling for fracture, and then with hands under Tanner's arm-pits drags him against wall or other prop in a sitting position. This shot is so close that if Hoey stands up his head will be out of picture. He does stand up.

Scene 64.
Foreground Hoey as he rises, puts two fingers in his mouth and whistles shrilly for police.

Scene 65.
Close foreground Tanner who seems able to register alarm at this action of Hoey's, for he says horsely:

513—Spoken title . . .

   "No cops! . . . D'ye want me pinched? Here, givus a hand."

Scene 66.
Foreground taking in the two, as Tanner speaks the above and Hoey turns in alarm. Tanner speaks some more to him and Hoey leans down and helps him up. Tanner it seems can stand. Hoey puts his arm in his as though to help him away. As he does so

Fade out.

Scene 67. (Tanner's room in cheap sailors' lodging house. Moonlight through window.)

Fade up wide view: The door opens and Hoey supports Tanner in and over to bed on which Tanner sits weakly. He motions Hoey to close the door. Hoey obeys. Then Hoey takes out a match and strikes a light. In a moment, with a hoarse cry, Tanner leaps at him and reaches him.

Scene 68.

A closeup of Hoey's hands with lighted match in them as Tanner's head comes swiftly into picture and Tanner blows out the match in Hoey's hand. (Note: Match-light effect, and then moonlight effect on Tanner's face and Hoey's hand.)

Scene 69.

Closeup Hoey's face registering surprise. Slowly his head turns and his eyes look down at his shoulder *out of picture.*

Scene 70.

Closeup Hoey's shoulder showing Tanner's arm ending in a steel hook which is caught in Hoey's sleeve cloth. (Note: This is the first time that Hoey or we have seen this hook. Make it clear and hold it long enough to put it over.)

Scene 71.

Closeup Hoey's face as it turns away from looking at shoulder out of picture full of wonder. He looks at Tanner out of picture.

Scene 72.

Closeup Tanner's face gazing tense and expressionless at Hoey's face out of picture.

Scene 73.

Wide view: The two stand gazing at one another as before, then Tanner, again registering a little weakness on his legs, disengages the hook from Hoey's shoulder sleeve and goes with unsteady craft toward the window. He gazes cagedly out of window and pulls down the blind. Nothing now but silhouette figures in the room. One of them moves to the door.

Scene 74.

Foreground by door, Tanner's silhouette in, opens door, looks out, closes it, locks it with key, turns out of foreground.

Scene 75.

Wide view: Hoey's silhouette still in room, that is no movement. Tanner's silhouette over to wall where it stops. He strikes a match. (Light effect) He lights a little brass gas jet on the wall and turns the light low. (More light effect) Then he staggers over to the bed as though all this exertion were too much for him, catches bed-post with his hook, and with his hand tears the scarf from his neck and pulls out the map. This he clutches tightly in his hand which he holds out in the air, as he says, dramatically:

514—Spoken title . . .

"Help me, boy, help me! . . . He must never get it!"

Continuing scene, he speaks out above and sinks back on bed clutching map. All this time Hoey has stood dumb with amazement, the very essence of romance crisping his nerves and holding him a statue. Now, as Tanner sinks back on the bed Hoey makes a few steps toward him and we

Close diaphragm quickly.

End of Part one.

1st Episode

"PIRATE GOLD"

Part Two

Marguerite Courtot is in danger again in the closing scenes of *Pirate Gold*. (Courtesy Joe Cuny)

514A—Subtitle . . . .
    The story of the map.
Scene 76. (Tanner's room as per 67)

———

Open diaphragm on a large closeup of Tanner's tattooed fist round the rolled map. There is movement of the hand with the map in it, as though the owner of the hand were talking and making slight gestures.
Scene 77.
Large closeup of Hoey in his best attitude of listening wonder and awe.
Scene 78.
Large foreground of Tanner propped up against pillows at head of bed and speaking to Hoey out of picture. Hold it a while to get over that he is in the midst of a story. He says:
515—Spoken title . . .
    "—and five of us, that had snug little bunks a day before, an' all we wanted

t'eat—an' you can say what you like, the vittles *was* tasty—"
Continuing foreground, Tanner speaks the above.
Scene 79.
Foreground of the engrossed Hoey assenting as though he had tasted those vittles himself.
Scene 80.
Foreground Tanner. He says:
516—Spoken title . . . .
"We found ourself now with nothin' t'eat an' lessen a belly full o' water between us ——"
Fade title into:
Scene 81. (The open sea. Rolling swells. Daytime.)

————

A wide shot of an open boat with five men in it. It is not necessary in this shot to distinguish particular persons. We're coming to that later. This is just a vivid impression of a small boat on a large sea.
Fade into:
Scene 82. (Tanner's room as per 67.)

————

Foreground Hoey and Tanner. Hoey all ears. Tanner goes on: "Well, the next night old Sloman gives up and we has to ——"
Fade into:
Scene 83. (Open sea. Moonlight.)

————

A long shot as before showing the four men easing one dead sailor, feet first, over the side of the boat and into the sea. (The writer believes that the best effect will be gained by shooting against the sun, as the silhouettes will be easily registered and the water very beautiful.)
Fade into:
Scene 84. (Tanner's room as per 67.)

————

Large foreground Tanner with tears coursing down his cheeks. He says "He was a good pal of mine, was Sloman, and I knew I would miss him dreadful. Well, the next day was clear an' hot an' ——"
Fade into:
Scene 85. (Open sea. Daytime.)

————

As close a shot as possible to register all of the occupants of the boat. Tanner and Kaidy very much exhausted and pretty weak propped up, one in the stern and one in the bow of the open boat. The third sailor sits gripping his oar with both hands and huddled over it asleep. The fourth sailor lies seemingly asleep at the bottom of the boat.
Scene 86.
Large closeup of water butt on which is stencilled in black letters:

Nancy Bowker
Water

(Note: This little barrel sets on two semi-circular wooden shoulders. For exact description see Mr. Millhauser.)

Scene 87.
A large foreground in the same place showing the head and shoulders of the sailor who was seemingly asleep at the bottom of the boat, stealthily working his way toward water barrel, which is in picture. His eyes are wide and cunning, and his parched tongue lops half way out of his mouth. A desperate man. His arms go out toward water barrel.

Scene 88.
Close foreground Tanner propped against stern of boat. Out of the pocket of his coat sticks telescope — the upper breast pocket. His eyes are half closed but he stealthily watches action of foregoing scene.

Scene 89.
Close foreground Kaidy in bow of boat. He, also, with half closed eyes, watches action of man and barrel. His face expresses physical weakness and burning hate for the water thief out of picture.

Scene 90.
Close foreground of sailor stealthily, shakily raising small water barrel to take out plug from bung hole, preparatory to drinking.

Scene 91.
Foreground Kaidy who weakly draws a gun and shoots.

Scene 92.
Foreground of man with barrel as in Scene 90. The bullet goes through the barrel and through him. He falls backward over boat into water, and the barrel falls into the boat.

Scene 93.
Closeup of barrel at bottom of boat with water pouring out of large bullet hole.

Scene 94.
Foreground Tanner who sees the foregoing and takes hold of the thwart with his hook weakly and tries to pull himself up to salvage the escaping water out of picture. It is too much of an effort, however, and he just sinks back. No facial contortions, just lack of strength.

Scene 95.
Closeup of barrel out of which the last bit of water runs.

Scene 96.
Close foreground Kaidy in the bow watching the last of the water disappear. His face distorted into a slight and horrible smile, as he works his dry tongue longingly around his baked lips. He, also, is too weak to salvage what few drops of water remain.

Fade into:

Scene 97. (Tanner's room as per 67.)

———

Foreground Tanner and Hoey. Tanner speaking on in his story. Hoey listening, his eyes, ears, heart and soul all open. As Tanner speaks, he shakes the fist with the map and says:

517—spoken title . . .

"That was Kaidy that done the shootin' . . . Him that's after the map."

Continuing foreground, Tanner speaks the above and goes on working himself into a paroxysm of rage as he shakes the map and says "But he'll never get it, understand? — Never!" Hoey is right with him. Now Tanner continues his narrative. He says:

518—Spoken title . . .

"We had rain that night which meant drink, which meant life. An' when it came mornin' again ——"

Fade title into:

Scene 98. (Open sea. Bright sunlight.)

————

As close a shot as possible showing just two men in the boat. In the bow, Kaidy seemingly asleep. In the stern, Tanner, seated up and facing another terrible scorching day.

Scene 99.

Closeup Tanner's hook resting on the thwart and alongside it the old shark skin covered telescope previously registered in his pocket. (Very bright sunlight on this scene.) As a result of the terrific heat, the shark skin on the telescope cracks and opens up a seam.

Scene 100.

Closeup Tanner's head and shoulders. He looks down for the cracking of the shark skin attracts his attention. Not a quick look, but a slow, lethargic, laboured look.

Scene 101.

Closeup of the telescope on thwart. The skin cracks further revealing parchment underneath.

Scene 102.

Close foreground Tanner as he reaches his fist down out of picture. The fist comes back with the telescope. He examines it closely, tears off the shark skin cover and pulls out the map, which curls up. He opens it with hook and fist and registers as much surprise as his weakness allows as we

Fade into:

Scene 103. (Tanner's room as per 67.)

————

Foreground Tanner and Hoey, as Tanner says:

519—Spoken title . . .

"Three hundred years old . . . No lenses in it . . . I just carried it as a keepsake . . . Got it offen a water-clerk for a ship chandler in the Chiny Sea . . . Name o' Dowson . . ."

Continuing foreground, Tanner speaks out the above, as he holds the map in his lap with one hand and uses the hook to straighten it out, and let it go again so it curls up. He does this all the time as he speaks and Hoey is fascinated by the map and would like to get a look at it. As he goes on speaking

Fade into:

Scene 104. (Open sea. Moonlight.)

———

Foreground Tanner in stern of boat seemingly asleep. Into this foreground, crawls Kaidy, who filches the telescope from Tanner's pocket. Kaidy softly withdraws from the picture and as he does so, we see Tanner's eyes open and we know that he has been conscious of the theft.

Scene 105.

Foreground prow of boat. Kaidy comes in with telescope. He stealthily removes map which Tanner has rolled up and put inside telescope, and flings the telescope overboard. Then he uncurls map and his eyes eat it up. Then he rolls it up and sticks it into his outside coat pocket as we

Fade into:

Scene 106. (Tanner's room as per 67.)

———

Foreground Tanner. He says:

520—Spoken title . . .

"I didn't want no trouble with him, then . . . But the next day he sights a steamer an' ——"

Fade title into:

Scene 107. (Open sea.)

———

Foreground Kaidy in prow. He is gazing off, very weak, but excited, and fumbling in his pocket pulls out a binocular, which he gazes through. Now he lowers the glasses and calls out of picture to Tanner, then he turns and again lifts the glasses. As this transpires, Tanner comes rather weakly into picture from other end of boat and also looks off. Although weak, these two men show an activity that is born of crazy excitement, now. Kaidy hands him the glasses. He gazes through them. Kaidy is eager to have them back again. He lets Kaidy have them. As Kaidy again adjusts glasses and uses both hands to hold them, Tanner, with a cunning smile, dips his one good hand into Kaidy's pocket — the pocket the map is in.

Scene 108.

Closeup Kaidy's coat showing Tanner's tattooed hand removing the map.

Close diaphragm and fade into:

521—Spoken title . . .

"That was four years ago. He ain't never laid hands on me until tonight . . . He'd 'a' murdered me if you hadn' a' come along!"

Scene 109. (Tanner's room as per 67.)

———

Foreground Tanner and Hoey as Tanner speaks the above and Hoey nods a modest assent. Tanner stops and looks down at the map which he rolls and unrolls. Hoey asks whether he may see the map. Tanner hands it to him. Hoey

takes it and spreads it on the bed. When he lets go of it it rolls up. He picks
it up again, and, holding the two ends, searches it avidly.
Scene 110.
Foreground of map in Hoey's hands. (Note: A very special job must be done
with this map. It should be well copied on old parchment from a photograph of
an aged map in some old book, Mr. Smith and Mr. Grot should confer on this
for it is important.)
Scene 111.
Closeup Hoey's wonder-ridden face as he gazes down at map.
Scene 112.
Foreground Tanner who is looking at Hoey and saying:
522—Spoken title . . . .
  "It ain't much T'look at, hey? . . . Well, it's a check for over a million in gold!"
Scene 113.
Close foreground Hoey as these words fall on his credulous senses, and he looks
a little bit away from map, breathing easily through the mouth.
Scene 114.
Foreground Tanner who says:
523—Spoken title . . . .
  "But it's only a piece o' paper to me. I'm gettin' old and tired, I'm lonesome. I
  don't want money . . . I want friends . . ."
Scene 115.
Foreground of the two as Tanner speaks the above. His voice sort of breaks, and
he would be the object of sympathy for a heart much harder and less impressionable than Hoey's. Hoey registers a quick response, for he goes impulsively toward
Tanner and lays his hand affectionately on Tanner's arm, as who would say, "It's
all right, old man. I'll be your friend." Tanner, not to be outdone, comes to
bat with his hand over the back of Hoey's, which he squeezes. A strong man's
deep and quiet emotion. Hoey is almost in tears. Finally Tanner looks up and
says:
524—Spoken title . . . .
  "You know, Boy, if I had about five hundred dollars what I'd do? I'd go to a
  sailors' home and lay up my old bones . . ."
Continuing foreground, Tanner wistfully speaks out the above, and goes on:
525—Spoken title . . . .
  "And I'd make a present of this little fortune to the first jack I took a fancy to!"
Continuing foreground, he speaks the above, and reaching up his hand, casually
takes the map from Hoey's, and sort of taps it with his hook. Hoey makes an
unconscious, half motion with his hand to recover it, but drops his arm. The
pulse in his temple thumps like a pile-driver. Finally, he says with timid eager-
ness, as one who is going to ask something which he hopes, but doubts, will be
answered "Yes": "If I gave you five hundred dollars, would you let me have the
map?" Tanner looks at him rather surprised and says, "You?" Then he thinks
a moment, as though making an important decision in his mind, and finally says,
"Ye-e-ess." Hoey can't believe his senses. "It's a go? You'll sell it to me?" Tanner

nods. "I won't be gone ten minutes," says Hoey, excitedly, as Tanner smiles sympathetically and Hoey dashes out of foreground and we

Fade out.

Fade up:

Scene 116. (Tuttle's Pharmacy as per 34.)

———

Foreground by cash register as Austin Tuttle has finished checking up the day's receipts, and with money in two little sacks is about to start for the safe. Before he goes he looks up to see the time.

Scene 117.

Closeup clock on wall. It registers a quarter to eleven.

Scene 118.

Medium wide view: Austin, a little bit worried that Hoey is not in as yet, goes over to safe with sacks and starts to unlock safe.

Scene 119. (Suburban street location. Moonlight.)

———

A long shot down center of the street as Hoey comes racing toward camera and past.

Scene 120. (Tuttle's Pharmacy as per 34.)

———

Wide view: Austin Tuttle with safe open as Hoey comes dashing in, breathing hard, and almost unintelligibly excited. Austin turns in surprise, and asks what's up. Hoey paws him in his urgent desire to transmit to his father in a moment what it has taken him over half an hour to learn. Austin looks at him curiously, as Hoey starts to tell the story of the attack, the rescue, and the wreck, Tanner, Kaidy and the map.

Close diaphragm on them.

Scene 121.

Open diaphragm on closeup of the clock which registers eleven o'clock.

Scene 122

Foreground by sales counter on which stands a couple of rolls of paper — one fat roll, and one skinny roll almost to the end. Hoey and his father in picture. Hoey still speaking excitedly to father who listens gravely. Hoey is saying:

526—Spoken title . . . .

"Tanner — that's the bird with the hook — says it's mostly old Spanish gold. And the map shows it's buried not eighty miles from here — Over a million!" Continuing foreground, he speaks the above. As he says 'over a million' he thumps the counter with his fist and looks down at it. He is not looking at Austin and that gives us an opportunity to show Austin's quick, eager look at the mention of a million in gold. It is a look of interested abstraction, for now Hoey turns his gaze to him and talks on. He is ardent, vigorous, eloquent, urgent in his argument. Austin listens. Finally, as a clincher to his argument, Hoey has an inspiration, for he pulls a piece of pill box wrapping paper about the size of the map — and lays it down. He shows Austin how the map curls up . . . very old . . .

Scene 123.

Closeup piece of paper on counter curling up, after Hoey has straightened it out with his hand.

Scene 124.

Closeup Austin's rapt expression as he gazes down at paper out of picture, and licks his lips.

Scene 125.

Foreground of the two. Hoey finishes with his paper and turns to Austin, as the lawyer who has summed up with a clincher turns to his jury. Finally, Austin looks down rather stealthily and says:

527—Spoken title . . . .

   "Promise not to tell Ma?"

Continuing foreground, he speaks the above very seriously. Hoey says "Yes." It's too good to be true. He goes on, kindly pointing out to his father the wisdom of such a decision, but Austin turns from him and exits foreground. Hoey watches. Hold it for a little. The expression on Hoey's face should make it worth while.

Scene 126.

Foreground Austin stooped before open safe and taking five old one hundred dollar bills from a battered old tin box that has a key and latch on it.

Scene 127.

Wide view: Austin rises after closing safe and advances to Hoey with the money. He gives it to Hoey who can't say thanks but says and expresses his jumbled excitement, as he turns and runs toward the door and out. Austin stands a moment as though he had changed his mind and then going to door calls Hoey back. He leans to Hoey's ear and says:

528—Spoken title . . . .

   "Be sure you get the latitude and longitude on the map!"

Continuing scene, Austin speaks the above, as Hoey at the door nods yes and exits. Austin watches him gravely. He stands a moment lost in thought and then goes over to the counter and picks up the curled up piece of paper — the map to him. His face is that of a boy who fingers his first rifle — one that really shoots. A boy who contemplates the wild beasts that will fall before his unerring aim. As Austin plays with this paper we can see that the map is his rifle, and buried treasure his game. This is very good business and should be handled by the director with a delicate appreciation of Ausin's feelings. If necessary, do this action in a foreground.

Fade out.

Scene 128.

(Tanner's room as per 67.)

———

Fade up wide view: Tanner propped up in bed as before. He registers a knock on the door and his hand flies under the pillow and pulls out a huge gun which he levels at the door as he calls "Come in." Hoey enters all a tremble. He is taken aback by the gun which Tanner quickly lowers and places beneath his pillow as he smiles a welcome. As he does so, he tells Hoey to close the door. Then Hoey comes to him and quickly takes out the money. He hopes Tanner hasn't changed his mind. He wants to change this measly five hundred dollars for that beautiful map. Shakes hands with Tanner and starts out. He is at the door again when he remembers about the latitude and longitude. Again he consults the map. The he goes back to Tanner and tells him that the latitude and longitude are not marked on the map. Tanner laughs as he says:

529—Spoken title . . . .
"That's right. I had forgot. I rubbed them latitude and longitude figures off, case o'accident; but I know 'em by heart."

Scene 129.
Foreground of the two. Tanner speaks the above and asks Hoey for the map. Hoey gives it to him and also gives him a pencil. Tanner thinks a moment, and then writes the numbers on the map. Hoey thanks him. Again takes map, shakes hands, and exits foreground.
Scene 130.
Wide view: Hoey exits with a last goodbye at the door which he closes behind him. Tanner yawns, and gets up from the bed. He's awfully steady on his feet now.
Scene 130A.
(Outside sailors' rooming house. A dingy, sinister waterfront location. Moonlight.)

———

Hoey exits house past camera.
Scene 130B.
(Tanner's room as per 67.)

———

Wide view: Tanner standing up. The door opens and Kaidy comes in, eagerly to Tanner in foreground. Tanner shows no surprise at seeing him. Kaidy says, excitedly:

530—Spoken title . . . .
"How much did y'get for it?"
Scene 131.
Close foreground Kaidy as he speaks the above eagerly.
Scene 132.
Close foreground Tanner as he raises his five fingers of his good hand.
Scene 133.
Foreground two. Kaidy whistles in glad surprise. Then Tanner tells him to give him a hand and help him take off his ear-rings. Kaidy takes off Tanner's ear-rings, and then unfastens the hook from Tanner's hand. Tanner's arm and

Having trapped Siebert and Kaidy (Harry Semels and Joe Cuny), Hoey and Austin Tuttle (George B. Seitz and Frank Redman) discussed what to do with their captives in Episode 5 of *Pirate Gold*. (Courtesy Joe Cuny)

hand come out after the hook and he rubs and flexes this member which has been cramped for a couple of hours. Then Tanner raises his other hand near his mouth and spits on the back of it on the tattoo marks. He uses a finger to rub the marks off.

Scene 134.

Closeup back of Tanner's fist showing the marks being obliterated by finger plus spit. Then the back of the hand is rubbed clean and dry on his clothes.

Scene 135.

(Suburban street location. Moonlight.)

————

Hoey comes trotting toward camera, out of breath, and holding his hand tightly over the pocket in which he has the map.

Scene 136.

(Tanner's room as per 67.)

———

Wide view: The men are seated smoking and talking. Tanner says:
531—Spoken title . . . .

"I was in good voice tonight . . .Added lots o'things that wasn't in the story before. He seemed to want it!"
Continuing scene, Tanner speaks the above and Kaidy and he both laugh. Tanner, proud of himself, goes on:

532—Spoken title . . . .

"I even give him latitude and longitude.
Made 'em up out of my own head!"

Scene 137.
Close foreground Kaidy as he hears this and a quizzical look comes over his face and he eyes Tanner suspiciously. He knows that Tanner is a boob and for a certain reason he mistrusts this extemporaneous stuff. He says, very clearly, "What did you tell him?"
Scene 138.
Foreground Tanner. He closes his eyes a moment, thinks, and then says:
533—Spoken title . . . .

(Insert here a latitude and longitude quotation. The writer is not familiar with them)

Scene 139.
Wide view: As Tanner speaks the above, Kaidy jumps up, whips cigarette from his lips, bounds over to Tanner and shrieks:

534—Spoken title . . . .
"You fool! You idiot! You bone-head!"

Scene 140.
Foreground of the two as Kaidy speaks out the above and Tanner registers simply, "Why, what's the matter with them figures? They don't mean nothing." And then, angrily, "What's the matter with you, you damn fool? What's biting you?" Kaidy throws up his hands to his head in utter disgust, and turns out of foreground.
Scene 141.
Wide view with Kaidy stumping around the room and Tanner watching. A couple of times Kaidy comes up to him and gestures and mumbles, but gives it up and goes on walking. The third time he comes up to him, he calms himself, and says:
535—Spoken title . . . .

"Imaginary, hell! You heard the Boss and me talking about the position of the big stuff — and *real* stuff that we had to sell this fake map in order to get

at – and the figures stayed in your mind!"
Scene 142.
Foreground of the two as Kaidy finishes the above, explaining with insulting precision and simplicity. Tanner is childishly penitent and rather frightened. He says "Maybe the kid won't go there, etc. etc." Lots of maybes. Kaidy registers that he thinks it is awful. He finally turns on Tanner and says:
538—Spoken title . . . .

   "We've got to keep this from the Boss, or he'll skin us both alive! And you've got to lay for that kid and get him away if he shows up!"

Continuing foreground. Kaidy speaks the above as Tanner, who is so frightened of the boss that he will agree to anything, agrees to this with alacrity and goes on agreeing to everything that Kaidy says:
Scene 143.
 (Tuttle's pharmacy as per 34.)
Wide view: Old man Tuttle pacing up and down and looking at the clock. Hoey enters and runs to him. Hoey quickly dives into his pocket and pulls out the map. Instantly, Austin pulls it away from him, shoves it into his pocket, looks wildly around as for a possible eavesdropper, and then registering a very earnest and theatrical "Sh" with his finger over his lips, looks outside, closes the door, pulls down the shades, switches off the electric lights, which leaves the place in darkness except for the light of the large apothecary's bottle of green water in the window, then he motions Hoey over to the window and the lighted bottle. Both advance. Austin takes the map out of his pocket, unrolls it and holds it as he and Hoey look at it with backs hunched. (Note Their backs in this scene are toward camera)
Scene 144.
Foreground Hoey and Austin, both holding the map and gazing at it, the green light on their faces, their backs hunched, the hot blood round their eyes and icicles pricking their spines.
Fade out and close diaphragm.

End of Part Two.
1st Episode
"PIRATE GOLD"
Part Three

537—Subtitle . . . .
   In which two romantic young men part company.
Scene 145. (Platform of station in Hoey's town.)

———

Open diaphragm on foreground Hoey and Austin. Austin is giving fatherly instructions to Hoey. Hoey is dressed in a changeable overcoat and a soft hat. He carries a duffle bag. He listens attentively to his senior.
Scene 146. (Tuttle Pharmacy as per 34.)

———

Mrs. Tuttle and two men engaged talking. The two men stand with their backs to the camera in this side shot. One of them is seen to ask a definite question.
Scene 147.
Foreground of the three. The two men are Tanner and Kaidy. It is Kaidy who is finishing asking the definite question. Mrs. Tuttle replies:
538—Spoken title . . . .

"Oh, no. Mr. Tuttle is down to the station seeing off my son, Ivanhoe, who is going to the Coast for a vacation."

Continuing foreground, she speaks the above. Tanner and Kaidy exchange glances. Business of "Oh, I see" from Tanner. They shake polite farewells and exit foreground.
Scene 148. (Platform as per 145.)

————

Foreground Hoey and Austin. Austin looks around, secretly, pulls small leather book from his pocket, and says:
539—Spoken title . . . .

"Secret code!"

Continuing foreground, Austin speaks the above and slips Hoey book, which Hoey puts in his pocket.
Scene 149. (Street location in Hoey's town.)

————

Tanner and Kaidy impetuously enter taxi-cab, giving driver fast order. Taxi out. Get sense of rush about this scene.
Scene 150. (Platform as per 145.)

————

Foreground Hoey and Austin talking. Austin is doing the talking. Hoey stops and says listen. They listen.
Scene 151. (Railroad tracks in country.)

————

Picturesque shot of train steaming around bend toward camera. Whistle blowing.
Scene 152. (Platform as per 145.)

————

Foreground Hoey and father. "That's the train." Again Austin looks around, puts his hand in his pocket and pulls out a heavy black mustache. He hands it to Hoey, who is about to take it as Austin says:

540—Spoken title . . . .

"Avoid recognition."

Continuing foreground, Austin speaks the above, as Hoey looks at the mustache a little bit puzzled. Nods his head and puts it in his pocket.
Scene 153.
Shot down tracks showing train coming toward station about a quarter a mile away, coming toward camera.
Scene 154. (Street in Hoey's town.)

————

Shot of taxi flying around corner. Lots of speed.

Scene 155. (Platform as per 145.)

———

Foreground Hoey and Austin. Austin is still giving important instructions. He says:

541—Spoken title . . . .

"And above all, watch out for this feller Kaidy. Remember what your friend Tanner says . . . He'd do murder to get that map."

Continuing foreground, he speaks above and Hoey nods assent.

Scene 156.

Wide view showing train pulling into station and Austin and Hoey shaking hands.

Scene 157.

Foreground Austin and Hoey saying a last goodbye, with hands clasped. Business of sympathetic understanding. Hoey breaks away and exits foreground.

Scene 158.

Foreground of steps of railway car. Hoey comes in, boards steps. Train starts out. Hoey turns and shakes goodbye.

Scene 159.

Medium shot of rather sad figure of Austin shaking goodbye.

Scene 160.

Shot down platform showing train out of platform.

Scene 161.

Foreground Austin watching, heaving a big sigh.

Scene 162.

Shot of train pulling away from platform, about an eighth of a mile out, going away from camera.

Close diaphragm.

Scene 163. (Inside a car of moving train. It is night now.)

———

Open diaphragm on length of the car with Hoey seated in foreground, riding opposite to the way the train is going. The conductor who has been taking tickets is near Hoey's seat. He comes to Hoey in foreground, takes Hoey's ticket, punches it and sticks it in the back of Hoey's seat. Hoey watches him rather suspiciously, as conductor moves past camera. Then Hoey looks covertly at his fake mustache, and up again at conductor out of picture.

Scene 164.

Foreground of conductor stopping at seat facing Hoey's. As he does so, a beautiful white, feminine hand and arm comes up into picture and hands him ticket.

Scene 165.

Foreground Hoey watching conductor *up* out of picture. He notes the hand and his eyes travel downward to its owner, out of picture. And then he looks as though somebody had punched him in the stomach.

542—Subtitle . . . .

A pretty girl.

Scene 166.

A lovely close foreground of girl seated opposite Hoey, the one who took the wind out of him. She smiles up at conductor out of picture as his hand comes in and hands her back her ticket. One of her nicest smiles. Then she resumes her magazine.

Scene 167.

Foreground Hoey gazing in frank and boyish admiration past camera at girl across from him.

543—Subtitle . . . .

 A very pretty girl.

Scene 168.

A lovely close foreground of the girl reading her magazine.

Scene 169.

A long shot down train with Hoey in close foreground gazing with rapt admiration past camera at girl. Kaidy comes down the aisle behind him, stops behind Hoey's seat, takes Hoey's ticket, looks at it, sticks it back in seat, turns and goes back the way he came, as smooth as silk.

544—Subtitle . . . .

 The prettiest girl in the world.

Scene 170.

Another foreground of the girl. She feels Hoey's gaze at her and looks frankly up and across at Hoey out of picture.

Scene 171.

Foreground Hoey confused at gaze. He quickly picks up newspaper and opens it up before him, hiding his face and body.

Scene 172.

Foreground of the girl, who raises her eye-brows a bit interrogatively, as at a curious person, and again, gives her priceless attention to her magazine.

Scene 173. (Another location in car.)

————

Foreground seat. Tanner seated smoking cigarette and waiting. Kaidy comes in and drops into seat beside Tanner. To Tanner's interrogation, Kaidy answers:

545—Spoken title . . . .

 "I made him. Simple young party . . . Ticket reads Coldbrook Junction . . .

 The damn fool is going right where he can make the most trouble for us!"

Continuing foreground, he speaks the above and Tanner is troubled. They start talking together.

Scene 174. (Inside car as per 163.)

————

Foreground large spread newspaper behind which we know Hoey to be. A finger comes through newspaper, making an eye hole. It is withdrawn and comes through again, making another eye-hole, both these holes represent Hoey's two eyes and are at the height of his head behind paper.

Scene 175.

Closeup of the paper showing Hoey's eyes behind eyeholes.

Scene 176.

Close foreground of the object of the subterfuge. You can't blame Hoey. She is very nice. Also, she is asleep.
Scene 177.
Long shot down train with spread paper in foreground. Conductor comes down train, and again inspects tickets. He comes to Hoey's place and stops. He takes Hoey's ticket from back of chair. Immediately the paper starts to come down from before our hero.

Scene 178.
Foreground by Hoey's seat. Conductor standing by Hoey's seat as before. Match up action with paper coming down from before Hoey's face. We are startled, for our hero has on the black mustache given him by his father. The conductor looks at him and is puzzled. He is very puzzled. He can't understand it. He cogitates a moment and passes on, past camera. Hoey furtively feels his mustache. Then he looks across at the girl, starts to put up his paper again, but cannot.
Scene 179.
Foreground of the girl asleep.
Scene 180. (Conductor's closet on train.)

––––

Conductor comes in. He wonders about the black mustache, for he is certain it was not a black mustached man he first took ticket from. He exits to go back and look again.
Scene 181. (Car as per 163.)

––––

Close foreground Hoey with black mustache on, looking across at sleeping girl.
Scene 182.
Close foreground girl who is uncomfortable with Hoey's gaze fixed on her. She wakes and looks across. A bit indignant.
Scene 183.
Close foreground Hoey. He sneezes mustache off and recovers it quickly, embarrassed.
Scene 183A.
Close foreground girl. She laughs as at a boob.
Scene 183B.
A wider shot of Hoey still embarrassed, and showing conductor approaching. He stops, looks at Hoey, notes his smooth face, is disturbed, and exits scene the way he came.
Scene 184. (Conductor's closet on train.)

––––

Conductor comes in, looks around him, takes half empty bottle of whiskey from bunk and, after regarding it for a second, flings it out of the window, straightens up, composes his face gravely, buttons his coat and exits. He'll never touch another drop.
Scene 185. (Car as per 173.)

––––

Foreground Kaidy and Tanner. Tanner is getting the little luggage they have together, preparatory to departure. He says:

547—Spoken title . . . .

"I just can't face the Boss while that kid has the map with those figures on it . . . He'd *smell* there was something wrong — and you know *him!*"

Continuing foreground, Tanner speaks the above. Kaidy nods gravely in assent and says:

548—Spoken title . . . .

"I was thinkin' about it . . . There's a bad stretch of road between the station and the hotel . . . I'll frighten the map out of him there."

Continuing foreground, Kaidy speaks the above and Tanner looks relieved. Suddenly Tanner says:

542—Spoken title . . . .

"Supposin' he refuses to be frightened?"

Scene 186.

Close foreground Tanner speaks the above to Kaidy out of picture.

Scene 187.

Close foreground Kaidy. He smiles sinisterly, takes out a large clasp knife, opens it, and lets the blade snap back significantly.

Scene 188.

Foreground Tanner who nods a slow and expressionless assent.

Scene 189. (Station platform at Coldbrook Junction. Moonlight.)

———

A wide view of station showing two distinct groups of waiting people and some stragglers about. In this shot, also show the train coming in, down the tracks toward camera.

Scene 190. (Inside car as per 164.)

———

Long shot down train showing people getting ready for exit.

Scene 191.

Foreground Hoey as we last saw him. He has his things ready and is watching girl opposite, out of picture.

Scene 192.

Foreground girl. She rises with her packages. The train comes to a sudden stop and she is thrown back into her seat. Again she rises and exits.

Scene 193.

Foreground Hoey who rises and exits after girl.

Scene 194. (Station as per 189. Moonlight.)

———

Foreground of one group of waiting people watching eagerly and anxiously off to recognize an expected arrival.

Scene 195.

Foreground steps of car. A few people get off and then comes the girl.

Scene 196.

Foreground group as per 194. Somebody recognizes her. "There she is!" . . . "Yoo-hoo!" And they rush out of picture.
Scene 197. (Another location on platform. Moonlight.)

————

Girl comes into picture, stops, recognizes folks coming toward her out of picture, and waves her hand, They come in and crowd around her.
Scene 198. (Another location on platform. Moonlight.)

————

Foreground Hoey looking off, watching. He has no makeup on now.
Scene 199. (Platform as per 197. Moonlight.)

————

Foreground group around girl. One kisses her, then another.
Scene 200. (Platform as per 198. Moonlight.)

————

Foreground Hoey. He is gazing off, fascinated and now moves slowly out of foreground.
Scene 201. (Platform as per 197. Moonlight.)

————

Foreground crowd around girl. She is kissed by two people in succession. Another person waits for a kiss. Hoey comes into picture. The person who waits for a kiss gets it, and now Hoey comes marching up. She knows no distinction in her excitement and, taking him to be one of her many friends, proffers her cheek to him, as to the others before. Hoey kisses and passes on.
Scene 202. (Another location on platform. Moonlight.)

————

Hoey comes in, his feet on the platform, but his head in the stars.
Scene 203. (Platform as per 197. Moonlight.)

————

Foreground group. The first group sort of makes way for another group which comes up and starts greeting and kissing business as before.
Scene 204. (Platform as per 202. Moonlight.)

————

Foreground Hoey who watches.
Scene 205. (Platform as per 197. Moonlight.)

————

Kissing business.
Scene 206. (Platform as per 202. Moonlight.)

————

Hoey watching comes to sudden decision. Puts on a vandyke beard, turns his coat inside out, with one thump changes the shape of his hat, and exits scene.
Scene 207. (Platform as per 197. Moonlight.)

————

Again there is only one person waiting to be kissed as Hoey comes into the picture. Hoey's turn comes and stepping up, he throws his arms about the girl, in a burst of great feeling and kisses her.

Scene 208.

Close foreground of Hoey and girl as he holds her in an unbrotherly embrace and hangs on to her lips longer than is good form on station platforms. The girl has to break loose from him. As she pulls way, she stares at him in amazement. She recognizes that she does not know him. She tears off his beard.

Scene 209.

Foreground group gazing at Hoey in righteous amazement. "Who is this person?"

Scene 210.

Foreground Hoey looking around rather sheepish. He has come down to earth with a thud. He is in the most embarrassing situation he could ever find himself. Suddenly, in a hysterical desire to get away, he stoops to pick up his bag and rising exits picture.

Scene 211.

Wide view showing Hoey racing away. Group in side fgd.

Scene 212.

Foreground of the group around the girl. She is explaining in a half crying way that she didn't know the young man. Isn't it terrible?

Scene 213. (Shot of road leading away from station into woods. Moonlight.)

———

Hoey runs toward woods, back to camera.

Scene 214. (Location near station. Moonlight.)

———

Tanner stands gazing off, sinisterly. He pulls his hat down over his face in a way that makes it difficult for any one to recognize him and exits picture.

Scene 215. (Woods location — path. Moonlight.)

———

Hoey comes on toward camera. Kaidy steps out of shadows and confronts him. He says:

550—Spoken title . . . .

"Give me that map!"

Scene 216.

Foreground of the two. He speaks the above as he tears Hoey's coat open and pulls out the map. Quick as lightning Hoey snatches it back from him, and breaking away exits foreground.

Scene 217.

Wide view showing Hoey breaking from Kaidy who springs at him. They fight. Let them fight for a while, and then Tanner runs up and jumps Hoey from behind. Hoey throws him off. He sees there's too much odds to contend against, so he turns and runs. They follow him out of picture.

Scene 218. (Location in woods with shack in picture. Light coming from window in shack)

———

Hoey runs into picture. Tanner catches up with him. Hoey turns, punches Tanner who falls back and as Kaidy comes up, Hoey again turns and runs pell-mell into house. The light from within promises protection. (Note: In these wood scenes get over the sense of a running fight as in the first episode of "Lightning Raider" on the beach)

Scene 219. (Inside lighted shack. Stairs with balustrade leading up to balcony.)

———

Hoey comes in, looks around, calls help and is about to bolt door when he is thrown back as the door is shoved open by the two men outside. They enter. From now on there is to be a terrific fight staged at the director's discretion and making use of the staircase with the balustrade and the balcony. Let the fight be a whopper and close the diaphragm on a shot of the three men rolling over in a tangled mass on the floor altogether. END OF EPISODE.

Index of Names

Index of Serials